*Death in the City*

VIOLENCE IN LATIN AMERICAN HISTORY

*Edited by Pablo Piccato, Federico Finchelstein, and
Paul Gillingham*

# Death in the City

SUICIDE AND THE SOCIAL IMAGINARY
IN MODERN MEXICO

*Kathryn A. Sloan*

UNIVERSITY OF CALIFORNIA PRESS

University of California Press, one of the most distinguished university presses in the United States, enriches lives around the world by advancing scholarship in the humanities, social sciences, and natural sciences. Its activities are supported by the UC Press Foundation and by philanthropic contributions from individuals and institutions. For more information, visit www.ucpress.edu.

University of California Press
Oakland, California

Library of Congress Cataloging-in-Publication Data

Names: Sloan, Kathryn A., 1961– author.
Title: Death in the city : suicide and the social imaginary in modern
    Mexico / Kathryn A. Sloan.
Description: Oakland, California : University of California Press, [2017] |
    Series: Violence in Latin American history ; 5 | Includes bibliographical
    references and index.
Identifiers: LCCN 2016043318 (print) | LCCN 2016044507 (ebook) |
    ISBN 9780520290310 (cloth : alk. paper) | ISBN 9780520290327
    (pbk. : alk. paper) | ISBN 9780520964532 (ebook)
Subjects: LCSH: Suicide—Mexico—History—20th century. | Murder—
    Mexico—History—20th century. | Death—Social aspects—Mexico—
    History—20th century.
Classification: LCC HV6548.M6 S56 2017 (print) | LCC HV6548.M6 (ebook) |
    DDC 362.280972—dc23
LC record available at https://lccn.loc.gov/2016043318

Manufactured in the United States of America

26  25  24  23  22  21  20  19  18  17
10  9  8  7  6  5  4  3  2  1

*For Kenneth Ray and Jack Kenneth*

# CONTENTS

# ILLUSTRATIONS

# ACKNOWLEDGMENTS

First and foremost I toast my partner in life, Jerry McCormick. He helped me stay sane while balancing the pressures of administrative appointments with academic research and writing. He made me coffee and breakfast in the mornings before I disappeared to my library carrel on Saturdays or while I carved out some writing time during the week before university offices opened. Every person should have such a generous partner and friend. Love and admiration also goes to my two adult sons, Ian and Orion. I marvel each day at the lives you lead.

I thank my colleague Elliott West, who generously shared his own research funds so that I could spend a summer in Mexico City to wrap up my archival sleuthing. My appreciation also extends to the dean's office of the J. William Fulbright College of Arts and Sciences for the year of research and writing time they afforded me before I took on the duties of administration in the college. Dean Todd Shields encouraged me to make time for the book as I polished the manuscript and prepared it for publication. Working alongside him and my fellow deans—Yvette Murphy-Erby, Jeannine Durdik, Steve Beaupre, Simon Chua, and Lisa Summerford—has been stimulating and rewarding.

The dean's office staff, which includes Debbie Powers, Sharon McFarland, and Dawn Fisher, have welcomed me warmly and been the model of professionalism and generosity. The staff of the history department—Jeanne Short, Brenda Foster, and Melinda Adams—made my initial foray into university administration a positive experience. Their innovation, good cheer, and senses of humor made coming to work each day a joy.

Successful research relies on the numerous archivists and librarians who allow us scholars to do our jobs. I am especially grateful to the staff of the interlibrary loan department at Mullins Library at the University of Arkansas for expediting the borrowing of multiple reels of microfilm and primary sources. Librarians Angela Fritz and Beth Juhl secured me access to important newspaper databases. The professional archivists at the Archivo General de la Nación, Archivo Histórico de Salubridad y Asistencia, and Fondo Reservado of the Hemeroteca at Universidad Nacional Autónoma de México made this book possible. Even the armed guards who stood a yard from me at Salubridad y Asistencia as I poured through asylum records played a role, as they made me ponder the sensitivity of conducting historical research. Family lineage and reputation still matter in Mexico. Documents in the hands of anyone with nefarious intentions have the potential to provoke scandal.

The consummate professionals at the University of California Press deserve my sincere gratitude. Acquisitions editor Kate Marshall showed enthusiasm for the project early on; Bradley Depew and Jessica Moll stewarded the book to production; and Genevieve Thurston polished the prose with her superb copyediting.

Finally, I extend my good cheer to a close group of friend-colleagues who have shared drinks, meals, conference trips, and snarky repartee. You know who you are! Performing the acts of a historian is blissful enough, but sharing work and play life with stimulating colleagues takes it to the moon.

# *Introduction*

POPULAR CULTURE HAS LONG CONFLATED Mexico with the macabre. Day of the Dead commemorations in early November find families gathered at gravesites feasting on tamales, festooning tombstones with marigolds, and toasting their loved ones. National icons include the bandolier-emblazoned bandit-cum-revolutionary, who populates the pages of history and T-shirts sold in tourist shops. Responding with rakish nonchalance to danger, the outlaw epitomizes stereotypes of Mexicans as reckless and violent. Roadside shrines to Santa Muerte (Saint Death) and Jesús Malverde, the protector of narcotraffickers and cops, further insinuate Mexico's intimacy with all things ferocious and deadly. The all-too-common drug cartel practice of hanging headless corpses from overpasses haunts the imagination and perpetuates the notion that Mexicans possess a culture of violence. Furthermore, some intellectuals persuasively argue that Mexicans have a special relationship with death, formed in the crucible of their hybrid Aztec-European heritage. Death is their intimate friend; death is mocked and accepted with irony and fatalistic abandon. The commonplace nature of death in Mexico desensitizes Mexicans to suffering. Death, simply put, defines Mexico. Essentializing a diverse group of people as possessing a unique death cult delights those who want to see the exotic in Mexico or distinguish that society from its peers. Examining tragic and untimely death—namely self-annihilation—reveals a counternarrative. What could be more chilling than suicide, especially the violent death of the young? What desperation or madness pushes victims to raise a gun to the temple or slip a noose around the neck? A close examination of a wide range of twentieth-century historical documents proves that Mexicans did not accept death with a cavalier snicker, nor did they develop a unique death cult for that matter. It was quite the reverse. Mexicans behaved just as their contemporaries did in Austria, France, England, and the United States. They devoted scientific inquiry to the malady and mourned the loss of each life to suicide.

This study moves between examining power—how the state and its representatives thought about and approached suicide—and subjectivity—how and why suicides committed a self-constructive performance in their act of self-destruction.[1] Observers, worrying about the fate of the nation on the cusp of the twentieth century, placed women and youth at the crux of the public dialogue confronting suicide. Competing voices in the conversation jockeyed for authority. Suicide had an internal logic, but it also presented multiple implications that changed with variables like age, class, gender, and the march of time. How the deaths of young Mexican men and women came to be viewed depended on these factors and the historical context. For example, prerevolutionary reporters romanticized many suicides, even going so far as to suggest that it was a noble sacrifice to save one's honor or to die for unrequited love. Although post-1920 commentators constructed the narrative of the suicide in poetic expressions, they were less sympathetic to youngsters who killed themselves for seemingly frivolous reasons. Committing self-murder out of tedium or because of juvenile love jeopardized the social order of the revolutionary state, an entity endeavoring to remake its citizenry in mind and body.

Analyzing suicide across the eras of the Porfiriato (1876–1911, the reign of President Porfirio Díaz) and the Mexican Revolution (1910–20) bears ample fruit. Modernization as a state goal triumphed in the hearts and minds of the revolutionary elite just as it did in the rational ethos of *científicos* (scientific technocrats) and President Díaz. Díaz focused on constructing markers of modernization like buildings, parks, railroads, and port facilities. Revolutionary politicians improved the built environment as well, but they also rehabilitated Mexico's citizenry to effect new ways of thinking and living. The transformation of the relationship of the individual to society and state figured prominently through both eras, but modernity as a concept remained a moving target as economic and social development as well as the function of capitalism proceeded unevenly, in fits and starts.[2] Indicators of modernization's successes included new buildings and public works, scientific advances like techniques to prevent epidemic diseases, and improve the health and order of families, meaning primarily women and children. Decades before President Plutarco Calles claimed children to be members of the "revolutionary collectivity" in 1934, his political forbearers assessed the health of children in order to gauge the progress of the nation.[3] Newspapers came alive in the early twentieth century with stories of young men and women who, at or just over the age of majority (age twenty-one), committed suicide in dramatic fashion. The extant body of suicide inquests from 1900 to 1930 also confirms that adolescents killed themselves at higher rates than younger and older citizens. The fact that youth, who were ostensibly full of promise, were self-destructing spurred national reflection and attempts to understand the roots of this unsettling pattern. Continuity of action and reaction, more than divergence, characterized the two eras and how different actors approached the social problem of suicide.

Mexico City changed dramatically from 1900 to 1930. Its population reached 471,000 in 1910, a 50 percent increase from 1895, and women made up 53 percent of the migrant influx.[4] By 1930, the population had surged to 1,029,068. The city had tripled in size since 1895.[5] Whether drawn by the capital's economic promise or propelled from their homes by the ravages of war, women came to Mexico City to take advantage of newly expanded employment opportunities and public activities. Many households lacked a male head, and women had to work to support their families. Young women in particular filled the demand for typists, shop workers, cigarette makers, and other positions in the urban economy. Modern leisure activities that found men and women mingling in department stores, cinemas, and cabarets threatened existing gender ideology that located honorable women in the home. This gender order gone awry correlated with the rise of suicides in the city. Journalists and editors discussed suicide and used the menace of the unnatural deaths to lament disturbing aspects of a changing world. Moreover, they shaped rational discourses on morality and honor to legitimize their position to forge public opinion. They even assigned honor or dishonor to suicide victims and used their sensational deaths to criticize their peers and rival newspapers. Instead of pistols, journalists wielded words as weapons in this discursive field of honor.[6]

Death was an inescapable reality of modern urban life. No matter how municipal planners attempted to separate the dead and dying from the healthy, *capitalinos* (residents of Mexico City) confronted the impermanence of life on a daily basis. Traversing the city by carriage, trolley, car, or on foot took inhabitants past rotting carcasses of stray dogs, diseased and infirm beggars, shops peddling caskets, funeral processions, cemeteries, and public memorials to heroes long since deceased but commemorated in uniquely Mexican fashion on the anniversary of their deaths.[7] Capitalinos paused in their everyday movements around the city to take in the sights. They might observe a state funeral or ride in the same streetcar as mourners destined for one of the public graveyards flanking the urban center. Modern city life brought with it "mechanized killings" in the form of railroad accidents,[8] trolleys derailing and careening into bystanders, and construction mishaps. Certainly, the spectacle of suicides committed in public spaces deepened residents' intimacy with their own transience.[9] Reporters played up the dangers of urban life by showcasing sensational suicides and murders on the front pages of major newspapers, complete with sketches or photographs of the deceased. Broadsides illustrated by José Guadalupe Posada depicted the coming apocalypse, serial murder, patricide, and the torture of children. It is no wonder that urbanites questioned their own existence when assaulted with words and images reminding them how vulnerable life could be. In fact, newspapers stood in for guides to committing suicide by outlining methods used, listing places deaths took place, and describing the particulars of leaving behind a suicide note. In effect, media coverage defined a cultural grammar of suicide.

At the turn of the twentieth century, Mexico had one of the lowest suicide rates in the world. Yet capitalinos who perused the numerous forms of media that proliferated at the time were receiving the message that suicides were rising at an alarming rate every day in Mexico City. By 1910, *El Imparcial* was selling one hundred thousand copies a day, and a satiric penny press was flourishing in the capital.[10] All classes had their dailies. Print media played a significant role in sparking a moral panic that exaggerated the frequency and pace of suicides. The practice of sensationalizing news to attract readers and, ultimately, advertisers, propelled a shift from reporting political views and commentary to chronicling violent death. A review of Mexican newspapers and medical journals in the early 1900s would convince a reader that suicide had indeed reached sweeping proportions in the nation's capital. Capitalinos shared this collective sentiment with the publics of New York, Vienna, Paris, and London—all cities with modern print media. Indeed, throughout the nineteenth century, city dwellers worldwide believed that their societies were sickened by suicide epidemics, and this opinion became more entrenched during this heady age of modernization that came as the next century loomed on the horizon. In their eyes, plagues of self-murder in urban centers were a result of technological and economic changes proving to be too much for some individuals. Suicide rates served as barometers of the health of a society but also as a gruesome badge of modernity. This sad indicator placed Mexico at the table of modern nations.

Modernity is a slippery and troublesome concept, especially when applied to turn-of-the-century Latin America, as it was "still a fantasy and a profound desire" at that point.[11] Theorists argue that modernity was not a linear progression from barbarism to civilization or a cataclysmic break between past and present. Rather, it was defined by watershed processes such as urbanization, secularization, industrial capitalism, rationality, scientific discovery, and the reification of the individual. Porfirian and revolutionary planners focused on modernizing the physical spaces of Mexico City. Porfirio Díaz favored Parisian-style boulevards and monumental buildings, while Secretary of Public Education José Vasconcelos commissioned artists like Diego Rivera to create murals that would rewrite history and instill revolutionary values in the citizenry. Part and parcel of Mexico's modernization efforts during both eras were the "civilizing missions" aimed at rehabilitating rural migrants, defining and redefining women's roles, and directing an empirical gaze at solving social problems like suicide, mental illness, and crime.[12]

The law did not punish those who committed suicide alone and of their own will. Assisting or coercing someone to commit suicide, however, was a punishable offense. In the late medieval period, a suicide might be denied a Christian burial and have his or her assets seized, but Enlightenment sensibilities that deemed suicide a rational choice or a result of insanity swayed juries and judges. Likewise, punishing heirs by confiscating the property of suicides also seemed less just in the modern era.[13] However, it is important to note that this shift in attitude was not clear-cut.[14] Cultural and legal leniency toward suicides and their heirs was indeed a sentiment of early modern Europe, but the harshness usually associated with medieval views was neither long term nor absolute.[15] Zeb Tortorici discovered that even priests in colonial Mexico did not view suicide in categorical terms. Priests buried in sacred ground one of their religious brothers who had committed suicide because they ruled that his body showed signs of regret. They read the body of the suicide and judged that their fellow priest had shown remorse, repented his decision, and struggled to free himself of the noose but that it had been too late.[16] Second thoughts and remorse allowed the priest a Christian burial.

Historians have paid meager attention to the phenomenon of suicide in Mexico, or in the rest of Latin America for that matter. One monograph treats the subject of suicide in Cuba, and there have been shorter essays and theses that examine the topic in other nations.[17] A Cuban sensibility accepted suicide as an escape route from a conflicted life. Cubans may have killed themselves for the same motives as people from other countries, but Cuban society viewed voluntary death as acceptable in many cases. Other studies focus on state and media responses to self-murder, paying little or no attention to the subjectivities of the suicides themselves. Suicide as a social phenomenon was truly an aspect of the modern era, emerging when states began to compile statistics on death, crime, and other measures that could disclose the fitness of society. The social meanings and interpretations of suicide reveal the myriad ways in which Mexicans experienced the world as liberal reforms and scientific advances impacted their daily lives. This study views the universal act of suicide from a historical viewpoint to understand the deed and its meanings in its cultural and temporal milieus. Although commentators romanticized suicide less often in the violent era of revolution than they had in the Porfiriato, both periods witnessed a transformation in the relationship of the self to society and the relationship of the citizen to the nation. The newspaper coverage was correct on at least one account: young, single men and women committed most suicides in these epochs.

Gender was a crucial factor in how people approached self-murder. Scholars have viewed suicide as a largely male event in Victorian and Edwardian London, imperial Russia, the post–Civil War U.S. South, and colonial and national Cuba.[18] Yet in the late nineteenth and early twentieth centuries, many Mexicans believed suicide to be a peculiar affliction of lovelorn youths and women. Official statistics, however, show that women did not kill themselves in especially large numbers but that young people did commit suicide more often than older individuals. Yet in a society preoccupied with the vicissitudes wrought by rapid social and economic changes, the spectacle of female and youth suicide magnified fears about the future. An expanded capitalist economy and workforce necessitated the employment of women. Social commentators argued that women had played important and sometimes very public roles in the revolution, but Mexican modernity in the 1920s and '30s prescribed "modernized patriarchy" or scientific motherhood as opposed to a republican motherhood of earlier times.[19] Both reified women's place in the home, although modernized patriarchy recognized women's capacity to be modern housewives who could apply science and technology to their domestic chores. Many believed family values steeped in religious mores were the best defense against suicide. Indeed, society believed that women ought to bear the travails of life's miseries with greater resolve than men because they had their traditional domestic refuge. Consequently, gender disorder—the perception that women increasingly transgressed norms by, for example, stepping out alone or challenging male authority—troubled some capitalinos. Specialists thought women committed suicide because they strayed from their prescribed gender roles. When men ended their lives, it was the "price of civilization." In prevailing gender ideology, madness or death awaited the woman who rejected the virtues of domesticity and piety.[20] The belief was that entering the world of men in work, politics, public spaces, and even art and literature would expose women to the same conditions that provoked suicidal impulses in men. The urban public space—its pace, sights, sounds, and dangers—provided the potential catalysts of self-destruction.

This is not a general study of death in Mexico. It is a study of suicide as a window on Mexican society and culture in a rapidly changing age. During the early twentieth century, Mexicans believed their nation to be in crisis. The specter of self-annihilation agitated the social imaginary of this dynamic society. Voluntary death spurred questions about the individual's relationship to the social whole. Louis Pérez argues that Cubans possessed a cultural understanding of suicide as self-sacrifice, especially in the defense of the nation. For example, Cuban politician Eddie Chibás shot himself on a live radio broadcast to protest corruption and political gangsterism, and his sacrifice resonates with Cubans to this day. Suicide could also be less heroic, however, and still be accepted by Cubans as a "plausible response to life."[21] Early twentieth-century Mexicans empathized with the motives or life circumstances that propelled individuals to self-murder, but they did not think it integral to what it meant to be Mexican (*lo mexicano*). Their responses to suicide echoed those of other urban centers: they worried about it, they studied it, and they wrote about it. Mexicans did not consider suicide to be an acceptable escape route or a measure to winnow the weak from the population. The act of suicide and the way it was interpreted by society reveal multiple meanings. Condemnation, sarcasm, empathy, and admiration were just a few of the ways that Mexicans responded. Argentines during the same time period viewed suicide to be an unpatriotic and antisocial act. Immigrants committed suicides at higher rates than native-born citizens, and experts viewed the scourge as a moral epidemic that could infect other social groups. Moreover, Argentine physicians regarded suicide as a European problem that immigrants planted on their soil. In other words, the "seed" of suicide had been rooted in immigrants before they planted their feet on South American soil and took the fatal steps to their deaths. Many also believed that an "excess of civilization" that was antithetical to the "psychology of the gaucho" led to self-murderous impulses in Argentines.[22]

Whereas scholars like Michael MacDonald, Terence Murphy, and George Minois[23] argue that the secularization of society led to the decriminalization of and greater forgiveness for the act of suicide, Susan Morrissey reminds us that religiosity persisted at the same time that societies became more secular. In early twentieth-century Mexico, even political leaders and intellectuals who embraced secularism still viewed suicide as a moral problem that ought to be condemned.[24] Likewise, Morrissey bristles at those who tell suicide as a story of modernity, arguing that scholars have been too influenced by Émile Durkheim's 1897 treatise on voluntary death, which placed its causes firmly in the alienating effects of modern society. Morrissey agrees that secularization was a top-down model of social change implemented by modern states, but she persuasively reasons that secularization coexisted with the religious: "The religious and secular are not opposing, however, but mutually complicit and highly political categories. Modern states continue to delimit the public domain of religion in a variety of ways; and secular powers have sacralized certain principles, such as the nation and the inviolable rights of the individual."[25] Morrissey examined suicide in imperial Russia, but her findings reveal many insights that also apply to the Mexican case. Secularization impulses began in Mexico during the Bourbon era and intensified in the nineteenth century as the country developed laws, civil codes, and political institutions. However, as several scholars have shown, liberal and anticlerical views did not equate with irreligiosity.[26] Morality and moral solutions to social problems like suicide prevailed among conservatives and liberals alike. Those improbable bedfellows believed that religion could inhibit self-murderous urges. Both political camps saw suicide as a crisis of morality. In other words, Mexico proceeded along a path of secularization like other nations of its time, but religious and moral prescriptions for individual and social problems did not fall away.

What set late Porfirian and revolutionary Mexico apart from Cuba and Argentina but in line with late imperial Russia was the preponderance of adolescent suicide. Statistical data from the time is rife with problems, but newspaper coverage supports surviving court records that show that young Mexicans under the age of twenty-five had the greatest likelihood of ending their lives. Regardless of the accuracy of statistics, Mexicans believed their young compatriots to be killing themselves at alarming rates. If a death wish infused the youth of the nation, what lay ahead for society? Émile Durkheim positioned suicide as the barometer to measure the vigor of a society. Suicide was another form of unnatural death, like homicide, that fueled the anxieties of urban residents and set the state apparatus to analyzing the phenomena and proposing remedies. However, whereas most believed that the compulsion to commit murder surfaced in the criminal mind, the impulse to commit self-annihilation was something more complex and unknowable. Journalists and medical experts vacillated between blaming atavism, degeneration, and environmental factors in the urban environment for propelling some individuals to leap in front of a trolley or gulp down rat poison.

The first part of the book presents the social and forensic context of suicide and death. Chapter 1 lays out the numerical and statistical context for the chapters that follow. It presents an analysis of the 157 extant suicide inquests from 1900 to 1930 collected by the Tribunal Superior de Justicia de Distrito Federal and currently housed in the Archivo General de la Nación. Statistics and statistics gathering at the turn of the twentieth century were inherently unreliable and subject to human error and values. However, the impulse to collect moral statistics in the late Porfirian era, with the rise of the sciences of sociology, psychology, and criminology, speaks volumes about what mattered to the intellectuals who governed the nation. It is clear that not all suicide inquests survived, as newspaper coverage of individual suicides very rarely coincides with case files in the archive. Furthermore, some families may have been able to have suicide files destroyed to protect their reputations. Moreover, incidences of suicide may have been still higher, as some suicides were likely deemed accidents or hidden by loved ones. The chapter discusses individual incidences of suicide and attempted suicide and examines such variables as age, gender, class, occupation, month, time of day, method, and origin.

Chapter 2 builds on the previous discussion to analyze the path of a suicide victim from body to corpse to cadaver. Some suicides undertook elaborate measures to prepare their bodies for death. Women, in particular, were likely to don their finest clothing and coif their hair. A few of them were determined to leave behind an exquisite corpse. Reporters and medical investigators had the first access to a corpse at the scene of death. Next, police station officials transferred the corpse to the Hospital Juárez for autopsy, and it essentially became a cadaver for scientific inquiry. Finally, it found its resting place in one of the many modern cemeteries or ossuaries that skirted the city. My analysis draws on the official forensic reports in the inquest files, newspapers reportage, visual sources like crime scene drawings and photographs, and popular culture to examine the scopophilic gaze directed at the female body. Officials read the suicidal body like a text and imbued it with multiple meanings informed by gender and class ideologies.

The next three chapters examine the meanings attached to suicide from multiple perspectives—the social, the medical, and the popular. A review of multiple newspaper articles and editorials from the secular and Catholic press, broadsides of José Guadalupe Posada, suicide letters, literature, and poetry provides the documentary base for chapter 3. The discussion analyzes the multiple narratives derived from numerous social imaginaries that competed and sometimes cooperated to make sense of the perceived suicide epidemic that shook Mexican society. The agents of suicide—those who succeeded and left a note behind, and those who attempted but failed to self-destruct—also interpreted their deaths in their own words. Fortunately for a researcher many years later, court officials investigated suicides to make sure they were not acts of homicide. They interviewed those who failed to kill themselves as they convalesced in hospitals or at home. Some claimed mental illness, but most said that they had sought the fatal escape because they had lost in love or had become estranged from loved ones. Others could not face the loss of their private or public honor and viewed death as a better alternative. Chapter 4 examines medical and forensic approaches to self-murder. Some Mexican scientists believed the causes of suicide to be biological *and* environmental. Others followed Émile Durkheim's arguments and placed the roots of suicide squarely in the urban environment. The environment was the modern city, its rapid pace, its changing technology, and the increasing alienation of the individual from family, community, and religion. Newspapers advertised a myriad of tonics and medicines to cure neurasthenia and other afflictions caused by excessive nervousness. Class and gender played significant parts in the interpretation and judgments of suicides, and these narratives acted out in media, judicial, and medical discourse. The documentary base of this chapter includes contemporary medical school journals, insane asylum intake questionnaires, case files of patients incarcerated in the asylums, and forensic medicine publications.

Theories of the production and everyday use of space to examine the public suicides of young men and women in symbolic public places of Mexico City in the first decades of the twentieth century take center stage in chapter 5. Individuals that opted for a public suicide made self-conscious decisions about how they would die, in particular choosing death sites for their personal and cultural meanings. Attempting to construct their selves in their suicides, young women in particular employed tropes of honorable death and conformed to a cultural logic of female suicide.[27] They took great pains to choose the site and method of their sacrifice in order to communicate significant meanings through their deaths. Men chose specific spaces in the city to author their deaths as well. Indeed, the locations of public suicides were not neutral geographies where life simply transpired. The production and the use of spaces in cities were constantly in tension. The people that designed public spaces and those that moved through them participated in their social construction.

Chapter 6 dissects how Mexicans processed and came to terms with death, especially tragic deaths of youth. It examines the moral panic that arose regarding the perceived propensity of youth to commit suicide and engage in other violent behaviors. The documentary base of this chapter draws mostly from editorials and media coverage that bemoaned the self-destructive impulses of adolescent Mexicans. The chapter also contrasts competing attitudes about death and how death ought to be commemorated in official and popular practice and discourse. I draw from the approaches of anthropologists and historians of emotions to read incidences of vernacular mourning and memorialization at suicide sites (popularly referred to as "stains of blood") for their political messages of marking untimely violent death and personalizing public issues like youth suicide.

# ONE

# A Social History of Suicide in Mexico City, 1900–1930

STATISTICS CONVINCE AND CONFUSE. Citing numerical data to back a claim lends it an air of legitimacy, but scholars acknowledge that the collection and interpretation of data can be problematic. Nonetheless, part and parcel of nation building in the nineteenth century was the establishment of institutions to collect data on everything from topography to mortality rates. Mexican officials first began assembling statistics to define the geographical and geological facets of the country. Description rather than determinism motivated early data collectors. As scientific politics took hold during the Porfiriato, a cadre of specialists expanded the scope of statistics gathering to population counts and number of marriages, births, and deaths. Not long afterward, counting incidences of crimes like homicide featured heavily in the mission of these experts. Statistics took a deterministic turn when Porfirian intellectuals started to wield them to rule society and gauge its advancement.

Statistical gathering and analysis were at the root of a scientific method to measure the march of progress. Indeed, the 1889 federal government publication, the *Periódico Oficial,* was prefaced with an 1888 directive that President Díaz wanted to present data at the 1889 Paris Exposition that showed not only the "material progress, but also the moral progress" that Mexico had achieved. The presidential order mandated that all states compile criminal statistics (including data on suicide) between 1870 and 1885 and send this information to the federal government.[1] Porfirian intellectual Antonio Peñafiel claimed that the use of statistics in Mexico began with the Chichimeca ruler Nepaltzin, who mandated a count of his people when they reached the Valley of Mexico after the conquest. To Peñafiel, it was natural that Mexicans would fancy statistics centuries later; it was in their DNA. He and his colleague Emiliano

Busto believed that statistics could accurately describe society, not with words but with numbers. Moreover, analyzing statistical tables would legitimate scientific approaches to social problems like epidemic disease and crime. They shared this sentiment with their European counterparts, who produced comparative statistical studies on crime, economic production, and disease. Comparative reports allowed states to gauge their levels of progress with others. As historian Mauricio Tenorio-Trillo noted, "only in a sea of numbers provided by all nations could the statistical picture of the ideal modern nation have emerged." [2] This keen worldwide infatuation with statistics could be seen most dramatically in exhibitions at world's fairs. What better way to portray the progress and splendor of a nation than through the display of products, photographs of engineering marvels, paintings, and statistical charts that could astound tourists, immigrants, and, especially, investors? Published statistics allowed nations to communicate their modern achievements to the world. Potential financiers could read statistical tables and decide whether a financial investment would likely bear fruit.

Like scientists, journalists wielded statistics to authenticate their arguments and claims. For example, *El Imparcial* and *Excélsior* printed statistical tables to lend authority to reporting in their pages. Numbers substantiated editorials that claimed rising crime or suicide rates in Mexico City. The collection of numerical data on population increases, railroad lines, and mining outputs signaled that Mexico was firmly on the track of progress. Journals like the *Boletín demográfico de la República Mexicana* published numerical and qualitative facts on the nation's advancement beginning in 1898. Directed by engineer José María Romero, *Boletín* published sections in French, Italian, and English. One stated aim of the publication was to prove Mexico's progress to potential foreign investors. The bulletin lauded the extensive networks of railroads in the nation and included statistics on kilometers of track laid, revenues enjoyed, and return on investment in railroad development. [3] Years later, the Mexican Academy of Jurisprudence and Legislation sponsored a series of lectures to celebrate Mexico's centennial in 1910. Francisco Barrera Lavalle delivered a lecture that same year on the history of statistics in Mexico from 1821 to 1910 that was subsequently published. [4] Barrera credited the intrepid officials of the Porfirian regime with expanding the types of data collected, which included demographic indicators like falling rates of epidemic disease. [5] The counternarrative to Mexican progress was also revealed in statistics. The average life expectancy of Mexicans was twenty-six-and-a-half years in 1900, twenty-nine years in 1910, and thirty-seven years in 1930. [6]

Infant mortality rates also concerned public health specialists, who worried that the death rate could stymie or even negate indicators of the country's advancement. A sick and dying population spelled disaster for Mexico. The physical and mental health of citizens consumed the energies of Porfirian and revolutionary statesmen alike. Statistics lent credence to stated claims about the public health of the city and legitimized the physicians and sanitation inspectors who developed programs to combat disease and raise hygiene standards among the city's population.[7] The collection and analysis of data found a home in institutionalized liberalism and gained renewed emphasis after the horrific death toll of the Mexican Revolution. Yet it is worth noting that, for all the promises of Pax Porfiriana, Mexico's population did not live longer or witness significant reductions in infant mortality rates during the reign of Porfirio Díaz.

## LIBERALISM AND SCIENTIFIC POLITICS

The late nineteenth-century ushered in a new era of liberalism among Mexican politicians and intellectuals. Scientific politics defined its divergence from the liberalism of early statesmen. The Reform Wars (1855–1861), the liberal triumph after the execution of Maximilian I (1867), and the ascension of Benito Juárez to the presidential seat signaled midcentury that the political tide had firmly shifted toward institutionalized liberalism. Instead of military men, a constitution, a body of secular laws, and professional politicians populated the halls of government. Porfirio Díaz seized the presidency in 1876, withdrew from office in 1880 to allow for a peaceful succession, and then reassumed the post in 1884—disregarding statements he made previously claiming he would not seek re-election. When he took office the second time, he surrounded himself with a cadre of educated professionals who promised to lead Mexico forward by relying on measurable scientific methods. According to historian Charles Hale, this generation of men rejected doctrinaire liberalism—what they sometimes called "metaphysical politics"—for a redefined positivist liberalism that required studying Mexican society to scientifically propose policies to correct social problems. Universal truths and doctrines fell into oblivion as experts studied social maladies in situ through empirical investigation. The findings allowed them to make procedural recommendations that they believed would regenerate society.[8] Their goals were to establish order, encourage progress, and, ultimately, secure Mexico's membership in the club of modern nations. These ideas and criticisms of the liberalism of Juárez found a voice in *La Libertad*, a newspaper supported by a government subsidy from Díaz. These experts garnered the moniker *científicos* (scientists), and among them were several intellectuals that will be mentioned throughout this study, including Justo and Santiago Sierra, Antonio Peñafiel, and Gabino Barreda.

French philosopher Auguste Comte provided the theoretical underpinnings of scientific politics. He refined his theory of positive philosophy, or positivism, in 1826. Comte believed that there was a hierarchy of sciences, from the simple and general to the more sophisticated and interconnected. Physiology (the study of the human body) and sociology (the study of such bodies as groups) were especially important to Mexican experts, and Comte ranked the latter as the most complex science and claimed that it was also undertheorized. Likewise, he considered human thinking to have a hierarchical positioning as well. Theological, or what Comte called "imaginary thinking," occupied the base range of complexity while the metaphysical made up the middle range. Scientific thinking was the most rarified and desired mode of knowledge and intellectual pursuit. Comte reasoned that scientists had abandoned the first two forms of thinking when they were analyzing the natural world but not when they were examining social phenomena. Ideally, a human mind would proceed in a positive direction from theological to scientific thinking. Metaphysical thinking (doctrinaire liberalism) was a sort of purgatorial knowledge state that científicos had passed through to reach a higher state of intellectual reasoning. Practically, this shift resulted in scientific liberals supporting the centralization of power and looking askance at popular sovereignty and other ideals of pure liberalism.[9] To men like Justo Sierra, Mexico was not ready for rule by consensus as suggested by Herbert Spencer. Public order would not emerge from a "natural strengthening of the social body."[10] A strong central authority like the Porfirian state had to be fortified, or Mexico would fail in its struggle to survive the process of evolution and extinction. Hale phrased it best: "The idea that society should be administered and not governed was an integral part of scientific politics at is origins."[11]

Although many would agree that statistics hide more than they reveal, Porfirian científicos thought that data gathering and the analysis of figures could yield answers to the etiology of suicide and other social problems, like crime. They believed that the individual made up just one part, albeit an important part, of the social organism, and thus statistics could yield information that would provide specialists the tools to combat moral diseases. Curing individuals—or, more importantly, preventing suicide—would improve the overall health of the social body. Contemporaries like criminologist Carlos Roumaugnac doubted the accuracy of statistics, but officials relied on them to make generalizations about the health of the body politic.[12] Data allowed experts examining the phenomenon of suicide to make generalizations about voluntary death, such as when it was most likely to occur, the most common reasons an individual would take his or her own life, where and how most victims committed the deed, and which categories of people (i.e., those of which age, gender, and social class) were most likely to kill themselves. Simply put, the state of society could be read through aggregated statistics—or in other words, moral statistics. Statistics are prone to human error when they are being collected and reported. Nonetheless, they are helpful in charting certain trends or patterns over time. When approached through the lens of social construction, the practice of gathering and using moral statistics reveals much about institutional concerns and priorities in their cultural context. Suicide is an apt example of a timeless act that gained enough urgency to be recorded and analyzed at the turn of the century.

## MORAL STATISTICS

*Statistique morale,* or the exploration of social phenomena (versus physical and natural facts), originated in early nineteenth-century Europe in the work of Parisian attorney André-Michel de Guerry and Belgian mathematician and astronomer Lambert Adolphe Quetelet. Both men posited that statistical composites "could strip away the particularities of the individual personality and come face to face with the essential properties of society."[13] Likewise, Italian physician Enrico "Henry" Morselli (1852–1929) reasoned that "official categorizers of suicides are always faced with many complex decisions to be made about these so-called psychological factors. Even the decision as to whether the individual knew the consequences of his actions is a very difficult psychological judgment in many instances."[14] Moral statistics were the fodder of sociological study at the time, and Mexican positivists like Barreda and Peñafiel embraced them as the best tools to define social problems and suggest solutions. Statistics revealed how certain measurable phenomena, like suicide and murder, recurred. Moral statisticians proposed that external factors rather than individual free will provoked suicide or murder.

Placing causality outside the individual defined suicide and violent crime as social rather than individual pathologies. If patterns of suicide and murder resembled patterns of natural death, then predictable laws "hidden from the naked eye" propelled individuals to kill themselves or others.[15] This deterministic viewpoint reasoned that, if free will operated in the commission of criminal and suicidal acts, then the rates of both would display randomness rather than regularity among certain social groups.[16] Likewise, if social laws determined behavior, then the environment could be changed to transform human beings and, ultimately, aberrant conduct.[17]

Employees working for the Dirección General de Estadística (General Board of Statistics), founded in 1882, collected, classified, and published data on a range of phenomena in Mexican society, including deaths, infant mortality, illness, crimes, and in some years, suicide. Published statistics lent legitimacy and authority to the state and its representatives, especially to public health specialists like doctors Eduardo Liceaga and Peñafiel. Rising premature death rates or incidences of epidemic illness allowed public health officials to implement policy based on what they considered the irrefutability of numerical indicators. Statistics gathering in combination with concerns about urban sanitation heralded a larger role of the state in individuals' lives, especially in the lives of the urban poor. In Mexico, public health specialists entered urban barrios to administer surveys, observe living standards, and make policy recommendations aimed at eliminating disease. The statistics they analyzed gave them the power "to impose order on most social and economic activities." Human bias interfered as well, in that most policy recommendations faulted "ignorance, backwardness and immorality of the urban population" as the root causes of disease.[18] These experts did not always comment on the fact that urban tenements often lacked methods to sanitarily dispose of human waste or the fact the infection spread quickly in crowded housing. Although believed to be objective, statistics were burdened with value-laden prejudice. Even in their collection and analysis, they could be seen as both quantitative *and* moral measures.[19]

European moral statisticians would dominate the way that suicide was approached until the early twentieth century. Their views and approaches culminated in the work of Émile Durkheim, a former student of Jean-Étienne Dominique Esquirol and the author of *Le Suicide* (1897). He argued that the moral aspect of suicide was paramount, even if external causes led individuals to self-murder. Moreover, any notion of an individual's right to extinguish his or her life was superseded by his or her subjugation to the rights of society.

In other words, taking one's life was a selfish and immoral action that had a negative impact on society.[20] Writing twenty years before Durkheim, Morselli proffered Darwinist analogies to argue that suicide, crime, and other social problems increased with the level of civilization. However, he contended that, like the linear progress of evolution, some elements fell away as societies evolved because they could not survive the process of natural selection. He did recommend education as a way to boost the wills of weak members of society, but he also took a Malthusian stance and argued that suicide and the death of frail humans were normal costs of the march of civilization.[21]

SEASONS OF SUICIDE

Many people today mistakenly believe that suicide rates spike during the holiday months. The stereotype communicates that those who spend holidays alone, when most people are enjoying the company of loved ones, are at an increased risk of committing self-murder. However, a recent article notes that the rates actually increase during springtime,[22] a finding first noted in the nineteenth century. Experts interviewed for the article theorized that semihibernation during the shorter days of the winter months exposed people to less human interaction and the accompanying frustrations that come with socializing. Likewise, work rhythms are less intense during that time, and agricultural activities come to a standstill. Spring heralds more work activity and human interaction and with it more potential for conflicts and stress. Morselli theorized that a "suicide belt" existed between latitude 47° and 57° north and between longitude 20° and 40° east. That range includes most of Western Europe. Mexico and the rest of Latin America lie outside of this alleged zone. According to Morselli, people residing in this belt possessed the strongest inclination to attempt suicide. He suggested that temperate climates, rather than extremely cold or extremely hot climates, provided the ripest conditions for self-destruction.[23] Mexico City's climate could be described as temperate, but it sat at the wrong longitude. Some researchers posit that climatic factors provoked by changing seasons trigger suicidal thoughts. Some believe that more sunshine and longer days are the culprits; others fault increases in temperature in the spring and summer months.[24] Nevertheless, historical trends seem to point to spring and summer months (no matter which hemisphere) to be the seasons of suicide. The statistics of

TABLE 1  Suicides and Suicide Attempts in Mexico City by Month and Gender, 1900–1930

| Month | Total | Men | Women |
|---|---|---|---|
| January | 9 | 7 | 2 |
| February | 10 | 6 | 4 |
| March | 20 | 9 | 11 |
| April | 10 | 6 | 4 |
| May | 10 | 6 | 4 |
| June | 8 | 5 | 3 |
| July | 18 | 9 | 9 |
| August | 11 | 9 | 2 |
| September | 15 | 11 | 4 |
| October | 16 | 7 | 9 |
| November | 14 | 10 | 4 |
| December | 16 | 6 | 10 |
| Total | 157 | 91 | 66 |

TABLE 2  Suicides and Suicide Attempts in Mexico City by Season and Gender, 1900–1930

| Season | Total | Men | Women |
|---|---|---|---|
| Winter (Dec-Feb) | 35 | 19 | 16 |
| Spring (Mar-May) | 40 | 21 | 19 |
| Summer (June-Aug) | 37 | 23 | 14 |
| Autumn (Sept-Nov) | 45 | 28 | 17 |
| Total | 157 | 91 | 66 |

suicide in Mexico City from 1900 to 1930 support this general trend. March drove the most women to suicide. September was the cruelest month for men. The suicide cases in Mexico City during this period show some patterns that mesh with studies of suicide in Mexico as a whole. In general, March, July, and September witnessed the most recorded monthly incidences of suicide among men and women (see tables 1 and 2). It was thought that the hottest months resulted in the highest incidences of suicide and crime.[25] Italian criminologist Cesare Lombroso supported this conjecture, and his Mexican peers agreed that high temperatures led to increased criminal activity.[26] Julio Guerrero wrote in 1901 that the number of fights and injuries diminished during the rainy season, when temperatures were also cooler.[27] For Mexico

City, October through May is the dry season, and June through September is the wet season. Interestingly, a 1968 study of the relationship between meteorological states and suicide found that reported suicides and suicide attempts skyrocketed in May as well. That month regularly produces the hottest temperatures nationwide.[28]

The statistics for Mexico City match national trends. Indeed, 72 percent (forty-eight) of the reported suicides and attempts among women occurred during the dry season. This statistic is of aggregated suicides and suicide attempts for the season; however, monthly peaks for women lie outside this period, in March, July, and September. The percentage of male suicide in the dry season was less striking, with 63 percent of all male suicides occurring during that climatological period. When broken down by conventional calendar seasons, the suicide rates distributed relatively equally for women, while autumn showed a spike for men. The statistics support the conjectures of theorists like Lombroso, Guerrero, and criminologist Alfonso Quiroz Cuarón, but the vagaries of reporting and archiving inquests mean that caution should be taken in making firm conclusions.[29] Mariano Ruiz-Funes García, a Spanish exile who taught at Universidad Nacional Autónoma de México, received the Lombroso prize (which celebrated the best works in medicine and criminology) in 1927 for his book *Endocrinología y criminalidad*. He theorized that climate impacted hormones, which in turn could cause immoral behaviors. A specialist in criminal law, Ruiz-Funes argued that a "primaveral crisis" struck from April to June and manifested in a rise in "blood crimes," like murder and suicide. Sexual crimes also rose during this season. He argued, "In this period of the year man, unable to control himself and dragged by the excitement of the psychomotor sphere, is in a particular state of drunkenness. These facts are attributed to red blood cells and also the endocrine glands."[30] Early twentieth-century criminologists and physicians considered crime and suicide to have physiological causes. They believed that the body and mind could be affected by patterns of temperature and rainfall.

The time of day that suicides occurred also interested scientists and jurists. Durkheim concluded that the majority of suicides in his study happened during the bustle of the workday. In her study of suicide in the 1960s and 1970s, however, Mexican sociologist María Luisa Rodríguez-Sala de Gómezgil found that most individuals killed themselves between the hours of 7:00 pm and midnight.[31] The surviving inquests examined in this study agree with the composite profile produced by Durkheim. By and large, men decided to kill themselves during the workday, with most committing suicide between the hours of 7:00 am and 9:00 pm. Women also chose the prime hours of the workday, from 1:00 pm to 9:00 pm, to commit suicide. In total, the hours between 1:00 pm and 3:00 pm, which correspond to mealtime and siesta, witnessed the most suicides. Many shops closed during this time. For men, it may have been the window of opportunity to leave their workplace and seek the privacy of the home to commit the deed. For women, it may have been an opportune time to find privacy while the household rested.

Most men and women committed suicide in the home—70 percent and 83 percent, respectively; 75 percent of all suicides took place at home. In this respect, Mexico's suicide demographics match those of other countries, with the private spaces of the home serving as the chosen site of most individuals bent on self-murder. The majority of suicides that did not occur in the home unfolded in other quasi-private spaces, such as a hotel room, a friend's home, or a bedroom in a brothel. Only 12 percent of suicides transpired in public places like parks, streets, and cantinas (see chapter 5). However a perusal of newspapers at the beginning of the twentieth century would make a reader think that dramatic public suicides were in fact commonplace. It is curious that most of the suicides reported in newspapers did not make it into surviving court records, suggesting that certain files may have been deliberately destroyed to protect family honor.

Minors (under age twenty-one) made up the bulk of suicides and attempted suicides by women, whereas most of the men who attempted or committed suicide were between the ages of twenty-one and twenty-five. Overall, individuals aged fourteen to twenty-five had the greatest rate of suicide, and it was also this age group that had the highest number of failed suicide attempts (see tables 3 and 4). The newspapers had it right when they lamented that suicide was a curse of youth in early twentieth-century Mexico. Other nations were also fretting about their young. For instance, suicide among adolescents panicked observers in the United States at the turn of the twentieth century. Reverend Samuel Miller of New York blamed the deaths on a weakening of moral values and a society that worshipped on the "altar of individual feeling." [32] This sentiment was not lost on the social engineers of the Porfirian and revolutionary eras in Mexico. Journalists had reported suicides on a regular basis since at least the 1870s, and they shared their international counterparts' estimation that suicides were on the rise in modern

TABLE 3 Suicides and Suicide Attempts in Mexico City by Age
and Gender, 1900–1930

| Age | Total | Men | Women |
|---|---|---|---|
| 14–20 | 53 | 16 | 37 |
| 21–25 | 42 | 26 | 16 |
| 26–35 | 30 | 19 | 11 |
| 36–50 | 16 | 16 | 0 |
| 51 and older | 5 | 5 | 0 |
| Total | 146 | 82 | 64 |

NOTE: Only 146 out of 157 case files noted the age of the victim.

TABLE 4 Suicides and Suicide Attempts in Mexico City by Success of Attempt,
Age, and Gender, 1900–1930

| Age | Total | Suicides | Suicide attempts | Suicides | Suicide attempts |
|---|---|---|---|---|---|
| | | Men | | Women | |
| 14–20 | 53 | 13 | 3 | 11 | 26 |
| 21–25 | 42 | 16 | 10 | 4 | 12 |
| 26–35 | 30 | 15 | 4 | 4 | 7 |
| 36–50 | 16 | 14 | 2 | 0 | 0 |
| 51 and older | 5 | 5 | 0 | 0 | 0 |
| Total | 146 | 63 | 19 | 19 | 45 |

NOTE: Only 146 out of 157 case files noted age of victim.

urban society. This led some newspapers, like *El Imparcial* and *El Nacional,* to lament the "suicide fever" that gripped the nation. What seemed to be especially upsetting to the public was the perceived rise in youth suicide, as the young were considered to be a social group that ought to be reveling in the joys of life. This was the era when adolescence as a special stage of childhood crystallized and the need to nurture, educate, and protect these youths gained currency. In some respects, Mexican society could understand that the mentally disturbed or the newly bankrupt might seek to end their lives, but the self-killing of seemingly healthy young on the cusp of adulthood seemed inexplicable and especially frightening to many. Debates ensued about why young Mexicans sought death over hope. In essence, the fear over the future of Mexico's youth sparked a moral panic over suicide.

More men successfully committed suicide than women (see table 5). This may have been in part due to women not being as determined as men to carry out the act, but women also employed less effective methods. In his study of suicide in 1930s Vienna, William Bowman notes that observers assumed men were more serious about taking their lives because they employed more violent methods, like the revolver or the noose. That more women failed in their attempts to commit suicide also led some to believe that they were actually seeking attention rather than death. However, statistics on attempted suicides are just as problematic as those on deaths by suicide.[33] Who knows how many attempts at suicide were concealed or how many victims were secretly treated by private family doctors? Attempted suicides might also be explained as accidents. For example, deaths reported as drownings may in fact have been suicides. The data from Mexico demonstrates that men employed firearms in 60 percent of suicide cases. Women used poisonous substances like mercury cyanide and strychnine in 64 percent of recorded cases. Poisons could certainly kill, but quick medical intervention could save lives. A well-placed gunshot, however, caused instantaneous death. The data for Mexico corresponds to what Louis Pérez found in his work on Cuba. Men and women in both nations committed self-murder with the instruments or substances they used in daily life.[34] Men were more likely to possess firearms, whereas women regularly used toxic substances in the home. Men and

TABLE 5 Suicide Methods Employed in Mexico City by
Gender, 1900–1930

| Method | Men | Women |
|---|---|---|
| Gun | 55 | 12 |
| Poison | 18 | 44 |
| Knife or cutting tool | 9 | 3 |
| Jumping off building | 5 | 3 |
| Hanging | 3 | 0 |
| Ingesting Matches | 0 | 2 |
| Drowning | 1 | 0 |
| Gas asphyxiation | 0 | 1 |
| Moving vehicle | 0 | 1 |
| Total | 91 | 66 |

women alike would have had access to arsenic and/or mercury-based medicines that were used to treat syphilis and other ailments. An overdose of those could easily bring death.

If you possessed resources, you would find it easy to purchase a Colt .45 or Browning pistol in Mexico City at the turn of the twentieth century. *Excélsior* advertised the sale of firearms in its pages. However, newspapers referred to suicide by gunshot as the elite male's method of self-murder. Before the revolution, employing the term "aristocratic revolver" signified that a suicide victim was a man or woman of the privileged classes.[35] However, soldiers and police also had guns at their disposal. Family members and friends could thus appropriate their pistols to commit the fatal act. During the 1920s, more women started to employ firearms to kill themselves. Some, like Olivia Rosenthal, already owned guns for protection. In fact, Olivia's husband testified that she slept with her gun under her pillow because of the frequent robberies in the city.[36] That Olivia used her gun to end her life did not surprise officials. Elvira Quintanar also shot herself with her own gun in 1923. She reported in her goodbye note that she worked in the mines as an interpreter and implied that she owned a gun to ensure her safety in that male sphere. Elvira wrote vaguely about her decision to commit suicide and suggested that a quick death was preferable to "many slow deaths."[37]

Poisons were easier to procure than firearms. Pharmacies, *boticas* (small drug stores), and hardware shops sold a variety of solutions and powders that could kill. Certainly, people bought cleaning supplies, disinfectants, rat poisons, and the like on a daily basis. Deadly poisons like the various cyanides and alkaloids could be easily purchased as these substances had applications in medicine in the late nineteenth and early twentieth centuries. Arsenic trioxide, famously featured in playwright Joseph Kesselring's 1939 *Arsenic and Old Lace,* was a favored poison of murderers as it could be administered in small doses that accumulated in the victim's body over time, eventually killing him or her. Arsenic taken in a large dose destroyed the gastrointestinal tract and caused a painful death. However, the poison could be readily dissolved in water and possessed no odor, color, or taste. Scientists figured out how to isolate arsenic in a body's tissues in the 1840s.[38] Arsenic was certainly the murderer's choice of poison in the nineteenth century. Rudolph Witthaus, a chemistry professor at Colombia University and author of *Medical Jurisprudence, Forensic Medicine and Toxicology* (1896), studied 820 deaths caused by arsenic poisoning between 1752 and 1889 and determined that at least half were murders. Accidental poisoning and suicide accounted for the other deaths. Arsenic is a heavy metal and a regular by-product of ore mining. In fact, medical treatments for infectious diseases like malaria and plague contained arsenic. Likewise, Salvarsan and Neosalvarsan, two drugs developed from 1907 to 1912 by Paul Ehrlich to treat syphilis, included arsenic and required weekly injections for a year or more. They seemed to be promising treatments, but unfortunately the side effects could be extremely disfiguring and painful, including liver damage, rashes, and general pain.[39] However, the treatment was a vast improvement over the mercury-based medicines, which caused ulcerations of the tongue and palate, swelling of the gums, and tooth loss. Veterinarians also used arsenic as a tonic to improve the health and stamina of horses.[40] When María Dolores Priego died after swallowing two spoonfuls of powdered arsenic in 1906, her friend Emilio Navarro testified that she lived in the home of a veterinarian who had the substance on hand to treat horses.[41] The inquest does not include an autopsy report, but surgeons would have employed a number of tests to determine which poison Dolores had ingested. Most tests required that tissues of the stomach or liver be macerated with a variety of chemicals. The heavy metal arsenic would leave behind a frosty layer of octahedral crystals on the test tube.[42]

Compounders included mercury, also known as quicksilver, in medicines and industrial products. Anyone would recognize mercury's silver globules from an old-fashioned thermometer or thermostat. It is toxic, although when it is ingested in this form it passes through a person's system. In fact, some people drank mercury as a cure for constipation in the mid-nineteenth century without it causing anything more acute than a sore mouth—although chronic ingestion could result in cancer.[43] Mercury bichloride, however, is an extremely lethal compound of elementary mercury and chloride in salt form. If consumed, it will lead to painful but (sometimes) quick death. Like its cousin sodium chloride (table salt), mercury bichloride absorbs readily into skin or any tissue it comes into contact with. Its corrosive properties loosen teeth and transform the stomach into a mass of bleeding ulcers. Autopsies of those poisoned by mercury presented telltale signs of damage to the kidneys, which had struggled to no avail to clear the lethal metal from the body. Since mercury bichloride was a prescribed cure for syphilis as well as a component of bedbug pesticides, laxatives, diuretics, and antiseptics, a person could easily get their hands on the lethal substance.

In 1929, Santa González Castro, a twenty-nine-year-old prostitute from Tehuantepec, traveled to Pachuca to purchase mercury bichloride from a pharmacy. She then returned to the capital, drank several bottles of beer and anise-flavored liquor, and ingested twelve pills. Roommates intervened, and Santa lived long enough to tell investigators that she had ingested the poison because her lover, Roberto Rivera, had deceived her.[44] Similarly, years earlier, in 1914, the Spanish madam of a brothel in Mexico City discovered that one of her prostitutes, Carmen Flores, had attempted suicide with mercury bichloride. The madam summoned physicians, who determined that Carmen was suffering gastritis as a result of poisoning. Carmen told investigators that her sweetheart had cheated on her and that she had decided to swallow the pills rather than face the heartache. She suffered for five days before succumbing to the ravages of the poison on her organs.[45] Although mercury bichloride was a common treatment for syphilis, Martin I. Wilbert, an official with the United States Public Health Service, called for the restriction of the compound in 1913. He cited large numbers of accidental poisonings and suicides resulting from its ingestion and advised that it only be available by prescription.[46]

Like mercury, cyanides occur naturally in nature. They can be found, for example, in plants, peach pits, and the secretions of millipedes. Chemists experimented with several forms of cyanide in the early twentieth century, and the compounds soon found their way into household and industrial products. Pesticides and disinfectants contained hydrogen cyanide, and sodium and potassium cyanides were used in mining, photography, and metal polishing. Famously, Nazis employed Zyklon B, which contained hydrogen cyanide, in German extermination camps during World War II. Cyanide was also the suicide agent for Third Reich officers, and Eva Braun and the Goebbels family used it to die rather than face capture by Allied soldiers in 1945. In fact, consuming food from a pot recently polished with a cyanide-based agent could kill a person. As journalist Deborah Blum puts it, "cyanides were useful, plentiful, easy to acquire—and astonishingly lethal."[47]

Those bent on suicide chose the poison for its rapid effect. Even low doses could kill within forty-five minutes. Cyanides bind with hemoglobin and basically starve the body of oxygen. Death by cyanide might be quick, but it is "brutal, marked by convulsions, a desperate gasping for air, a rising bloody froth of vomit and saliva, and finally a blessed release into unconsciousness."[48] Murderers seeking to poison their targets usually avoided cyanides because they left telltale signs. Forensic investigators were able to recognize cyanide poisoning by a bluish mottling of the victim's skin and a faint scent of almonds emanating from the body. Regardless of the gruesome effects of cyanide, many chose to ingest it anyway. Seventeen-year-old Carmen Díaz had been living in a consensual union with Homero García for six months in 1925 when he informed her that he was planning to leave the capital without her. Carmen then bought some pink pills at a botica on the pretext of killing rats and rented a room in the Hotel Juárez. The maid there testified that the young woman summoned her to deliver a note to her house at noon. When she returned to the room at midday to pick up the letter, Carmen grabbed a glass off the table and declared, "Look, I am going to poison myself." The maid fought her for the glass, but it was too late. She called other employees of the hotel, and an ambulance transported the ailing woman to the hospital. Carmen left behind letters to Homero, her mother, and her friends. She died almost a month later in the hospital.[49] Men were less likely to use poison in their suicide plans, but when they did, they also employed easily obtained chemicals. Alfonso Vallejo, a thirty-nine-year-old member of the *rurales* (rural police force), admitted before he died that he had consumed mercury cyanide, a medicine he used in the treatment of his horses. He wrote a letter specifically informing his surgeons, "I think there is no need for autopsy nor medical study. The drug I took is mercury cyanide."[50]

Other toxic chemicals and corrosives employed in suicides included iodine, cleaning fluids, kerosene, and chloroform. The last mentioned was a revolutionary anesthetic for surgeons in the nineteenth century, but at the turn of the twentieth century the American Medical Association requested that hospitals cease using it because of accidental overdoses. However, anyone could find chloroform on pharmacy shelves for many more decades. Chloroform was an ingredient in cough syrups, a common sleep aid, and a cure for seasickness, hiccups, colic, and diarrhea. It is an unpredictable mix of carbon, hydrogen, and chlorine; a small amount might kill one person but not another. Carlota Alatorre mixed it with laudanum in 1914 in an attempt to kill herself when her lover accused her of infidelity.[51] She survived. Some years later, in 1927, investigators found Luz María Berlín on the floor of the Santa Catarina church at the corner of Brasil and Nicaragua streets with an empty bottle of chloroform beside her. She died without leaving testimony.[52] Others chose potassium permanganate, a substance sold sometimes as Condy's crystals or powders. A popular and effective disinfectant in the home, potassium permanganate was also used by photographers in flash powder.

The cheapest poison could be extracted from matches. Sometimes, a carton of cigarettes came with a free box of matches, and the phosphorus tips of the matches could cause death if someone ingested enough of them. The white phosphorus causes intense gastritis and literally burns through the stomach or intestines. The handling of phosphorus could even poison the workers making matches. There was so much concern worldwide about accidental poisonings and suicides via match eating that the U.S. Congress held hearings in 1912 on white phosphorus matches.[53] In 1911, eighteen-year-old María Concepción Avendaño, who had suffered the jealousy and suspicion of her boyfriend, cut the phosphorus tips off two boxes worth of matches, dissolved them in water, and drank the fiery liquid. She survived after treatment at the Hospital Juárez.[54] Phosphorus poisoning allowed time for the victim to be rescued or even have a change of heart.

MOTIVES AND SUICIDE

A social angst seemed to have settled over Mexico City at the turn of the twentieth century. Newspapers and broadsides reminded residents of this cultural malady daily. What drove men to pick up a revolver and fire a shot into their body? What compelled women to swallow mercury cyanide and suffer a painful and gasping death? The reasons provided in goodbye notes and testimonies of those who committed or attempted suicide were clear-cut for women. Thirty-seven percent stated that they had been deceived in love. Twenty-eight percent claimed that *disgustos* (displeasures or conflicts) with a spouse, a parent, or another loved one drove them to end their lives (see table 6). Men blamed mental illness, deception in love, financial hardship, or physical illness; however, no particular motive claimed by men stands out as the most popular. From 1900 to 1930, dishonor drove three men and three women to suicide, but the motive did not always communicate deception. For men, dishonor could be a slight to their financial reputations. The majority of women clearly asserted that emotional strife caused by conflict with loved ones or deception in romantic relationships was the cause of their morbid impulse. Men killed themselves for emotional reasons as well. Only thirteen of the fifty-nine recorded suicides and suicide attempts with a recorded motive listed the male suicide motivations of financial hardship or physical illness.[55] Emotional reasons were the leading motivations for suicide for the subjects of this study. Adolescents with little life

TABLE 6  Reasons Reported for Suicide in Mexico City
by Gender, 1900–1930

| Reason | Men | Women |
|---|---|---|
| Deception in love | 7 | 19 |
| *Disgustos* | 5 | 16 |
| Mental illness | 9 | 2 |
| Tired or bored with life | 5 | 6 |
| Financial hardship | 7 | 0 |
| Dishonor | 3 | 3 |
| Love | 5 | 1 |
| Physical Illness | 6 | 0 |
| Death of a loved one | 1 | 4 |
| Despair or sadness | 4 | 1 |
| Moral failings | 4 | 1 |
| Alcoholism | 3 | 1 |
| Totals | 59 | 54 |

experience may have felt lost love or public slights more deeply than older people. For example, in 1911, José Díaz claimed in a letter to Francisco Vega that he would rather die than live with a public assault on his honor. A cantina owner had called him a "petty thief without shame" (ratero sin verguenza) in front of several patrons. Díaz felt so much shame that he swallowed strychnine at his workplace.[56] The surviving suicide inquests from 1900 to 1930 in Mexico City mesh with the newspaper reporting on suicide. Unrequited love or deception in love was what drove most young Mexicans to suicide in this period.

Newspaper coverage of suicides had society believing that the very rich and the chronically idle were at a higher risk of killing themselves. Others who were likely to attempt suicide included those who were not able to achieve social mobility after they moved to the city from the provinces. The suicide inquest documents remaining in the national archive today rarely line up with newspaper reports on individual suicides. Newspaper editors found that the public was most fascinated by the suicides of prominent members of capital society or aspiring migrants from the provinces. Of the fifty-five cases that reported occupation, 38 percent listed the victims as artisans. Another 20 percent were identified as *empleados,* an expansive category that included civil servants, business employees, and the like. *Comerciantes* (traders or merchants) made up 18 percent (this group also had

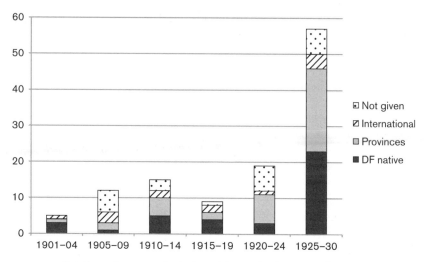

FIGURE I. Suicides and attempted suicides in Mexico City by origin of victim, 1900–1930. Source: Suicide case files from 1900–1930, Tribunal Superior de Justicia de Distrito Federal, Archivo General de la Nación, Mexico City.

a 100 percent success rate at completing suicide). A smattering of students, professionals, soldiers, and unskilled laborers made up the remainder, 24 percent of the total.

Civil status also played a significant role in who might or might not seek self-destruction. Single men made up 76 percent of all cases. The birthplace or origin of suicides did not always make it into the documents. However, 93 of the 157 cases recorded origin. Although newspapers relished romanticizing the suicides of people that hailed from the provinces and were not able to achieve their dreams in the bustling city, in reality just as many Mexico City natives killed themselves as migrants. There was no marked different in the gender of native and migrant suicides either. However, as figure 1 demonstrates, there was some variation in the proportion of migrant suicides depending on the decade. For example, after the battles of the revolution had ceased, the number of migrant suicides outstripped the number of Mexico City native suicides. The revolution displaced rural inhabitants, especially those that had resided in villages to the north and south of Mexico City. Rural migrants flooded the capital, which saw little violence during the conflict aside from the Ten Tragic Days (La decena trágica) in 1913, when a military coup ousted President Francisco Madero and installed Victoriano Huerta. Fierce fighting broke out throughout the city, mayhem and looting ensued, and capitalinos strived to avoid stray bullets.

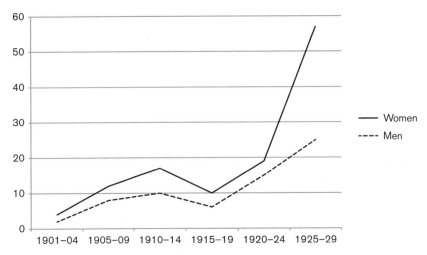

FIGURE 2. Suicides and attempted suicides in Mexico City, 1900–1930. Source: Suicide case files from 1900–1930, Tribunal Superior de Justicia de Distrito Federal, Archivo General de la Nación, Mexico City.

After a week and a half of pitched battles, residents finally had some peace, but the streets were filled with "rubble, jumbles of wire, dead horses, and dead people, and a harsh wind scattered dust and disease in all directions."[57] Migrants had been cut from their familial bonds and found themselves in a city teeming with strangers. Unrealized goals, the insecurity of daily life, and dislocation may have caused the spike in migrant suicides from 1920 to 1930. Figure 2 shows a spike in suicides after 1920, especially among women. However, the increase could be explained by the establishment of more careful archiving and the better preservation of inquests that followed the revolution, as the post-conflict peace allowed for orderly court business and recordkeeping.

Surviving archival records indicate that more suicides and attempts at suicide occurred in working-class and lower-middle-class neighborhoods of the federal district. Neighborhoods to the west and southwest of the central historical district housed more prosperous families, and these zones saw a smaller incidence of suicide than lower-class areas (see chapter 5 for a discussion of this). The greatest number of suicides hailed from barrios like Doctores and El Centro, two areas that had a majority of working-class residents. The newspapers reported plenty of suicides and attempted suicides among the more prosperous classes as well; however, inquest files have not been found for most of them.

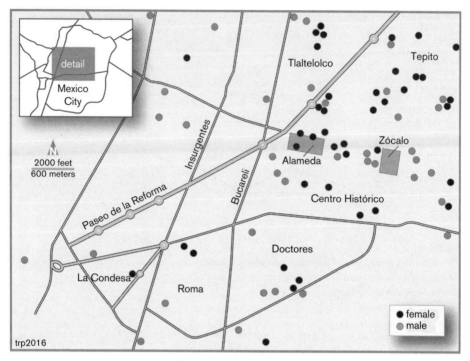

MAP I. Locations of suicides in Mexico City, 1900–1930. Map by Thomas Paradise.

CONCLUSION

The statistical conclusions in this chapter are based on available archival data and are thus not definitive. However, artisan, empleado, and comerciante were clearly aspirational occupations, and since 76 percent of all suicide investigations extant in the archive recorded victims as having these trades, there may be some credence to the notion that having one's chances for social mobility blocked could weaken the will to live. Mexico enjoyed material and social improvements after the revolution, but there were economic troubles in the country. Most artisan and middle-class workers could not secure mortgages to purchase houses in the modern housing developments that sprung up around the city. Although the revolutionary battles had ceased and Mexico had an elected president, the Cristero rebellion raged on from 1926 to 1929, and the Catholic Church encouraged economic boycotts. The Mexican economy started its downward decline in 1926, three years before the New York stock market crashed. By 1930, unemployment had increased 350 percent, and the economy had contracted by one-fifth.[58] Daily pressures of securing a living must have confronted many capitalinos and led a fraction of them to seek a final exit. The eternal problem of love gone awry remained a constant through historical eras, and it especially affected women.

The government's decision to collect statistics on social problems like suicide, murder, and infant mortality also suggests that politicians desired to analyze social conditions in order to prescribe prophylactic measures to improve the moral and physical health of the social body. Statistics could also prove progress. Through keeping statistics, Mexicans would find that they were right to fear that suicidal impulses most infected the young. They would also discover that there were "seasons" of suicide for men and women alike. More generally, the collection of statistics fostered and legitimized public health campaigns to evaluate the capital's population and formulate social theories about the causes of mental illness or premature death.

# TWO

## *From Corpse to Cadaver*

### SUICIDE AND THE FORENSIC GAZE

THE ADVENT OF HIGH MODERNITY and capitalism fastened social identity to the body, bringing about what theorists have called "embodied self-identity."[1] In other words, modern consumer culture and its shaping of clothing styles, grooming, and public conduct located the body as a central and dynamic element of self-identity.[2] The body became another component of the self, inseparable from the interior self. One inhabits the body and subjectively feels and moves that body.[3] However, discourses of power that shape social norms might also act on that "docile" body.[4] Bodies are both active and acted upon. Language, or discourse, becomes another facet of "being-in-the-world."[5] The embodied self becomes a body and a self in crisis in the event of sudden and unnatural death. The body after death transforms from a fount of self-identity to an object of social identity that is reflected on from outside by mourners, doctors, and spectators. The self-conscious suicide that methodically planned for death reflected on his or her self in the final preparations. Choosing the clothing, grooming, setting, material objects, and even weapon of choice served as last self-reflexive actions of the individual devoted to self-murder. Just as death became more ritualized beginning in the early modern era, some suicides followed scripted practices to achieve death as well.[6] Once the body expired and became a corpse, it remained a text that could be read for information. Readers of the corpse also inscribed meaning on it *and* the circumstances that led to death. For example, reporters who gazed at a well-dressed corpse or investigators who surveyed the scene made certain judgments about the personal biography of the victim and what factors might have propelled him or her to suicide. Likewise, the body lying on the dissection slab of the morgue became a cadaver to be probed, cut, and analyzed by forensic specialists responsible for determining cause of death and advancing medical science. Through the trajectory from live body to corpse and finally to cadaver, varying meanings were inscribed on the body, and this was especially true of the female body, as death and the feminine have been linked for centuries in Western culture.[7] Examining the female body from its preparation for death to corpse at the death scene to cadaver on the cold slab of the morgue and finally to burial allows the scholar to glean much about Mexican society during the first decades of the twentieth century.

Margaret Higonnet theorizes, "To embrace death is at the same time to read one's own life. . . . In their deaths, many are obsessed with projecting an image, whether to permit aesthetic contemplation or to provoke a revolution in thought." Although far fewer women commit suicide than men, Higonnet contends that a "mythic vision of suicide as feminine" exists.[8] Indeed, in early twentieth-century Mexico, nothing titillated authors and readers more than the young female suicide. Readers of dailies devoured the details of such stories. Reporters narrated the tragic biographies of these women for capitalinos, describing them as having been in the flower of life, full of so much promise and innocence. Reporters even acted as lay forensic experts, especially when writing about young women who hailed from the middle and upper classes and presumably had promising futures before them. They sought to figure out why these women had chosen to end their lives. They also endeavored to describe the death scenes in as much detail as possible, dedicating particular care to the lifeless but still beautiful female body. They interviewed the victims' loved ones and made bold conjectures about the emotions and motivations of the young women. Journalists' extensive access to crime scenes and morgues would shock us today. Positivist ideologue and physician Gabino Barreda wrote of a "fin-de-siècle pornography of violence" and "the masculine obsession for dead women."[9] The words of naturalist writer and diplomat Federico Gamboa epitomized both the public access to the recently deceased and the male fascination with the dead female body. Writing in his journal, he described his visit to the morgue in the Hospital Juárez to view the corpse of Esperanza Gutiérrez, a first-class prostitute more commonly known as La Malagueña (the woman of Málaga, Spain). Another sex worker, María "La Chiquita" Villa, shot her in 1897 because she believed that Gutiérrez had stolen her suitor. Gamboa professed to have attended a dance that La Malagueña had been at the night of her murder, and he said that he had even chatted briefly with her. The murdered prostitute served as one of his muses for his wildly popular naturalist novel, *Santa* (1903). In his diary entry describing the morgue scene, he teeters between contemplating her stone-cold body and reflecting on the impermanence of his own life.[10] Jean Franco described Gamboa's tone best:

> He meditates on the decomposition of the body, a fate that awaits us all. Most of all he is "fatally attracted" to "the scar of her wounded eye, the diminutive scar over which fell her proud, disordered blonde hair, now disheveled and dirty." What fascinates him? Is it the fact that she cannot return the look because there is no eye? The dead Malagueña makes Gamboa uneasily aware of the scopic power of the male look because here the object offers no barrier, no distance. There are no clothes, no lowered or defiant gaze. For once, the powerful male eye hesitates. But only for a moment. The diary becomes the place of public penance where sexual guilt can be exorcised as a meditation before the *mementi mori*. In other words, the transcoding of the low sexual into the social allows Gamboa to reaffirm traditional values.[11]

Elisabeth Bronfen might surmise that Gamboa, in reflecting on the murdered woman's body, experienced "death by proxy," dying with La Malagueña but then having the fortune to "return to the living." Bronfen argues that death and femininity are disruptive forces that are culturally constructed and serve as "ciphers for other values, as privileged tropes."[12] The suicidal body, in contrast to the murdered body, takes the position of subject and object. In other words, self-murder is a "communicative act" that allows a woman to "gain the subject position only by denying her body." Dying by her own hand positions a woman to refute "social normative debates" on the link between the dead feminine body and inferiority. Bronfen states, "Staging disembodiment as a form of escaping personal and social constraints serves to criticize those cultural attitudes that reduce the feminine body to the position of dependency and passivity, to the vulnerable object of sexual incursions. Feminine suicide can serve as a trope, self-defeating as it seems, for a feminine writing strategy within the constraints of patriarchal culture."[13]

A woman who exterminates herself as an act of agency may seem to be committing a self-defeating deed in many ways, but suicide has always been a political act.[14] Although suicides become objectified after death as journalists gaze at and describe most intimately their corpses and scientists probe into the mysteries of their tissues and organs, these women took great efforts to contour the postmortem narrative. The preparation of the body and scene was a key component of this strategy. When they left letters behind, most suicides asserted that they alone were responsible for their deaths. These statements were intended to save loved ones from unnecessary interrogation but also to save their bodies from the cut of the scalpel. Nonetheless, the state required autopsies in cases of unnatural death.

## LEGAL MEDICINE AND FORENSIC PRACTICE

The official connection between police investigation and medical science in Mexico began in 1833. The Establecimiento de Ciencias Médicas (Establishment of Medical Sciences) appointed a team of professors to make up the Departamento de Medicina Legal (Department of Legal Medicine) in Mexico City. Agustín Arellano was its first appointee, and he also worked with the Comisión de Higiene Pública y Policía Médica (Commission of Public Hygiene and Medical Police), which was also part of the Establecimiento de Ciencias Médicas. The Departamento de Medicina Legal experienced some tumult in its early years, but by 1849, Luis Hidalgo y Carpio had ushered in an era of pioneering forensic medicine. Hidalgo y Carpio served as president of the Sociedad Médica de México (Medical Society of Mexico), the precursor to the Academia Nacional de Medicina (National Academy of Medicine). The attorney Rafael Roa Bárcena, another pioneer in forensic education, wrote the first textbook that combined law, criminal procedure, and legal medicine. His *Manual razonado de práctica y médico-legal forense mexicana* (1860) provided Mexican legal-medical students and practitioners with the first guide to understanding how medicine linked with criminal proceedings. Before this, they had had to consult Spanish and French textbooks and then revise that knowledge based on Mexican penal law. Roa Bárcena's 529-page book defined and classified crimes, discussed criminal process, and classified forensic categories such as injuries and lesions, autopsies, poisoning, and insanity, among others.[15] Hidalgo y Carpio was one of Roa Bárcena's contemporaries. A professor at the national medical school, the Escuela Nacional de Medicina, he specialized in the toxicological analysis of blood and published a book that provided forensic experts guidelines for determining poisonous elements in the body. Hidalgo y Carpio joined other experts on a committee to draft Mexico's first penal code, which President Benito Juárez enacted in 1871. Hidalgo y Carpio collaborated with physician Gustavo Ruiz y Sandoval to write *Compendio de medicina legal: Arreglado a la legislación del Distrito Federal,* which was published in 1877 and assigned in the Escuela Nacional de Medicina. The illustrious physician died in 1879, but his legacy for legal medicine and investigation persisted. Later criminologists like Carlos Roumagnac were likely influenced by his writings on free will and the individual study of criminal types and their physical and mental abnormalities.[16] Twentieth-century specialists had myriad forensic publications from the late nineteenth century to draw on. In their study of forensic science in Mexico, Mario Alva-Rodríguez and Rolando Neri-Vela list more than fifteen theses in legal medicine written at the Escuela Nacional de Medicina before 1900.[17] Indeed, the late nineteenth century was the era of putting positivist science into practice to study and solve social problems.

Medical personnel assigned to police stations accepted the bodies of victims of fatal crimes, including alleged suicides, from the eight district courts beginning in 1880. Live and wounded victims were quickly transported to hospitals. The station's physicians worked closely with prison doctors and the medical personnel at Hospital Juárez, the official site for autopsies. The courts also housed a forensic council and a cadre of legal-medical experts, who participated actively in the administration of justice and its investigations. The 1903 Judicial Organization Law (Article 114) delineated the Forensic Service as a collaborative enterprise between hospitals, police stations, prison doctors, and legal-medical experts. Article 119 of the law required Mexico City's forensic team to include two chemists, a practicing physician, four forensic experts, and two porters. The districts of Tacubaya, Tlalpan, and Xochimilco also housed one forensic expert. Forensic experts had to meet certain criteria, including having a morally upright reputation, having obtained the status of professor with a combined degree in surgery, medicine, and obstetrics, having completed five years of experience, and having reached at least thirty years of age.[18]

Ruiz y Sandoval and Hidalgo y Carpio included a section on suicide in their 1877 *Compendio*. The authors began by noting that it would be useless to judge the morality of the act because suicide was not a crime. They wrote that, in cases of self-murder, physicians and judges should determine if mental illness had played a role and if the suicide acted alone, pointing out that Article 559 of the 1871 penal code mandated five years in prison for any person who ordered another to commit suicide, one year in prison for anyone who instigated suicide, and a fifty- to five-hundred-peso fine for anyone who acted as an accomplice.[19] The physicians wrote that some argued that suicides lacked reason, but they disagreed with this, stating that reason separated humans from animals. They argued that violent passion and ordinary reason could drive someone to self-murder. Mundane motives included financial difficulties, and emotional motives included covering shame. Mental illness

may have propelled some to self-murder, but the physicians argued that suicide letters proved the rationality of many who chose death over a lifetime of
moral or physical suffering. The rationale smacked of individualism and of
one's right to dispose of one's life as one saw fit. Ruiz y Sandoval and Hidalgo
y Carpio surmised that the suicide rate was highest among those aged forty
to sixty; however, the cases considered in the present study do not support
that conjecture. They claimed that women were afraid that losing their hair
or having no eyelashes would render them unattractive to men and noted
that this made them vulnerable to suicidal impulses.[20] The authors could
only see frivolous reasons for female suicide. In the cases I examine in this
study, however, mental anguish rather than vanity propelled women to kill
themselves.

The *Compendio* discussed causes of death and delineated the different
methods of suicide and how investigators might determine the difference
between a self-inflicted injury, a murder, and an accident. They explained
that a medical investigator would find that a self-inflicted wound left by a
cutting instrument was generally made from left to right and had ragged
borders, whereas in cases of homicide the wound went from right to left and
had clean borders. A later forensic medicine manual written by Alfonso
Quiroz Cuarón agreed that wounds left by a cutting instrument exhibited
cleaner borders in homicides.[21] The presumption was that a suicide's hand
shook violently and thus made a ragged cut. Death by hanging almost always
indicated suicide. However, murderers had been known to strangle their
victims and then hang them to make it look like self-murder.[22] Firing a gun
into the mouth had the best chance of achieving death, as the bullet would
usually make a fatal course to the brain. Investigators suspecting suicide by
gunshot ought to look for signs of gunpowder on the hands of the victim, but
they should not rely on this observation to make a conclusion of suicide. Ruiz
y Sandoval and Hidalgo y Carpio credit Alexandre Jacques François Brierre
de Boismont for instructing forensic investigators to also look for burn marks
on the clothing. Brierre de Boismont reasoned that a murderer would fire a
gun from a distance, and this would not result in any burning of the victim's
clothes. Death by falling from a high elevation could confound investigators.
A person could be pushed, jump on their own, or simply lose their footing
and fall. In the case of potential homicide, investigators needed to determine
whether the victim had suffered a fatal injury before he or she fell or were
thrown from a high elevation. If an accidental fall was assumed, specialists
were instructed to examine the digestive system for signs of inebriation and

the brain for indicators of apoplectic attack.[23] The chief objective of medical experts was to advise the judge on who perpetrated the fatal act: the victim or someone else.

Autopsy was the destiny of a suicide's corpse. A formally staged dissection allowed physicians to determine cause of death and, at the same time, furthered medical knowledge. Two medical experts were to conduct each postmortem. The process was laid out simply in the *Compendio*. Curricular changes at the Escuela Nacional de Medicina in 1907 required that practical exams like dissection replace written tests.[24] The school's provost at the time, Dr. Eduardo Liceaga, led the innovation. He believed that students would learn more with their surgical tools, eyes, and hands than they could by reading a textbook. The *Compendio* instructed surgeons to disrobe the cadaver and take special care to preserve the clothing for further scrutiny. It tutored experts to determine gender and look over the body for scars, deformities, birthmarks, and signs of previous injuries. The specialist should also observe the hands, feet, and chest for signs that the person had practiced a certain occupation. Signs of putrefaction and rigor mortis ought to be noted, as they could reveal how long ago the death occurred. Doctors should examine all natural orifices, including the anus and vagina, for signs of injury and/or sexual activity. It should be noted if a male cadaver exhibited an erect penis or signs of ejaculation or if a female cadaver displayed a loose and wrinkled belly. Physicians wanted to know if a woman had recently given birth or if a man or a woman had had sex shortly before death. Finally, before taking up the scalpel, experts were to approximate the subject's age, though the authors noted that drowning caused a cadaver to look older than it was.[25]

Once forensic experts completed the exterior examination, they began the dissection. If the body showed a visible wound, they started there. If no visible wound existed, the autopsy began at the head. Surgeons first cut laterally from ear to ear and longitudinally down the face and then carefully lifted the skin to examine the skull and tissues beneath. A strong scalpel and tapping instrument allowed the surgeons to gently open the skull to scrutinize the brain and its cavity. The *Compendio* detailed which hand to use or which fingers to probe with as the autopsy continued. Doctors were instructed to carefully observe all parts of the brain and note bleeding, bruising, or other injuries that might have caused death. Once the brain matter was surveyed in the cranium, surgeons removed all of it, setting it on the operating table and then severing the nerves and removing the pituitary gland. They then cut the brain on a longitudinal axis to reveal the ventricles, glands, and other parts of its structure. Next, they cut down the neck from the lower lip to the sternum of the cadaver with lateral incisions and peeled back the skin to reveal the muscles and tissues below. Cutting deeper, they exposed the diaphragm, lungs, and pericardium. Next, they turned their attention to the organs. The goal of this stage of the autopsy was to get under the exterior shell of the cadaver to reveal the mysteries of the organs, tissues, and muscles beneath. At this juncture, the cause of death might be evident to doctors, but forensic practice required removing the intestines to better examine the liver and kidneys. When autopsying a female cadaver, surgeons would cut through the pubis to examine the uterus and reproductive organs. Next, the cadaver would be flipped face down so that the spinal column could be dissected. The removed stomach was emptied of its contents for inspection and chemical analysis if poisoning or inebriation was suspected. Finally, all organs and other parts of the body were returned to their proper places, the skin was sewn up, and a sheet was placed over the cadaver before it was set in a box for transfer to family members or the cemetery.[26] The surgeons were exacting and thorough in their dissembling and scrutiny of the body. No wonder suicides pleaded in their goodbye notes for their bodies not to undergo autopsy!

Forensic experts could readily determine death by asphyxiation or gunshot. Poisoning could produce telltale signs on the corpse as well. However, specialists endeavored to determine the type of poison that resulted in death. As discussed in chapter 1, women preferred poison as a method of suicide. The *Compendio* instructed experts to examine the esophagus, stomach, and intestines in place. They were then directed to remove the stomach, empty the contents into a vessel, cut through the stomach walls, and lay the flayed organ on a clean sheet of glass. All particles left behind on the stomach walls and mucous membrane were to be removed for further inspection. Experts recorded any discoloration or abnormalities in the stomach and then placed it in a glass jar. The same procedure was undertaken with the intestines. In cases of possible poisoning, the liver, kidneys, spleen, and brain were placed in glass jars as well. The experts also collected as much blood as they could recover from the body for chemical analysis. The manual warned that the contents of the various specimen jars should be treated carefully and sealed with soaked parchment paper and corks rather than sealing wax, which sometimes contained metals that could interfere with a chemical analysis. The specimen jars were sent to medical experts associated with the court, who used microscopes to analyze their contents. The section on autopsy procedure in the manual ended with a warning that exhumed corpses might show traces of arsenic and/or mercury in their tissues because both occurred naturally in soil and agricultural products and were also common ingredients in medicines.[27] In other words, victims may have absorbed arsenic and mercury in their tissues from the natural environment or through their ingestion of common medicines. The presence of these compounds in bodily tissues may not always mean intentional poisoning.

Faced with an array of organs and tissues in jars but no other forensic evidence, legal-medical experts had to determine if poison caused the death. Ruiz y Sandoval and Hidalgo y Carpio reminded their readers that experts would often not see the entire body of a patient or possess knowledge of the symptoms, so they had to make their conclusions from analyzing individual organs. Poisons of a vegetal nature were more difficult to discern than mineral-based toxins, which could be determined by chemical analysis. To ascertain which toxin had been used, a doctor would cut the target tissue into small pieces, submerge them in alcohol, and heat and agitate them until they dissolved. After twenty-four hours, he poured the contents through a filter to capture any solids. He then strained the liquids a second time to form a soft extract that could be administered to a test animal like a dog, frog, or rabbit. If the animal died, the victim had indeed been poisoned.[28]

The manual instructed legal-medical experts to assume poisoning if they observed a victim that showed symptoms that could not be explained by other illnesses. If the victim was still alive, experts collected his or her vomit and urine to test in a lab. If the victim was already dead, experts checked for signs of poisoning, such as foamy spittle or deep reddening of the face. Forensic investigators sometimes collected vomit and other bodily fluids at the scene of death, but only by extracting the poison from the organs could a poison's identity be confirmed. The three steps in poisoning investigations were recording and evaluating professed symptoms, cataloguing anatomical injuries, and conducting a chemical analysis of bodily organs and/or fluids.[29]

Legal-medical experts were often able to inform judges which type of poison a suicide had employed and the amount consumed. Judges also wanted to know how the poison was administered. Had it been combined with another substance that activated its toxic properties? Had it been mixed with food? Judges wanted to know whether the quantity of poison ingested was enough to have caused the death. For example, how many grams of arsenic does it take to kill a person? The *Compendio* reminded experts that it was difficult to determine dosage from a cadaver that had absorbed much of the poison into its tissues, but with live subjects, the contents of the stomach as well as any vomit could be tested. Some amount of toxins that were found in everyday household items like arsenic-based medicines or pesticides was expected in bodily tissues, but high levels of these toxins indicated homicide or suicide. Judges asked forensic experts to inform them of the approximate time of ingestion as well. Noting that ingesting matches, toxic mushrooms, or *colchico* (a toxic tuber) produces delayed results, the manual advised that doctors could not be certain about the time of poisoning. Many organic-based poisons disappeared quickly from the body but could leave behind ulcerations in the stomach or gastrointestinal tract.[30] The task of the forensic expert was indeed complex.

Legal-medical experts delineated five groups of poisons. Corrosive substances, including bleach, bromine, iodine, and certain purgatives, comprised the first group. Many of these substances could be found among household cleaners and medicines. Investigators could determine whether the poison was acid or alkaline based by testing vomitus. If it produced effervescence when poured on clay bricks, the substance was acidic. Alkaline toxins produced no bubbling. The primary symptoms include intense burning in the throat and stomach, and when these were encountered in a potential suicide, investigators noted them in the judicial record. Other symptoms include bloody stools, a bloated belly, unquenchable thirst, and the cessation of urination. A painful event, poisoning by corrosive agents produces death after several agonizing hours. The manual warned doctors to take care in diagnosing poisoning by caustic agents as the symptoms could be confused with a strangulated hernia, acute gastro-enteritis, or an intestinal perforation.

Choleraic toxins made up the second group. Arsenics, phosphorus, copper salts, digitalis, and bismuth are some of the poisons of this group. Many suicides had access to these toxins. Symptoms mimic poisoning by caustic agents, but choleraic toxins lead to convulsions and paralysis of thinking and movement. Victims cease being able to talk, begin sweating, and develop patches of bruising on different regions of the body. Those who actually survive this class of poison can recover full intellectual capacity, but convalescence can be long and painful.

Carbonic acidic gas, carbon oxide, ether, chloroform, belladonna, and tobacco made up the third group of poisons, classified as narcotics. Having few symptoms in common with corrosives, narcotic poisoning produces a suppression of the nervous system, bloating of the stomach, frequent vomiting, dilation of the pupils, and coma. These symptoms could, however, be confused with meningitis and convulsive hysteria. The order a patient experienced the symptoms could assist doctors in assessing whether he or she was suffering from one of these illnesses or from a narcotic overdose.

Opiates, though also considered narcotics, comprised the fourth group of poisons. When ingested, opiates produce those symptoms described in the paragraph above, but they also cause exaltation of the senses, intense itching, deep sleep, a fixed gaze, and, if taken in large doses, death after eight to twelve hours. Opiate overdose could be confused with cerebral bleeding, carbon monoxide poisoning, or pulmonary apoplexy.

The fifth and final group of poisons included tetanus and pseudo tetanus toxins like strychnine, prussic acid (hydrogen cyanide), quinine sulfate, cantharides, and camphor. Hydrogen cyanide is a precursor to sodium and potassium cyanides and was employed by mining operations to separate gold and silver from ore. Cyanides are extremely toxic and, in high doses, can kill a human in one minute. Strychnine is a base for many vermin poisons. Cantharidin is derived from pulverizing the bodies of blister beetles (also known as Spanish flies). Although a poison, cantharidin had been ingested as an aphrodisiac since ancient times because it irritated the urinary tract and mimicked the voluptuous sensations of sexual arousal. Death by any of these toxins is usually rapid, but symptoms could be confused with illnesses such as epilepsy, hysteria, and angina.[31]

Habitual ingestion of any class of poison over time has long-term deleterious impacts on health. For example, many of the medications for syphilis before 1945 contained arsenic or mercury, and ingesting these over long periods harmed overall mental and physical health.

The collaboration of judges and medical experts in the nineteenth century solidified the high status of medicine and its practitioners as authoritative voices in court cases. Judges relied on forensic medical experts in their rulings, signaling science as an integral component of jurisprudence. However, medicine has never been infallible. Indeed, there must have been many misdiagnoses of cause of death. When the law mandated an inquest for an unnatural or suspicious death, judges relied on medical and social discourses of death. Medical experts determined the material cause of death; witnesses and loved ones provided testimonies to narrate the circumstances surrounding the death. The body of a suicide no longer belonged to the family but to the legal-medical experts who conducted postmortems. It was also up to the experts to determine when a body could be returned to relatives for grieving and burial rituals. Once a corpse was in the hands of physicians or coroners and family or others had visually identified it, it became a cadaver, an object to be probed, analyzed, and inscribed with medical meaning.[32] Following a body from live individual on the mental precipice of self-murder to freshly expired corpse to studied cadaver and finally to its burial in one of Mexico City's modern cemeteries illuminates much about life, suicide, death, and the multiple meanings of embodied self and social identity.

## THE SUICIDAL BODY

Some suicides took methodical steps in preparing themselves for death. A "chic" script of suicide popularized in France guided the style-conscious in leaving behind an exquisite corpse. A reporter for *El Imparcial* noted in 1898, "A person who boasts of being elegant loses his or her reputation if dressed in improper attire for the kind of death they have chosen." [33] It went on to state that a woman who kills herself and hopes to die gracefully and with honor must not leave behind a disfigured and sloppily composed cadaver. Therefore, the chic suicide avoided firearms and virulent poisons that might result in gaping wounds, a protruding tongue, or a contorted face—in other words, an ugly corpse. Moreover, the elegant suicide script demanded impeccable clothing. The chic female suicide donned dresses of luxurious, richly embroidered fabric with cascades of lace. Unexplained deaths required autopsies; therefore, the suicide should take care to wear her finest and most attractive undergarments, preferably finely embroidered petticoats, dark silk stockings, and delicate slippers.[34] Indeed, nineteenth-century reporters commented on how corpses were clothed. Much of their judgments of the suicide's class and honor centered on the quality of his or her clothing and attention to grooming. Journalists were more deeply moved by the suicides of people from their own social group or higher. Laborers or poor farmers who killed themselves received far less print devoted to their biographies and motivations. They lacked the luxurious clothing and accessories that journalists enjoyed describing in detail. It seemed evident that romantic conventions of self-annihilation were culturally sanctioned, and these conventions provided suicides with a script and grammar they could use to construct their selves in their deaths. The script dictated the drama of the act and the letters and material objects suicides left at the scene, as well as where a suicide chose to die and what they wore when they died. Newspaper coverage of female and youth suicides implied that their actions could be rational, even justifiable, when committed to protest unrequited love or to avoid shame, especially if the public judged the suicides to have been virtuous in life. The plots of newspaper articles during the Porfiriato followed the narrative structure of fiction, a fact not lost on some critics of the press. Revolutionary-era commentary romanticized young suicide less but still published sordid details of spoiled love and financial futures. A couple of decades into the twentieth century, death scene sketches gave way to photographs of corpses.

Regardless of era, the body held symbolic meaning in Mexican society. A person could use his or her body to convey respect and disrespect or act on other bodies to enforce subordination. Slander and insult cases abound, with testimonies of citizens being slighted by others by a glance, a gesture, a turned back, or pulled hair. As Mexicans moved through private and public spaces, their demeanor communicated multiple messages. At the core of this communication was the fact that "the body served as a metaphor for social order and honor." [35] Therefore, it isn't surprising that the preparation of the body before carrying out self-murder and the condition of the body after death mattered to many suicides. A sensational double suicide by two young women in 1909 that shocked the capital's residents demonstrates the importance of the body and comportment in suicide scripts. According to family members, María Fuentes and Guadalupe Ortiz had risen from their beds on the morning of the suicides just like it was any other day. The girls walked to the public baths, groomed and styled their hair, and dressed in their finest clothes. They tucked their suicide notes in their bodices, carried a bundle of letters and portraits neatly wrapped with satin ribbon, and boarded the trolley at the Zócalo on Friday morning for Chapultepec Park. Allegedly, they loved the same man and chose to consume deadly poison together rather than have him choose one or the other. Two points are important here: the young women hoped to both guide the interpretation of their suicides and control the destiny of their corpses. Committing suicide in the middle of day guaranteed that their purposeful walk through the park would not be considered out of the ordinary for two young women, as being on the streets in daylight did not label them as dishonorable. Chapultepec was a favored destination of many residents, who strolled through its forests and boated on its lakes, so the girls would not be out of place there. Moreover, undertaking the deed during the day ensured that their remains would be found quickly and not left to decompose or become food for the city's numerous stray dogs. Taking care to go through the rituals of civilized, honorable citizens—bathing, grooming, and dressing in their best clothes before entering public space—

also constructed the girls as honorable young women. Wrapping their letters and photographs with ribbon and depositing them at the scene also linked the girls to a long pattern of romantic suicides. Young people in particular killed themselves for love, and society accepted this as a sometimes honorable, albeit tragic, motive. Death scenes were often littered with *prendas* (romantic gifts), such as love notes and portraits. In fact, in criminal cases, the existence of sentimental keepsakes like love letters, locks of hair, or portraits connoted a formal love relationship. This was a grammar that society understood. These details also allowed journalists and medical experts to make suppositions about the suicides and their reasons for choosing death over life.

When reporters gazed on the corpses of María and Guadalupe, locked in an embrace, they surmised that the two girls hailed from the best class, as they wore suits from the city's best tailors.[36] In fact, one reporter even went so far as to read the tags on the clothing to verify its quality.[37] When Guadalupe Ponce swallowed poison in Chapultepec Park in March eight years later, journalists from *El Demócrata* flocked to the scene to scribble notes for the paper's front-page article. Park-goers found the young women's corpse just after noon near the picturesque Calzada de Violetas (Path of Violets). The reporters devoted a section of the article to describing her cadaver. She had dark brown hair and was dressed in elegant clothes, including a "tailored suit of black cloth, a green blouse underneath, patent leather shoes, stockings of sheer silk, and a black velvet hat with feathers all around." The description allowed readers to imagine what Guadalupe looked like and visualize her death, especially when the reporter followed the description of her clothing with the line, "Besides, her mouth was open and her tongue stuck out."[38] The three young women who chose to end their lives in the historic city park paid careful attention to their grooming and made sure that they dressed in as fine clothes as one would expect from respectable women. As chapter 5 will reveal, María Fuentes and Guadalupe Ortiz lacked the status that their clothing conveyed, and when journalists discovered this, the reporting on their deaths lost its romantic tone.

María de los Ángeles Santacruz also upheld feminine propriety when she carried out plans to kill herself in 1930. She called a chauffeur from her home at 7:45 pm and entered the hired car wearing a black suit and shoes. Driver Raymundo Sánchez took her to Dr. Luis Chávez's office, but, finding him absent, she asked him to drive her instead to the Avalos family's home, on the sixth block of prosperous Avenida Madero. The driver stopped in front of the home, but the young passenger refused to get out because she had not put on stockings before she left her house. They sat in the car for twenty minutes until Guillermo Avalos arrived home from work. Communicating with him through the car window, María asked to borrow a pistol for mutual friend Juan Lomelí, claiming that he had been threatened by someone and wanted to be ready to defend himself. Guillermo resisted at first but ultimately acceded to her plea and went into the house to fetch the pistol and bullets. After they said their goodbyes, the car traveled down Madero toward Calle Lafayette. At this point, the driver heard a gunshot, and María exclaimed, "I just killed myself." Raymundo turned the car around and returned to the Avalos residence with the bleeding woman. Seeing that she was still alive, they called an ambulance, but she died on the way to the hospital. She left no note or motive for her tragic resolution. Curiously however, even though she traveled to her friend's home to borrow a gun, knowing full well her intention to commit suicide, she refused to reveal her bare legs in public.[39] Propriety and gender norms of how to present oneself in public spaces as an honorable woman, especially on the stylish Avenida Madero, superseded the fact that she would be a corpse soon enough, one scrutinized and discussed in medical and public discourse.

## THE CORPSE

When a passerby discovered the corpse of Guadalupe Ponce in Chapultepec Park in 1916, watchmen secured the area to await police investigators but allowed three editors of *El Demócrata* to survey the scene and the young woman's belongings. The editors acted as amateur forensic specialists. In the article they wrote, they described "the place in which the suicide slept her last dream."[40] Half a meter from Guadalupe's fallen hat lay a purse of dark yellow leather with the initials G. P. painted on it in greenish-blue ink. Under the purse, they found a pottery cup adorned with artistic scenes, but they noted that it contained no vestiges of poison. Next, they described the position of the nineteen-year-old woman's corpse, observing that her arms were in varying stages of flexion. Her feet were pronated and there were "traces of wet clay" on the bottom of her shoes. They zeroed in on her small hands, describing them as "fine and delicate" and noting that the right hand was clutching—almost convulsively—a white handkerchief. They then turned their scrutinizing eyes to the ground around her. Four meters from the body, they discovered a small perfume bottle with a crystal stopper and the label

"Sweet Pea."[41] The editors noted a milky white residue on the sides of the vessel. Next to the bottle lay a rolled-up page of *El Demócrata* with a white powder stuck to it. Determined to find out the type of poison Guadalupe had used, the editors visited a medicine shop and asked to see a vial of mercury cyanide pills. They informed readers that the residue on an ampoule of such poison resembled that found on the objects at the suicide scene. Not content to let the story rest, they suggested that the white stains on Guadalupe's skirt and the white drops on a rustic bench twenty-five meters from where her body dropped were in fact mercury cyanide dissolved in water. They recounted the scene for readers, surmising that Guadalupe sat down at the lakeside on the bench, ingested the poison, spilled some on her clothes, and then stumbled twenty-five meters away to her final resting place. Footprints left by high-heeled shoes signaled her trajectory. They theorized that she had walked to the lake, filled the perfume bottle with water, mixed in the cyanide pills, and met her death shortly afterward. Sensationalizing her suicide even more, the article proceeded to describe the last seconds of her life: "Dominated by convulsions caused by the venom, and in the throes of agony, she tried, without a doubt, to stand up, and not succeeding, turned on her heels and fell in the position found by our editors."[42] The portrait of her alleged death throes was not pretty but rather dramatic, a tone that may have resonated with certain city residents, especially those interested in having their own stories narrated for more than one hundred thousand readers.

After examining the site, the intrepid editors did not immediately return to the offices of *El Demócrata* to write their article. Instead, they rode in their carriage to the Eighth Division of Police. An ambulance was dispatched to Chapultepec Park, and the editors invited Police Chief Pedro Medina to accompany them back to the scene. The watchman who guarded the corpse and scene told authorities that the editors had discovered the objects that now lay close to the corpse. Police opened Guadalupe's purse and discovered some Veracruz currency, various small cartons, and a photo of the deceased in an oval frame. The back of the portrait contained some writing that the editors attempted to read over the shoulders of the authorities. They could only make out some of it: "My name is Guadalupe . . . I live in the fifth block of Altamirano . . . Rafael: I killed myself for . . ." Other small pieces of paper contained the name Pepe. The article asked, "Who is he? Rafael or Pepe?" It went on to lament what infidelity might have driven the girl to take the fatal decision. The editors gazed at her corpse on the stretcher and described her face and hands as "ravaged" by the poison: her face was "totally bruised," and "her gleaming fingernails scrupulously cut." The bruising conformed to the description of cyanide poisoning in a forensic handbook; cyanides starve the body of oxygen, causing the corpse to take on a bluish cast. They noted that dried blood stained her mouth because she bit her tongue in the final death throes. Rounding out the description, they described her very white face, once beautiful but now contorted in pain, covered in dirt and dead leaves.

The difference between the reporting of this death in 1916 and that of the double suicide of María Fuentes and Guadalupe Ortiz in 1909 was the focus on the macabre details of poisoning. The reporters agreed that Guadalupe Ponce must have been beautiful, but death left ghastly signs on her once vibrant body. Perhaps reporters were aiming to deter other suicides by describing the realistic ugliness of self-murder, or perhaps they were trying to sell papers, knowing that readers ate up these kinds of sordid details. Certainly, reporters were not sanitizing violent death in the same era in which burial regulations had been enacted to move processes of death, dying, and burial from public view. Stories of revolutionary violence also filled the front pages of the capital's newspapers. This form of sensational reporting on violent deaths undoubtedly produced shock in readers and likely brought those from all classes of society together in recognition of their collective humanity. Reading the horrific details of suicides elicited empathy rather than casual indifference to death.

Once personnel had hoisted Guadalupe's lifeless body onto a stretcher for her ambulance ride to the morgue, the three editors of *El Demócrata* sped to her house. Invited in by her sister, whom they described as beautiful and elegant, the editors commented that fine furniture filled the parlor and portraits of Constitutionalist Army officers lined the walls. A younger sister rushed into the room, crying, to inform her sibling that the police had summoned them to the station. The family members quickly changed their clothes and were accompanied to the station by the editors in their carriage. Understandably, the younger sisters exhibited extreme grief and, according to the article, exclaimed that Guadalupe had warned them, "You will rue the scare I will give you when I kill myself." The sisters disagreed on whether she had a boyfriend, but they concurred that she did not kill herself because of a man. They said that she had spoken of killing herself before, but they had dismissed it as mere "banter" (*guasa*). The article ended by stating that much light would be shed on the case if it could be discovered who Rafael was. They presumed that deception in love had driven the young Guadalupe to end her life on the poetic Calzada de Violetas.[43] This hypothesis conformed to popular opinions that had been held about female suicide since the Porfiriato. Love matches torn asunder were enough to drive some women to self-murder.

A journalist similarly behaved as amateur forensic investigator in the 1919 death of Hilaria Moreno, a working-class woman, whom the reporter for *Excélsior* described as "bohemian."[44] Police officers on the scene wanted to determine if Hilaria shot herself in a clear case of suicide or if she had been murdered. Reporters often looked over the backs of official investigators, studied evidence, and drew their own conclusions. Clearly, the reading public devoured the quasi-scientific analysis of crimes as they unfolded in the headlines of city papers. The reporter for *Excélsior* started his article on the suspicious death of Hilaria by noting that newspapers were accustomed to covering the "dramas and tragedies" of the prosperous classes with "great sensationalism" but not the daily "chronic crime" that resulted from the "intense passions" of the popular classes. He went on to claim that the tragedies and dramas of the proletariat were just as interesting but lacked the "theater of sumptuous bedrooms with paneled walls, and the murder weapon did not shred lace and silk."[45] Hipólita Hernández shared a rented room with Hilaria. Reporters described their living conditions, noting that they had 225 square feet of living space, a contiguous kitchen area, and a passageway that opened to the street. The barrio was occupied mostly by workers employed by the flour mill La Harinera, and they were on strike at the time of Hilaria's death. Police had a heavy presence in the neighborhood because of the "agitation and disorder" of the strikers.[46] Hilaria's husband had been rounded up in one of the mass arrests the day of her death. During the evening of March 2, 1919, residents of the building heard a thud, a strangled cry, and a gunshot. Hipólita ran from the building to summon police and shouted, "Blondie has been killed. She has been shot in the head."[47]

Reporters surveyed the crime scene in the presence of police investigators. Hilaria's body was on the floor, her head resting in a pool of blood, and a Browning pistol lay twenty centimeters from her right hand. The chamber held four bullets; one more was on the bed. The scene appeared like a suicide, but several clues led the reporters to surmise that Hilaria had been murdered. Hipólita testified that she had been sitting with her back to the door sewing when she heard her friend run into the room. Before Hipólita could turn around, she perceived a blow, a cry, and a gunshot. One reporter explained that if Hipólita had shot Hilaria as she came into room, the trajectory of the bullet would have been different, and if Hilaria had committed suicide because her husband had been arrested three hours before, she would have to have experienced a rapid and unlikely episode of insanity. The reporter implied that there must have been a murderer who had escaped without being seen by Hipólita. Police officers could not find the shell of the bullet that caused her death, and reporters noted that it appeared she had been shot from a distance of two to five meters, which ruled out suicide. No burn marks were found on her clothing or skin. Besides, the reporters also interviewed the building's porter, who noted that she had also heard a blow or thud, a shout, and then a detonation. The article informed readers that, if Hilaria had pulled the trigger herself, the noises would have occurred in the opposite order—a gunshot, then a cry, followed by a thud as her body fell to the floor.

Noting their careful and methodical investigations, *Excélsior* proceeded to make their judgment of homicide. Moreover, *Excélsior* concluded that a Browning pistol would have been out of financial reach of a working-class woman. Costing eighty to one hundred pesos, such a pistol could not even have been purchased by her spouse, who worked at the factory. After reporters and police left the crime scene, the newspaper received a tip-off from an informant who said that four *rateros* (petty thieves) known as Los aguacates (the Avocados) lived in the *vecindad* (tenement) and alleged that one of them had had amorous relations with Hilaria. *Excélsior* gloated that it informed police of these findings, noting that the perpetrator must have been one of the rateros, as "they go about, usually, well armed."[48] Readers expected journalists not only to report the facts of crime but also to seek justice. Journalists tutored readers on the correct response to violent death—which was shock and a demand for social change.

Reporters, it seemed, could carry out unofficial forensic investigations, and their readers demanded it. Certainly, reporters were often the first to a crime scene, and seasoned newspapermen no doubt observed many such scenarios in their careers. Reporting also frequently paralleled official police investigations, down to including calculations of firing distances, details of the location of entry and exit wounds, and, importantly, the position and condition of the corpse. For example, *El Demócrata* provided a sketch of the trajectory of the bullet that had gone through the skull of Señora Cobada de Lozada when the court decided to exhume her body to reinvestigate whether she had committed suicide or been murdered (see figure 3).[49] Newspapers routinely described in detail the bodily manifestations of death, including signs of death throes such as contorted and flexed limbs, gaping mouths, and the expulsion of bodily fluids. Journalists used wording that mimicked the

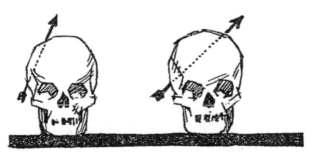

FIGURE 3. Sketch of bullet trajectory in the forensic investigation of the death of Señora Cobada de Lozada. *El Demócrata,* November 13, 1920, 1.

semantics of forensic reports in inquests. When writing about the suicides of women, especially elite women, reporters fixated on other minute details as well. Like the *El Demócrata* reporter who noticed Guadalupe Ponce's manicured fingernails, journalists tantalized readers with minutiae so that they could visualize the corpse.

When a soldier noticed water bubbling in a ditch and, moments later, saw a female corpse float to the surface in 1930, the newspaper reporting paralleled coverage of violent deaths of women from decades before. Calling the unidentified woman "a butterfly of the cabaret," [50] police and reporters surmised that the approximately twenty-three-year-old woman had been strangled and tossed in the ditch. Her dress suggested that she worked in one of the neighborhood cabarets. Judging by the condition of the body, forensic experts guessed that she had been dead and submerged in the water for three or four days. Nevertheless, *El Universal* claimed that her facial features showed her to be a beautiful woman, suggesting that the construct of the exquisite corpse resonated with journalists.[51] As Edgar Allan Poe famously stated, "The death of a beautiful woman is, unquestionably, the most poetical topic in the world." [52] It seemed that feminine death made male journalists and observers, like Federico Gamboa, feel more deeply their mortality. Bronfen writes, "Even as the woman as desired sexual object undoes the work of death by promising wholeness, her body is also seen as the site of a wound, its sight a source of death for man." [53]

The sketches and photographs of female corpses in the newspapers support this conjecture. While male suicides were also drawn or photographed, newspaper editors made the choice to illustrate female death more often. Coupled with text that described the death scene, commented on the condition and beauty of the female corpse, and made conjectures about the thought processes that led to suicide, the illustration zeroed in on the face of the dead woman. In fact, the image of the victim frequently dominated the frame. Gaping wounds, pools of blood, grimacing faces, and broken bodies were accompanied by shocking captions intended to draw readers in. Even illiterate individuals could understand many elements of a crime from the image of the victim.

Other images portrayed the entire scene. Newspapers employed sketch artists to provide illustrations for all types of stories. When Eduardo Velázquez, the former inspector of the Federal District, fell from grace and allegedly committed suicide in prison in 1897, the case captured headlines and even inspired a *corrido* (ballad), which was illustrated by José Guadalupe Posada.[54] Inspector Velázquez had set out to reform and modernize the city police force, but rumors circulated that his officers routinely used torture. His downfall came in 1897 with the arrest of Arnulfo Arroyo, who had attempted to assassinate President Porfirio Díaz on September 16, Mexico's independence day. Police questioned Arroyo that evening, but after midnight, facilitated by a deliberately calculated slip in security at the police station, an angry mob entered and stabbed him to death. What followed was a farce of justice. Police arrested twenty-one bystanders and passersby for the murder of Arroyo. Men who had been passing by after attending the theater, a roast-chicken vendor, and a journalist were some of the suspects detained for seventy-two hours. Understandably, rumors and anger circulated in the city as many residents questioned how an angry mob of common men could have gotten into Velázquez's headquarters and stabbed a detainee to death. Velázquez resigned on September 18, and authorities arrested him, coconspirator and head of secret police Miguel Cabrera, and others and transferred them to Belem Prison. The warden provided Velázquez a luxurious cell. It included a piano, a desk, a small library, and a statue of Díaz. Less than a week into his incarceration, the once esteemed official shot himself with a British-made pistol that he owned. No one heard the gunshots, and his corpse was discovered in his bed by a guard the next day.[55] An illustration of the deceased Velázquez graced the front page of *El Imparcial* on September 25, 1897, a day after his suicide. The sketch artist did not emphasize the ghastly wound in Velázquez's temple, instead depicting him as seemingly asleep. A sketch of the recently fired pistol and a drawing of the floor plan of his prison cell accompanied the article. Less than a year later, another *El Imparcial* sketch artist drew the corpse of another male suicide victim and the revolver he used to end his life. This time, the artist graphically depicted

# Victoriano González, el último suicida

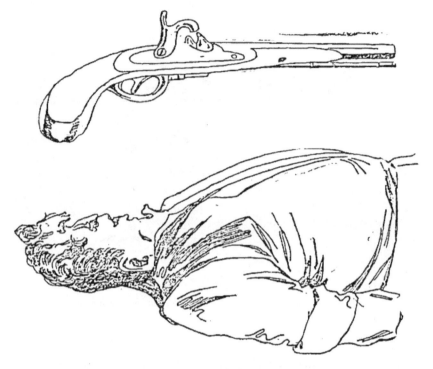

Horrible aspecto que presentaba poco después del suceso, y pistola con que se dió la muerte. (Apuntes del natural por nuestros dibujan tes.)

FIGURE 4. Sketch of revolver and male suicide victim. *El Imparcial,* June 2, 1898, p. 2.

the victim's injury, showing that he had blown away a good part of his face and skull (see figure 4). These early sketches were rough and lacked detail, but they allowed readers to visualize the corpse and the scene of death.

Etchings accompanying stories of violent death became more detailed in later years. A double suicide carried out in 1911 by two young women married to the same man received a careful and detailed sketch by an artist employed by *Ilustración Popular* (figure 5). The drawing supplemented an article by Gonzalo de la Parra discussing how the women made their deadly pact when they could no longer support living in sinful bigamy with their deceiving husband.[56] The image bears the title "The Eternal Tragedy of Love" and shows the two women side by side on the same bed. An overturned chair in the foreground of the etching, a bottle of poison, and a glass presumably shared by the

FIGURE 5. Sketch of double suicide of two women married to the same man. *Ilustración Popular,* April 30, 1911, p. 1.

young woman to drink the toxin round out the death scene. The women are dressed respectably, but the sketch displays their morbid postures: the arm of one of the women dangles off the bed, and the other woman clutches her head in pain. The image, meant to invoke shock and concern from readers, appeared on the journal's front page. Readers could come together in a community of emotion to lament and try to understand why the two young women would choose death. Displayed in a kiosk in the plaza, this sort of image must have attracted passersby to purchase the publication.

A less romanticized etching of a murdered woman in 1921 contrasts with the Werther-like scene of the double suicide ten years before (figure 6). The later image centered on a young woman who had been violently murdered. Her body floats in a fountain with a frightening skeleton of death menacing her corpse from above. Two suspicious men in the background flee the scene under the cover of night. The gruesome etching shows a rope tied around the victim's neck, and the caption informs readers that the murderers used rocks in an attempt to keep her corpse submerged in the fountain. The image was meant to provoke horror and fascination in readers. As with other crime

EN FORMA MISTERIOSA FUE ESTRANGULADA
EN TOLUCA UNA BELLA Y ELEGANTE MUJER

LOS ASESINOS ARROJARON EL CADAVER A UNA FUENTE DEL "PARQUE REFORMA,"
CON DOS PIEDRAS ATADAS AL CUELLO, PARA IMPEDIR LA FLOTACIÓN

FIGURE 6. Sketch of female corpse in fountain. *El Demócrata*, April 13, 1921, p. 1.

stories, journalists promised to stay on the trail of the crime and bring the beautiful woman's murderers to justice. The artist drew the victim floating in the modern fountain, her wet evening dress clinging to her curvaceous form, her feet in stylish shoes, and her bobbed hair still coifed and in place. The image shocked and titillated and even fetishized the eroticism of female death. Yet readers were not simply curious gawkers that looked upon death with cold indifference. Rather, these sorts of images united readers in an emotional community that crossed class and gender.[57]

When the corpse left its last resting place and ended up on the cold marble slab of the morgue, it fell under the medical gaze. The success of the self-construction attempted by the victim rested on the judgments of medical specialists, who interpreted myriad discourses from witnesses, family members, and medical science. The self projected by the suicide was transformed into multiple selves as forensic specialists interrogated the body. Multiple agendas informed this process, from those of loved ones coming to terms with the death to those of physicians determining the cause of and circumstances leading to the death.[58] The case of María Luisa Noecker, the daughter of a German businessman, who shot herself in her bedroom on the morning of December 3, 1909, is typical. The alleged provocation for her suicide centered on the famous bullfighter Rodolfo Gaona, one of the suspects in the case. Police also arrested his brother, Enrique Gaona, and Cirilo Pérez, an egg seller who had escorted Luisa to a party the night before her suicide. The story bounced back and forth between rival newspapers, and Mexico City exploded with daily stories about the investigation, moral outrage from elite residents, and popular street demonstrations by the bullfighter's supporters. What began as a tragic story of a girl's seduction, deflowering, and suicide turned into a media witch-hunt against the bullfighter and "his kind," as well as a brawl of words between the semiofficial press (which received government subsidies) and the independent press. This isolated event in 1909 Mexico City illuminated societal tensions about youthful despair and suicide, sexuality and honor, the proclivities of the lower class (as symbolized by the certain aficionados of the savage bullring), and the processes of reporting and criminal justice in early twentieth-century Mexico. Rodolfo Gaona was an immensely popular celebrity in the capital, but there were some that disparaged his indigenous, working-class background. Dandies heckled him with shouts of "indio bolero" (Indian bootblack) from the elite section of the bullring.[59] Many could not accept that a humble Mexican had been able to climb to such heights of fame and wealth. Until Rodolfo's rise, most elite fans favored Spanish matadors, while the working class supported homegrown toreros. Editors and writers took turns maligning one other's coverage and opinions and, at the same time, expressed their fear that justice for Luisa would not prevail. A few papers, including *El Abogado Cristiano,* refrained from blaming the young bullfighter, pointing out that there was nothing more than circumstantial evidence, and called for due process.[60] The papers never called into question the young victim's reputation, as it was assumed that she was a virginal daughter of elite society, although a reporter for *El Imparcial* described her as "nubile."[61] Luisa was simply at fault because of her youth and inexperience, and this meshed with the gender ideology that underpinned sexual crime laws of the era.

Certainly, the fact that one of the alleged perpetrators in the case was the famous bullfighter rallied attention to the tragic affair. The newspaper accounts spent more ink on his travails and presumed guilt than on the struggles of the young Luisa. However, the more than three hundred pages of the inquest, now stored in Mexico's national archive, devoted substantial attention to the forensic investigation of the young woman's body, the crime scene, and her alleged seducers. When forensic experts arrived at the Noecker home, on the corner of Avenida Balderas and Calle Nuevo México, they set about looking for clues that a crime had taken place. Doctors determined that Luisa had been deflowered recently because her cadaver presented a newly torn hymen and her clothing and genitalia revealed bloodstains. They did not see signs of violence, however. She had suffered two gunshot wounds, one to the head and the other to the abdomen. Once investigators transported her body to the morgue in the Hospital Juárez, they used a microscope to examine stains on her clothes. Later, they took the same microscopic approach to the clothes and bedding of the suspects. This use of scientific instruments marked a new practice in criminal investigations, which previously had relied on perceptions of the naked eye. Doctors conceded that it was possible that the girl's hymen had been torn by a finger or an object. However, they insisted that an erect penis had caused injury to the hymen, although they only found traces of blood and urine, not semen, on Luisa's clothes. Investigators also searched the hotel room where the alleged crime occurred and the home of Rodolfo for clues of Luisa having been deflowered in either setting. Servants at the Hotel Venesia testified that they had not seen any bloodstains that might have signaled the defloration of a virgin when they had collected the sheets, towels, and pillows in Rodolfo's room on the day in question. When asked about the washbasin, they noted that they had found it containing only dirty water. The laundress confirmed that she had found no signs of blood on the sheets either. Investigators then proceeded to the home of Rodolfo's manager, Saturnino "Ojitos" (Squinty Eyes) Frutos, and discovered suspicious stains on his bed. His wife explained to authorities that her menstrual blood had sullied the bed covers and that no crime had occurred there.

The inquest included the notes from the autopsy, which was conducted by legal-medical experts Dr. Tomás Moreno and Dr. Jacinto García. Their tasks were to determine Luisa's age, whether she had been deflowered, if violence was evident in the crime, and whether drugs or alcohol had played a role in her death. Age was important because if a young woman had consensual sex under the age of sixteen, her partner could be charged with *estupro,* a crime akin to statutory rape. Luisa had been born in St. Louis, Missouri, and her parents lacked an official copy of her birth certificate. The experts surmised that Luisa had reached fifteen years of age. They found dried blood on her face, her head, the back of her neck, her trunk, and around the entry and exit wounds of two bullets. The wounds also showed vestiges of gunpowder and burn marks, known markers of suicide by firearm. Doctors moved on to her genitalia and noted that her hymen had been recently torn into four flaps and showed signs of bleeding. Dried blood also marked her vulva and inner thighs. Finally, physicians submitted a portion of her brain and stomach for chemical analysis. They concluded that her recent defloration had not been life threatening and that the bullet wounds had led to her death. The judge continued the case to decide if the crimes of *rapto* (abduction by means of seduction) and/or estupro (deflowering of a minor) had occurred.

The medical analysis turned to the three male suspects of the crime. The bullfighter's brother, Enrique, had confessed to having had sex with Luisa, and Cirilo Pérez had befriended Luisa earlier and accompanied her to a party the night before she died, allegedly promising to introduce her to Rodolfo. Each male suspect was given the same examination. The doctors inspected each man's pubic hair, testicles, and thighs for signs of semen or blood and then decided whether he was capable of deflowering a virgin. Doctors examined Enrique first and then refuted his confession of having had sex with Luisa, noting that he had a physical impairment that prevented him from achieving an erection. It seemed Enrique suffered from suppurating chancres, signs of the first stage of syphilis. Medical examiners conceded that he might be able to copulate with an experienced woman of "ample" vagina but never with a virgin. In effect, they ruled that he would not be able to achieve a hard enough erection to penetrate a virgin's hymen and, furthermore, that he would not be able to do so without suffering debilitating pain. He countered their claim, insisted that he had had consensual sex with Luisa and had found her not to be a virgin. A loyal brother, he seemed determined to protect his famous sibling from imprisonment. Medical experts ruled the same for Cirilo, diagnosing him as being in the primary stage of syphilis, identified by chancres, which connoted an inability to have sex with a virgin with a resistant hymen. Rodolfo did not escape a physical exam either. Doctors found no vestiges of any secretions on his clothing or body that might indicate he had deflowered a virgin. Of course, a few days had passed since the alleged sexual encounter, and any of the suspects could have bathed and washed their clothes during that time. Experts determined the torero to be young and healthy and reported that he had "perfectly formed genitalia with no infection." They concluded that the bullfighter possessed the virility to deflower a virgin. At this point, it fell on the court to prove beyond a doubt that he had been with the young Luisa. He claimed to have been at the theater in the company of friends when the alleged sexual relations occurred. Several friends corroborated his alibi. According to witnesses, he never showed up at the banquet and party where Luisa had hoped to meet him. Newspapers emphasized Luisa's obsession with the handsome torero. She had plastered her room with playbills of his fights and had his image framed in a locket.

The reading public, including various medical experts, offered their help in the case. Chemist L. K. Koley wrote to the director of *El País* and admonished the legal-medical experts for not looking for other substances besides alcohol in Luisa's cadaver. He offered to examine the girl's viscera for cantharides and stimulant plants on behalf of the "unfortunate victim of the *mafia de coleta*." [62] Armed with their medical training and experience in criminal cases, medical experts continued to be arbiters of honor and shame, fact and fiction. In other words, while they sought hard evidence (e.g., blood stains, bodily fluids, the ability of the male perpetrator to gain an erection and engage in sexual intercourse) in cases involving sexual crimes, medical experts still had to assess the reputation of each party and even judge whether consensual sex had occurred or not. Forensic investigators performed the law by examining potential crime scenes, the bodies of victims, and even the bodies of the alleged perpetrators, but they also made judgments about the honor or morality of all parties. Character was important and could steer the course of an investigation. For example, many doctors (and the chemist Koley, mentioned above), noting that Luisa hailed from an elite, honorable family, thought that she might have been drugged. Why else would she go to a party with strange men or take a gun and shoot herself? At the time of her death, her father had been out of the country on business, her mother had been recuperating from typhus in the hospital, and her inattentive uncle had not been keeping proper tabs on her whereabouts. Only the broadside *Sufrimientos, reflexiones y consejos de la suicida de María Luisa Noeker* [sic]:

*En la otra vida* (Sufferings, reflections, and advice from the suicide María Luisa Noeker: In the other life), illustrated by José Guadalupe Posada, faulted the reckless girl for going to a party with strange men. The broadside depicted Luisa speaking from beyond the grave, cautioning readers "to exercise vigilance over their children and to teach them right from wrong." [63]

The judge released Rodolfo on December 30, 1909, on a five-thousand-peso bond, but the press continued to call for justice. The *Mexican Herald,* an English-language daily read by expatriates and businessmen, covered his bullfight on January 17, 1910, and gloated when he failed to kill the bull and "wept like a woman." [64] On January 28, Luisa's father still did not have the necessary documents to proceed with the case and asked the judge for an extension. The *Mexican Herald* encouraged the court to grant him time, warning, "It will be seen whether to be a 'torero' constitutes a 'fuero' [immunity] before the law." [65] The case file notes that a bundle of cantharides (Spanish fly) was entered into the evidence and secured in a strong box; the implication was that it had been found in Rodolfo's house, but this is not clear. By March, the court came to its final judgment and dropped charges against the Gaona brothers, Cirilo, and María Guadalupe González, the family maid. The father had not been able to establish his paternity. Defense lawyers pointed out that only the victim, her husband (if she had been married), or her parents could instigate a charge of rapto because of the ramifications it had for the honor and reputation of the aggrieved parties. Mr. Noecker could not establish that he possessed *patria potestad* (paternal authority) over his daughter as his documents proved that he was the father of "Lucia A. Noecker" and not "María Luisa Noecker," [66] and lawyers noted that his patria potestad had ceased anyway with her death. When the German consul general attempted to intervene, both the judge and the defendants' lawyers cited various treaties and international laws to block their interference. They asserted Mexican sovereignty and the obligation of Germany not to flout the nation's laws. In the final ruling, the judge concluded that there was not enough evidence to prove that Rodolfo had attended the party and met Luisa. Cirilo could not be charged with rapto as he did not take Luisa "from her house" to satisfy "fiendish desires" (deseos torpes). [67] Similarly, it was determined that Enrique took her to a hotel to have sex with her but did not remove her from her house, as she left with him from the party. Finally, the maid could not be an accessory to rapto if no rapto had occurred. Three months after the tragic suicide, the judge acquitted all defendants in the case.

Luisa's tragic story disappeared from the front pages, and Rodolfo enjoyed an illustrious public career into the 1920s. The scandal did little to impair his reputation.[68] Even just three years after Luisa's death, a famous photograph showed Rodolfo standing with President Francisco Madero at the bullring. Nonetheless, the case revealed several tensions in late-Porfirian Mexico City. If one believed the newspapers of the day, a suicide epidemic gripped Mexico. Multiple lovelorn youth killed themselves each year. Most garnered one short article in the papers or inspired an editorial on suicide fever, whereas Luisa's death captured headlines for three months. However, her suicide got less coverage, even in a time of "suicide fever," than her alleged seducer—the bullfighter Rodolfo Gaona. Calling for justice for the young woman veiled an underlying motive of forging moral discourses on bullfighting, judicial process, and responsible journalism. Newspapers like *El Imparcial* were quick to indict Rodolfo with nothing more than hearsay and prevailing stereotypes. *El Imparcial* was also the semiofficial paper of the government because it received the largest subsidy, a fact that made it affordable to the masses and contributed to its daily circulation of 117,000 copies. Independent papers, perhaps spurred on by their resentment of the governmental support given to their competitor, used the Luisa Noecker case to criticize *El Imparcial's* propensity for yellow journalism. *El Abogado Cristiano* and *La Iberia* admonished the paper to temper its opinion and allow the judge to investigate without undue influence. *El Abogado Cristiano* recognized the seediness of the bullring milieu, but it laid blame on the media for promoting bullfighter idols. Trinidad Sánchez Santos, the owner of the Catholic daily *El País,* had a contentious relationship with the Díaz regime, and Porfirio Díaz later stated that the paper did more to damage his presidency than northern revolutionary leader Pascual Orozco's bullets.[69] Fiercely pro-Church, the paper used the suicide to criticize liberal-positivist public education, which conservative Catholics asserted bred the impulse to kill oneself.

Rodolfo Gaona crystallized the fears and uneasiness that elite capital residents had with the lower classes. Criminologists went from blaming heredity for the pervasive crime and perversity in certain Mexico City neighborhoods like Tepito to faulting lower-class culture and environment. The liberal tradition was to expose and study lower-class dissipation and criminality in order to call for social reform—a task that many científicos embraced. Some considered drinking *pulque* (an alcoholic beverage made from fermented agave plant and favored by the popular classes) and "bloody spectacles" like bullfights to be fundamental causes of urban violence.[70] This ideology allowed journalists to disparage the lower classes, especially the *gente de coleta,* or undesirable aficionados of the bullring. Journalists seized on these sentiments, trying to knock Rodolfo, known popularly as El Indio Grande, off his pedestal and calling into question the whole sport. Yet even the elite were not keen on outlawing bullfighting, especially as ticket sales brought tax revenues to the state, and benefit fights allowed charities to raise funds for flood victims, the poor, and other causes. Changing gender roles also compounded uneasiness about the future of Mexican society. Luisa Noecker had been left without firm parental control and had managed to attend two parties with men unrelated to her. This situation certainly foreshadowed fears about gender disorder in the years after the revolution. Women had been traversing public spaces for many decades, but they increasingly took on public roles and public occupations during the revolution as men fought in the north and many perished in battle. Nonetheless, while Rodolfo rose to even greater heights after the Luisa Noecker scandal, the young suicide faded out of residents' consciousness.

The morgue repelled and fascinated. Reporters delighted in warning potential suicide victims that they could end up lying on the cold slab of the dissecting table at the Hospital Juárez. Reporters utilized vivid language to describe a room that most residents hoped never to see. For example, a 1919 article commenting on a rash of violent crimes in the city noted, "The slabs of the commissariat were stained scarlet, and the morgue of the Hospital Juárez was populated with cadavers showing torn flesh, ravaged entrails, and faces disfigured by terrible and violent agonies." [71] Trafficking in cadavers was also a common fear that was sometimes based in reality. Even medical students, who used corpses to further their education, seemed suspect. The provost of the Escuela Nacional de Medicina in 1905, Eduardo Liceaga, discovered that medical students had paid staff members to not return study cadavers to storage after class. The attendants earned a few pesos in tips, and students gained much needed practice time by having the cadavers available outside class hours. [72] An article in *El Univeral Gráfico* charged the Hospital Juárez with trafficking in cadavers. Apparently, Brígido Varona Salazar arrived at the hospital on July 9, 1929, with multiple wounds. He died eleven days later, and physicians performed an autopsy on July 21. His widow received his body a day later and had to pay the hospital twenty-six pesos to claim it. The reporter expressed alarm that a public hospital had the nerve to charge the bereaved family a fee to collect the remains of their loved one. The mission of Hospital Juárez was to provide free assistance to the indigent sick without discriminating by race, nationality, or religion.[73] The hospital director responded to the charge, noting that the fee covered the coffin and the transportation of the body to the family home by a third party.[74] An article in *El Universal* protested conditions at the hospital because an informant who went to pick up the remains of a loved one who had been "tragically killed" had noticed that, besides the horrible surgical seams left by the autopsy, the cadaver showed animal bites. In fact, this individual reported that "there were bodies whose faces were totally eaten off" by rats as big as hares that relished a "macabre feast on the flesh of the dead." The article noted that the Departamento de Medicina Legal planned to go after the "abominable rodents" because they impeded its forensic investigations.[75] The headline described the crisis of vermin in the morgue: "Monstruous Plague of Rats in Juárez."

Indeed, Mexico City seemed to be drowning in cadavers, and the morgue could not keep up the quick pace of autopsies. Hospital Juárez established a laboratory to embalm cadavers to slow decomposition in 1919. In 1920, the director of the insane asylum La Castañeda gave permission for medical students to practice dissection and autopsy on cadavers not claimed and picked up after twenty-four hours.[76] All unclaimed cadavers were donated to the Escuela Nacional de Medicina, which also had the responsibility to make sure all unwanted remains found a resting place in the cemetery.[77] Generally, autopsies occurred within twenty-four hours of death, but the administrators of Hospital Juárez petitioned the Federal District in 1929 to construct a cadaver depository on lots near the general prison. The morgue at the hospital had no more room, and bodies needed to be stored for two to four days while they awaited autopsy and subsequent burial or cremation. The petition stated that the depository would be hygienically controlled, noting that, at present, cadavers at the hospital decomposed, attracted flies, and emitted foul odors. The document also noted that the proposed location near the prison would be convenient and that there were sufficient trucks to transport cadavers back and forth between the depository and the hospital.[78]

## ASHES TO ASHES: BURIAL OF THE BODY

Once medical investigators completed an autopsy, the civil registry provided family members of the suicide with a burial ticket that indicated where the body would be buried. There were five classes of tickets, and each denoted a different section of the Panteón Dolores (Dolores Cemetery). Bringing a body to the cemetery without a ticket resulted in a fine, potential imprisonment, and the holding of the cadaver in a depository until all proper paperwork had been arranged and fees paid.[79] Most of the suicide cadavers found their final resting place at Dolores. Mexico City's first true public graveyard, Dolores was built in 1876 to serve all classes and included paupers' graves for unidentified corpses and for the poor. In contrast to the old cemeteries in the city center, Dolores was designed to follow the guidelines prescribed by cemetery reform movements worldwide. Modern cemeteries mimicked parks and included trees, gardens, and fountains. Death and burial rituals became secular enterprises distanced from religion.[80] Likewise, cadavers no longer found their final resting place on sacred church property but in the modern, hygienic, and secular graveyards that skirted El Centro. Besides the public health issue of having decaying flesh pile up in the city center—which was prone to flooding—the secular cemetery was expected to project an image of the progress and modernity of a liberal nation. The public cemetery movement occurred in most Western nations during the early nineteenth century, and the change in Mexico from religious to civil burials was just one step in secularizing everyday life; another was the implementation of civil registries for births and marriages. The modern nation no longer had subjects but rather citizens, and politicians hoped to inculcate a sense of civic belonging among them.[81] Along with shifting burials to city limits came energetic critiques of "baroque funerary pomp."[82] Indeed, liberals desired less ostentatious burial rituals that were also more private and in tune with their modern religious sensibilities.[83]

By the nineteenth century, after Benito Juárez and Miguel Lerdo de Tejada promulgated a series of laws to privatize corporate lands and establish a civil registry for births, marriage, and deaths in the 1850s, the handling of the dead had been sanitized and relegated to scientific processes. The dead who lacked family to claim them from area morgues were transported to public cemeteries, where they were buried or deposited before the cemeteries opened to prevent mourners from coming face to face with the nameless, and often coffin-less, corpses. Exhumations as well could only occur during off-hours, when the public had no access to the gravesites.[84] Modern cemeteries in the bucolic countryside were "sites for contesting and making manifest the underlying cultural infrastructure of modern capitalism."[85] Trading in death (by selling different classes of burial, for example), exhuming bodies and bones for medical science, and enforcing sanitation and hygiene laws to limit a period of mourning signaled "the end of the cultural autarchy of the parish."[86] However, this secularization impulse did not mean that religion or spirituality ceased to exist in graveyards and mourning practices. Strict regulations would govern cemetery operations, and death and burial would be orderly and hygienic. Located in Tacubaya, to the south of El Centro, Dolores had a troublesome history through the Porfiriato and the revolution. The cemetery was developed to alleviate sanitation concerns and overcrowding at federal district cemeteries, but few residents chose to bury their loved ones there in its first several years of operation. The poor could not afford to transport coffins to Dolores, and the elite shunned its green spaces because the majority of graves there held the wretched poor, accident and epidemic victims, or remains delivered from hospitals that lacked the decency of clothing and coffins.[87] The plan placed first- and second-class graves nearest to the entrance and the Rotunda of Illustrious Men. The rotunda housed the remains of major statesmen, which had been exhumed and reburied in Dolores with eulogies, speeches, and great pomp. Paupers' graves were relegated to the perimeter of the cemetery, near a ravine that sometimes flooded in the rainy season. Families that purchased gravesites chose between paying for a temporary or permanent burial. Those that failed to renew their "lease" had their loved ones' bones deposited in a common ossuary once the flesh had decomposed away from the skeleton. Elite families usually purchased permanent gravesites and erected large monuments, marble chapels, or other structures that attested to their wealth and piety.[88]

Transportation to Dolores could be tricky for some families. The government offered indigent families free transport to the cemetery on trolley car lines. Early on, these were mule-drawn cars; later, they were replaced by electric cars. Families with more means outfitted carriages and rented trolley cars with funereal wreaths and decorations to escort their dead to Dolores in style. First-class cars were steered by smartly dressed drivers wearing black gloves and top hats with crepe bands. Bystanders customarily removed their hats when a coffin car passed.[89] Wealthy families sometimes rented private cars. Even the illustrator José Guadalupe Posada mocked the transportation of the city's dead in a broadside showing the collision of a funeral carriage and a train. The illustration portrays shocked passengers staring at a corpse that has fallen out of its broken casket and onto the track. Sometimes, the traffic was so bad that coffins did not arrive at the cemetery until sunset, which meant that families had to wait until the next day to bury their deceased because regulations only allowed interments during the day.[90]

Corpse deposits existed in different parts of the city near rail lines so that bodies could be stored, although state officials made every effort to move cadavers to burial as quickly as possible. Elite residents of Colonia Cuauhtémoc, on the southwest, modern side of the city, complained in 1909 about these corpse trains, which moved through the neighborhood taking bodies from deposits to cemeteries. Their odorous passengers in varying stages of decomposition made elite residents fear for their health. Certainly, scientific knowledge had debunked miasma theory by that point, but decomposing corpses raised health concerns nonetheless. These wealthy residents continued their clamoring protests and even hired an attorney, eventually forcing the city to construct another corpse depository in Cuauhtémoc and consider rerouting the electric tram to avoid its passing near fancy homes. El Departamento de Trabajos Públicos (The Department of Public Works) arranged for mule-driven carts to collect the cadavers of the urban poor from depositories around the city and transfer them to Dolores Cemetery via tram lines that ran away from elite barrios.[91] All of this changed a year later, when the state gave the Electric Tram Company exclusive rights to transport the dead to cemeteries around the city. The company designated two cars that could transport ten coffins each as official funereal transportation to Dolores. Soon, suburban communities like Churubusco asked for electric tramlines to deal with their unhygienic corpse problems, noting that cadavers from the military hospital were piling up in cardboard boxes.[92]

However, even burial did not guarantee that a body had finally found its last resting place. Medical students sometimes secured corpses destined for the potter's field or bones from ossuaries to further their studies. Some students collected individual bones to reconstruct a full skeleton, especially when they could not afford to purchase one.[93] The deceased urban poor thus provided anatomical fodder for many medical students in early twentieth-century Mexico.

## CONCLUSION

Bodies, dead or alive, with or without flesh, hold considerable meaning and power in a society. An entire book has been written about the political impact of mortal remains in Latin America.[94] Physicians look for signs of disease on corpses. Journalists judge a dead person's class by their dress and hairstyle. Some suicides planned the presentation of their body after death.

They designed death scenes, bathed and dressed in their finest clothes, and left notes that pleaded with physicians to skip the disfiguring autopsy after death. Literally, the body transformed into a corpse at death and into a cadaver as a doctor lowered a scalpel to cut the cold flesh. Once surveyed, flayed, and sewn back together, families collected the body to further prepare it for burial. The bones of the deceased remained important and never lost meaning. They could even cause conflict between towns or political factions that were attempting to control their people's historical narrative. In 1842, President and general Antonio López de Santa Anna ordered the exhumation of his lower leg, which had been buried in Veracruz, placed it in a glass box like a saint's relic, and transferred it to its own mausoleum in Mexico City with eulogies, tributes, and great pomp and circumstance.[95] The leg continued to hold special meaning for anti–Santa Anna protesters, who exhumed the "relic" once again and dragged it unceremoniously through the streets of Mexico City to shouts of "Death to the cripple."[96] The alleged cadaver of fallen revolutionary Emiliano Zapata still provokes comment today. Contemporaries doubted that the corpse was Zapata's, and they scrutinized photographs of it for telltale warts, birthmarks, and a missing finger. Myths and corridos materialized, claiming that Zapata had not died at the hands of the Constitutionalist army but rather lived on.[97]

Remains of famous Mexicans were treated as secular relics that deserved stewardship and commemoration. Manuel Acuña was a noted poet and medical student, and he had many friends and readers in Mexico City. Many believed he had a bright future ahead of him as a philosopher poet, with medicine as his practical profession. Like many professionals of the time, he merged science with humanities and was truly a man of letters. One afternoon, however, he ingested prussic acid and died quickly of hydrogen cyanide poisoning. He did not reveal a reason for his suicide, but many suspected it was the result of an unrequited love for Rosario de la Peña.[98] *El Eco de Ambos Mundos,* a daily dedicated to politics, literature, science, arts, industry, commerce, courts, theater, fashion, and news, devoted its front page to the poet's tragic death, funeral, and eulogy. It recalled Acuña's genius, discussed his promising career in the wake of initial reprobation and shock, and compared his death to the suicide of Spanish satirist and liberal Mariano José de Larra in 1837. The reporter described Acuña's funeral in great detail. Mourners and spectators gathered at the patio of the Escuela Nacional de Medicina, where he had resided as a medical student and poet. A sumptuous funeral car arrived to transport his body to the cemetery. But instead of loading his coffin into the car, his closest friends hoisted it onto their shoulders and set off on the route to the cemetery, followed by the car and fifty carriages carrying mourners. A lyre with broken strings and a crown the poet had won for one of his poems topped the funeral car. The article lamented, "It seemed the image of glory shuddered over the remains of his son."[99] The solemn procession wound through the streets of Pila Seca, Esclavo, Manrique, San José el Real, San Francisco, San Juan de Letras, and Hospital Real, finally arriving at Campo Florido. The reporter took the opportunity to fault the Church of Santo Domingo for not allowing the eulogies and speeches to occur on its threshold, although this had been permitted for another poet who had died recently. The implication was that the sin of suicide prohibited Acuña's profaned corpse from being near sacred ground.[100] In 1889, sixteen years after his funeral, the state exhumed his bones and reburied him in the Dolores cemetery in the Rotunda of Illustrious Men. In 1917, his remains were dug up again, this time by fellow Sonorans, and Acuña found his final resting place in his hometown of Saltillo, Coahuila.[101] The organization that lobbied to repatriate his body to Coahuila made claim to their rightful stewardship of his bones and erected a statue at the site of his reinterment.

Poor families may have been unable to extend their leases on the gravesites of their loved ones, but many commemorated their dead in Mexico's cemeteries on All Saints and Souls Day during Day of the Dead celebrations. Irrespective of class, the body held significant power, even after it inhaled its last breath. Families, communities, and nations wished the remains of their loved ones—be they national heroes or beloved kin—to remain close by.

THREE

# Media, Moral Panic, and Youth Suicide

BEATRIZ NORMAN, WHO WAS BY all accounts a modern Mexican woman, penned the following two phrases in her goodbye note before she shot herself in 1927: "Don't think I killed myself for romanticism or love. I did it out of cowardice and nobody but destiny is at fault." She followed these lines with pragmatic instructions, bequeathing her coats, hats, and other articles of clothing to her maid Micaela.[1] Prior to the Mexican Revolution, romanticism and lost love were commonly acknowledged reasons for why young, single people, especially women, chose self-murder. In fact, young female suicides were even eulogized and romanticized in the press. But that overwrought romantic sentiment faded as Mexico endured violent upheaval during its social revolution, from 1911 to 1917. Beatriz hoped to shape the interpretation of her death in her own words. She dismissed love as a reason for her self-destruction. Perhaps she did not want to be seen as a silly young girl who had offed herself for frivolous reasons. She communicated plainly when she insisted that she had taken a weak person's exit. Perhaps she hoped that newspapers that reported on her death would not sentimentalize her biography to make claims about honor and the folly of youth. Like Beatriz, people who wrote suicide letters made their private acts public and behaved as "arbiters of the self."[2] It was expected that a suicide letter would be read not only by loved ones but also by the authorities that investigated the death. Investigators had the mandate to sleuth out a suicide's motive. They needed to determine if the victim had actually been murdered or compelled by another to end their life. Newspapers had a tradition of printing the contents of these *despedidas* (goodbye notes) verbatim during the Porfiriato. This practice was less common later, although the real or fictional content of suicide letters were published from time to time in the 1920s and stunned readers.

Newspapers, police bulletins, broadsides, fiction, poetry, and religious tracts all attempted to make sense of suicide. Each offered explanations of the act that more often than not coincided. Really, there were only subtle changes in suicide habits between the eras of the Porfiriato and the revolution. Youth killed themselves more than any other age group, and their reasons for doing so included unrequited love, dishonor, and boredom. However, the place of the individual in the suicide act was at the crux of differing interpretations. Did the self-murderous impulse derive from psychological or sociological factors? Did the motives for suicide conform to some commonly acknowledged social logic? These questions confounded both medical experts and social commentators, just as they did journalists. Media, literature, and the words and writings of suicides themselves help us understand the cultural meanings and motives imbued in the fatal act. Importantly, the perceived rise in suicide—the epidemic—during the early twentieth century corresponded to the birth of modern journalism during the Porfiriato, when there was a move away from signed opinion and political tracts and toward reporting on world news, local politics, and everyday crime and scandal.[3] Suicides, like sensational murders and robberies, figured prominently on the front pages of newspapers during the Porfiriato but lost urgency during the Mexican Revolution, when news on Pancho Villa's Northern Division, the Constitutionalists, Zapata's movements in the south, and World War I consumed the front pages of most Mexico City dailies. However, newspapers like *El Universal* and *Excélsior* continued to showcase sensational crime in the style of *la nota roja* (literally "red news," the term for Mexican crime reporting that included publication of explicit images of victims of violence), occasionally on the front page but more commonly on the first page of a second section, which was devoted either to crime, sports, or the visits of Hollywood stars like Lupe Vélez.

The urgency and importance attached to suicide in any given time and place is culturally constructed. Beginning in the nineteenth century, nations viewed suicide as an "epic crisis of western civilization."[4] The perception that suicide was on the rise and infecting the Mexican body politic coincided with the country's independence from Spain and its struggle to achieve political identity and stability. In his study of suicide from 1830 to 1875, Francisco Javier Beltrán Albarca found that newspapers such as *El Siglo Diez y Nueve, La Iberia,* and *El Derecho* claimed a suicide epidemic gripped Mexico. As early as 1837, an article penned by physician Manuel María Andrade y Pastor (1809–48) had the provocative title "Imitative Fever." He argued that a man lost his sense of self when grouped with other men who influenced him, that this transformed his mind, and that he in turn could propagate the same behaviors and thinking, even across long distances. Those most susceptible to this mob mentality and power of suggestion included the apathetic, the indolent, and those of obtuse sensibility. The results of this nefarious social influence, according to Andrade y Pastor, included homicidal monomania, duels, and suicide. In essence, suicide was considered to be akin to cholera, a contagious ailment with grave social consequences.[5] He and other Mexican physicians took their clues from French specialists; many had visited France and studied medicine there. Yet, while Andrade y Pastor theorized causes of suicide, it would be Porfirian specialists who took action to understand and make recommendations to curb its occurrence. The medical explanations of suicide will be explored in more detail in the following chapter. However, it is important to note here that newspaper reporters acknowledged medical explanations for the rising suicide rates in Mexico. The suicides themselves even utilized medical lingo to describe their states of mind. In fact, medicine and the nascent social sciences of psychology and sociology provided the suicides with the vocabulary and analogies to make sense of the deadly act.

The causes and meanings that different groups attached to suicide varied, but they all centered on the individual and whether a person had a "right" to end his or her life. Likewise, most commentators adopted a secular approach in their interpretations of suicide. Suicide ceased being a crime after Mexico won independence, but prosecution for the act had been uneven since the late colonial period. Secularization was an impulse of late nineteenth-century nations that endeavored to build state institutions and develop loyal and modern citizenries. Separation of church and state excited some nation builders, but that did not mean that they ceased believing that religion was integral to a healthy society. In her study of suicide in imperial Russia, Susan Morrissey argued, "The religious and secular are not opposing, however, but mutually complicit and highly political categories. Modern states continue to delimit the public domain of religion in a variety of ways; and secular powers have sacralized certain principles, such as the nation and the inviolable rights of the individual."[6] As the following discussion reveals, secular liberals believed, just like their colonial counterparts had, that religion had a place in curbing self-murderous impulses. In fact, liberals and conservatives agreed that suicide was a moral issue with moral remedies. However, they had difficulty in defining and prescribing therapies that were generalizable. Gender, class, and the personal circumstances of each suicide's life informed the attitudes and meanings that he or she ascribed to self-murder. The tone of the public commentary ranged from sentimentalism, to concern about the plight of the working poor, to sarcasm, to comedy. The victim's honor, which most reporters related to class, often worked itself into the discussion as well. All parties agreed that a suicide epidemic gripped Mexico and that the nation's youth were suffering the most. They believed that modernization and urbanization had sparked the epidemic and that the high rate of suicide among Mexico's youth was the unfortunate but treatable side effect.

### THE VIEWS FROM THE PRESS

Most commentators at the cusp of the twentieth century believed suicide to be an inevitable consequence of modernity. Some liberal writers felt compelled to defend the march of civilization. They accepted that Mexico was suffering from a suicide epidemic, but they did not want to see the country's impressive trajectory of progress under Porfirio Díaz stall out. Liberals also felt the pain of having to constantly defend the tenets and values of liberalism against their religious rivals. However, they were not irreligious themselves, and many of them contended that the state had a moral mission to heal society. Laureana Wright de Kleinhans, the founder and director of a periodical for female readers, *Violetas del Anáhuac,* wrote a two-part, front-page editorial on suicide in 1888. Her opening statements read, "This terrible disease, so widespread in modern societies, has always existed, everywhere and in all epochs; but never with such profusion as now."[7] She asked how such a crime against human nature could occur in the advancing age of knowledge and reason. She refuted those who saw everything from the perspective of "timidity and fear" and stated that suicidal impulses arose from not fearing God and his ability to punish sinners. She criticized those who impugned civilization—"mother of all light, creator of all good"—and its forward march. On the contrary, Wright de Kleinhans speculated, "The more a man knows, reason is nourished ... [and] his morale is strengthened." She discussed the famous heroic suicides of Lucrecia, who died to save her sexual honor; Cato, who would not submit to Caesar; and Mithridades, who chose not to suffer the treachery of his son. She reminded readers that most humans did not kill themselves when they suffered the same circumstances. Wright de Kleinhans mentioned that the Druids chose suicide to enjoy an exalted afterlife, but she concluded that their reasons for suicide were different from those of individuals in nineteenth-century Mexico. She surmised that the common reasons for suicide were excessive suffering, desperation, fear of the future, and boredom with life. She claimed that an individual's lack of righteousness, intellectual energy, and conscience were to blame for allowing suffering to drive that person to suicide and unruly passions, and she declared that a lack of reason or temporary dementia was responsible for pushing someone to the point of self-destruction. As for the motive of fearing the future, she blamed victims for not waiting out the threat. Wright de Kleinhans had the least amount of empathy for those who killed themselves out of boredom, noting that a "refined egoism" separated the personality of this type of person from others and that a lack of fraternal and humanitarian education made these people unable to understand that living was not just for oneself but also for others.[8]

In the second part of her editorial, Wright de Kleinhans censured romanticism and its adherents, who relished in tragedies of the heart and chose death over life, likening them to Cervantes's Man of La Mancha, with his vainglorious enthusiasm for lost causes.[9] In the end, she placed religion and science on twin pillars, noting, "When religion and morality walk together with exact, abstract, subjunctive, and rational science, creating the august triumvirate of reason; when one provides man proven and solid education, logical and satisfactory theories . . . his judgment will be grounded, his soul will be strengthened against inherent weaknesses, and suicide will disappear from criminal statistics, [suicide] finally becoming impossible in educated societies."[10] Florid in its prose and forcefully intellectual in its argumentation, Wright de Kleinhans's essay put her on a par with men of letters, who valued their "literary virility." Unlike them, however, she could not combine her journalistic talents with political or legal ambitions.[11] In fact, Wright de Kleinhans founded *Violetas* to provide women writers a venue to display their intellect and their skills at poetry, history, and social commentary.

The journal was initially published under the title *Las Hijas de Anáhuac,* and it was under this name that it published a poem in 1880 by Lucia G. Herrera, the niece of prominent científico and diplomat Francisco Díaz Covarrubias. Herrera's poem, titled "El suicidio," followed the romantic trope of a deceived woman seeking to drown herself. It told the tale of a troubled woman whose blood burned with a suicide fever as she walked under a very black night close to the sea. She eventually walked, arms outstretched, into the deadly waves and succumbed to the salty water. The next morning, town residents found her corpse washed up on the beach.[12] Tragic yet romantically intoned, the mysterious female suicide no doubt intrigued minds with a penchant for the melodramatic. Herrera's intention was most likely to use the poem as an antidote to suicide by portraying the macabre side of self-destruction and thus warning impressionable readers against the act.

*El Imparcial* showcased suicides on its front pages and served as the archetype of sensational journalism in the late Porfiriato. Founded in 1896 by Rafael Reyes Spíndola, the paper received the largest government subsidy and was therefore viewed by many as the voice of the Porfirian government. *El Imparcial* ushered in modern journalism for a diverse reading public that included people from all classes and of both genders. The daily had something for every reader: news from abroad, business news, advertisements, crime reports, and articles for women. Like its French peer, the *Petit Journal*, *El Imparcial*'s hyperbolic style made perfect sense in a society led by positivist thinkers. Sensationalist reporting of violent crime and suicide shocked sensibilities, stirred emotions, and "stood in close relation to a positivist vision of an ordered world. It generated a way of talking about the world and demanding change." [13] Newspapers gave examples of social problems wrought by rapid modernization and provided residents with the language to debate them. *El Imparcial* and other dailies that sensationalized "news" spoke to the empathetic reader who responded with horror to violent deaths and felt sympathy for victims. Gregory K. Shaya argues that sensational newspaper coverage provided primers on how the reading public ought to respond to violent death: not with cool indifference but rather with shocked concern. [14]

Independent newspapers filled columns with overt and veiled attacks on *El Imparcial* for its close relationship to the Díaz regime. Rival newspapers viewed *El Imparcial* as the mouthpiece of the presidency and criticized it for accepting money from the government. An opinion piece in an 1898 edition of *El Imparcial* voiced a view similar to Wright de Kleinhans's, criticizing those that linked the rise in suicide with the inevitable march of progress. The writer contended that the rising suicide rates were in fact related to the upsurge in population. A burgeoning populace, especially in the capital, meant that suicide was more noticeable. Moreover, he wrote, suicide "does not have its roots in one cause, but a group of causes, all inherent in certain spirits that drive the state of the conscience. This disgust for life, this desire to escape reality, when reality does not correspond to an internal vision that can be achieved." He placed fault clearly with the psychology of the individual, not with modernization and progress. [15]

Ramón L. Alva, a gadfly editor of *El Monitor Republicano*, a newspaper that criticized the perpetuity of the Díaz regime, asked on the front page,

"Why has this act, before uncommon, become common and frequent? What is the cause of this evil, always worthy of grief and emotion?" He credited the change in "ideas and customs of the times, the defective education of children at home and in school, education in which little is done to fortify the spirit and prepare one to struggle against adversity, to resist the blows of misfortune with resignation and bravery, to triumph over the pains and penalties of life." Alva believed that suicide resulted from "social corruption" and that only a "moral remedy" could be effective in preventing it. More specifically, he called for a strictly moral education in the home and school and a severe crackdown by state institutions on vices. Police and courts should be emboldened to punish debauched behaviors. Alva prescribed a moralization of society to build the "brakes" to help individuals bolster their instincts for self-preservation.[16] Perhaps couched in his rhetoric there was a message that Porfirian liberalism fostered the "relaxation of customs." [17] Indeed, it seemed that reporting on social problems and crime held hidden messages that criticized the Pax Porfiriana. A corrupt government bred corruption in all the nooks and crannies of society.

The notion that suicide was a contagion or that the body politic could be infected with the disease of suicide informed many opinions at the turn of the century. Youth were especially apt to become young Werthers, staging they own stylistic deaths because they had lost in love. Werther, the doomed protagonist of Johann Wolfgang von Goethe's 1774 book, *The Sorrows of Young Werther,* falls in love with a woman named Charlotte but cannot have her because she is engaged to another man. Rather than suffer an impossible love triangle, the sensitive artist shoots himself in the head. The book reputedly led to the first rash of copycat suicides in Europe. Many believed that reading about suicide led to more suicides. *El Nacional* reported that editors of capital newspapers had convened in 1899 to discuss methods to combat suicide in Mexican society. *El Imparcial* also followed the story and agreed that reporters should not narrate suicides as if they were novels. Although they acknowledged that readers might purchase newspapers for the sensational reporting on violent deaths like suicide, the editors urged newspapers to "present suicide in its awful nudity and comment on its crime against nature with reason and philosophy so that a natural repulsion will be inspired in the minds of readers." In order to convince youngsters not to commit suicide, "Why not present to the eyes of the readers the cadaver of the desperate young man who in a moment of insanity took his own life, naked, spread-eagled among other soiled cadavers on the morgue slab, giving fuel to the malicious taunts of the practitioners, reporters, and workers of the hospital?"[18] Ironically, *El Imparcial* combined this true-crime, realistic approach with hagiography in much of its reporting on young suicides, especially those of single women. Newspapers preferred elite women, who presumably had so much promise ahead in their lives, to those of working women crushed by economic hardship. A 1900 editorial in *El Nacional* lamented that suicide had moved down the social ladder into the humble classes. The poor had caught suicide fever! The author warned, "The poor need faith, hope, and charity to live . . . and the spread of suicide among them infallibly reveals that this set of virtues that applies brakes and lifts the spirit is losing, and this is very grave. People without this will always be as miserable as they are dangerous."[19] The underlying message was that suicide was fast becoming a social problem and could unleash the dangerous and criminal impulses of the miserable poor. This was frightening news for Porfirian científicos and urban residents alike, and violent and petty crime was on the minds of criminologists and reformers.[20]

On the other hand, the workers' press argued that it was actually the progress that benefited the educated and elite that led to suicide. To them, modernization meant decreasing morality and rising suicide rates. An 1897 article in *La Convención Radical Obrera* discussed Mexican society and the rise in homicides and suicides in the nation. The writer noted that both crimes rose in tandem with the advancement of society and that although Mexico had achieved material progress, "Can we say the same with respect to morality?" He described what he called a common scenario: a man of the comfortable class enters a cantina at 11:00 am for a light lunch and has one drink after another, at which point conversations turn ugly, a fight breaks out, and a murder is committed. "This is what occurs daily between the people that one calls educated and illustrious," smirked the author. He contended that drunkenness led to immorality, which in turn led to homicide and suicide; in other words, progress fueled alcoholism and criminality. He opined that workers were more "temperate, relatively, in their habits, compared to the wealthy" and that if immorality was "ostensible" in workers, it was "scandalous" in the comfortable class. The editorial continued: "Besides: the working man has a brake, the mutualist association, no matter how much their enemies deny it, . . . they continue being schools of education for many, and the source of moralization for all that belong to them." The author concluded by advocating for temperance because "it will prevent infinite crimes."[21] An 1881 editorial in another workers' paper, *El Hijo del Trabajo*, asserted that drunkenness provoked workers to commit suicide.[22] Liberal commentators agreed that suicide was a social problem that could be solved with moral remedies. However, "moral" in this sense should not to be confused with "religious."

Reporters and editors writing for religious newspapers sometimes agreed that suicide was a social problem, but they differed from liberal outlets in that the only remedy they supported was a return to religious education in schools and the home. Nineteenth-century liberal politicians in Mexico had endured a lengthy battle to secularize education and relegate the Catholic Church to ministering to its parishioners. The advent of liberalism and separation of church and state had many religious leaders decrying the moral corruption that resulted from secular and public education. The religious take on suicide placed fault on the individual, as taking one's own life was an act of free will, albeit a sick will. For example, in 1890, *La Caridad,* whose masthead read, "A daily consecrated to defend the Catholic religion," published a front-page editorial titled "Social Cancer." The writer lamented that the social body was in a state of "rot" that corrupted youth: "In the study of the wise, the privy of the young, the workshop of the laborer, everywhere are noted naked Venuses, provocative groups, impure statues, praising the indulgences of the imagination, engendering the hedonisms of thought. Truth flees; material corruption grows at an appalling rate. It is the coming of the empire of lies." The editorial proceeded to focus on modern society and how it had corrupted, in particular, the youth of Mexico:

> If we look back to youth, we find it muddied in vice; it wallows in the hot-bed of passions, stunning itself with the sound of feasting: life hastens in the fruition of pleasure. At each step we find mobs of the young, aged by the premature abuse of pleasures, looking down at the ground as if ashamed of their conduct, as fearful of looking to the heavens because of their depravities; they carry trembling hands, reddened eyes, a nerveless thought and will without vigor: the seal of the Divinity has marked them with the sign of the reprobate.[23]

For the writers for *La Caridad,* modernity equaled corruption of the youth because it encouraged them to seek excessive freedom and indulgences, and their parents allowed them this. Faulting a "senseless" society for crooning a "hymn of admiration" to the suicide and "revering his memory" as a hero, the writer blamed the profaned home, in which adolescent brains had grown accustomed to alcohol.[24]

Less than two weeks later, the paper published another front-page editorial placing culpability for the corruption of youth more squarely on liberal newspapers, charging that they had forgotten proper decorum and "employ their pens to describe scenes that do nothing more than stoke the passions of inexperienced youth, inflaming their impure desires with pages full of sensuality right before their eyes, under the futile pretense of teaching those who do not know the consequences of evil." The article emphasized the hypocrisy of journalists who argue against the death penalty because "society has no right over a human life, and who are the same who consider the duel necessary, stealing their privileges from the law, and [they] excuse suicide, contrary to the laws of nature."[25] *La Caridad* continued the theme of blaming Mexico's social sins of prostitution, gambling, and suicide on anti-Christian education and alcoholism.[26]

An 1880 editorial in *El Hijo de Trabajo* aligned closely with the Catholic view on suicide. Shunning an unfettered individualism and a belief in full sovereignty over one's person, the article began, "No one can dispose of what does not belong to him." Signed simply "Silvio," the opinion piece argued that humans were the only creatures in the animal world that committed death by their own hands. It described the act as going against natural laws of human preservation and argued that a man did not possess the right to end his life. His life was not his own to dispose of how he saw fit; it belonged to nature. The writer concluded that suicide was, in fact, the worst sort of crime that could be committed and that the act depreciated the dignity of all.[27] Thirty years later, this sentiment had not changed. *El Diario* commented on an editorial in *El Imparcial* penned by Luis G. Urbina, a modernist writer and journalist. Urbina recognized that many had advocated the belief that "your life is yours alone; you can have all that is yours. Then you can throw it away when you want, like you toss your handkerchief in the middle of a stream." Reasoning that even Robinson Crusoe did not give up when stuck on an island populated with savages, the reporter for *El Diario* argued that suicide emphasized the dark times of present days. Urbina empathized with individuals who ended their lives because they feared pain, had lost faith, and given up hope. The writer for *El Diario* begged to respectfully differ: "We believe that one who rightly thinks of life never ends it; one who fears pain does not understand pleasure; one who loses all faith has never believed in it; one who hope has scorned has never been dependent on charity."[28]

The public seemed aghast and worried about the self-murderous impulses of Mexico's youth. However, some editorials poked fun at the inanity of the young and their penchant for self-destruction. Satire or dark humor in these cases also communicated disapproval for the immoral act of suicide, or perhaps satire served as an available coping mechanism for a society in a philosophical crisis. Signed simply "Pitou," a front-page editorial in *El Popular* with the title "Suicide: Fashion Plague" began seriously enough, "There are almost no days that the press doesn't recount a new case of suicide." The reporter admitted that he had seen many cases of suicide in his long career, and at this juncture the sarcasm flowed. He chose the most bizarre examples (most likely fictional) of self-pity and suicide. For example, Pitou described a woman who was seduced by a *tenorio* (womanizer) and then drank a potion of four boxes of match tips dissolved in alcohol. When questioned by the police, she opened her mouth to speak and blue flames launched out of her mouth, eyes, and nose, terrifying the officers, who thought she had unleashed the devil. Safely cured, this same unfortunate woman went on to eat a statue of Sappho (who had been deceived by Phaon) and drink the contents of an inkwell on another occasion. This time she succumbed, leaving a "whiff of sulfur and a black tongue like a parakeet." Or what reader could forget the young man "gummed by a curly, waxed moustache, who believed himself irresistible"? Only brown freckles spoiled his comely visage, and he tried all sorts of concoctions to fade the spots. "The young Adonis" washed his face so much that he developed a flaming dermatitis that made him inconsolable. He decided that suicide was his only way out. His family feared his "dangerous inclination" and removed all sharp objects from his reach. The young "Narciso" persisted in his death wish, however, swallowing a toothbrush and thrusting his face into a basin of water. He survived but suffered a "devilish gastritis." His body "yielded some shaggy strands believed to be from the brush .... The handle took up residence in his body, but the man lives happily, subject to a regimen of hydrotherapy." [29] The tone must have provoked laughter and smirks from readers, but the fact remained that Mexico suffered a suicide epidemic among its sensitive youth. While Pitou ridiculed the death wishes of Mexico's youth, Mexicans mourned the deaths that occurred around them.

Religious newspapers like *El País* published lengthy editorials that condemned liberalism and modern philosophies like positivism. *El Nacional* stopped short of blaming ideology but surmised that only religion could combat materialism, that without God there could be no ideals to govern society. [30] A 1900 editorial on the front page of *El País* also blamed liberal papers for reporting on two suicides of the day before—a young woman who swallowed strychnine and a young man who shot himself in the chest. The writer argued that the reporting provoked neurotic youth with weak souls to be infected by this "suicide fever." He pleaded his readers to save three pesos monthly so that they could afford to send their children to religious schools and instructed parents to prohibit their children from reading liberal newspapers that contained daily crime exposés.[31] Sensational news of suicide and murder ought not to fill the papers or be consumed in the homes of religious households, he argued. Just a few weeks later, *El País* published a similar editorial, titled "Suicide, Regicide, and Barbarity," which noted that suicide had previously been uncommon in civilized societies but had now become a fever like malaria. The writer implied that suicide rates correlated with efforts to destroy the importance of religion and the Church in society and that the rights extended and practiced under the anti-Christian Mexican Revolution had led to barbarity and destruction. The moral "don't do to others what you would not want done to you" had been replaced with the "law of natural selection," under which all the rights belonged to "the most able, the strongest, the most astute and least scrupulous."[32]

Later that month, another article in *El País* reported that there had been three suicides of young Mexicans in one day and ridiculed the official diagnosis of "degeneration." The writer insisted that suicide never occurred when Catholicism dominated society, only when Jacobin education corrupted the minds of children.[33] In other words, both editorials offered a spirited critique of positivism and its main proponents, the científicos, who populated the halls of government and the medical school. *El País* lamented changes in Europe as well, noting that assassins had murdered Empress Elizabeth of Austria in 1898, King Umberto I of Italy in 1900, and other regents in an irreligious and modern era of anarchy. Ridiculing the notion that the present century was more civilized, *El País* argued that the current course of society would lead to barbarism.[34] Simply put, positivism rested on the assumption that civilization was an inevitable march forward, and the writer disagreed with this. In his eyes, the current scenario of a modern, irreligious society would take Mexico backward. Modernity and its worship of democratic institutions, the free market, and individualism would be the undoing of Mexican society. Commenting on the three suicides, the editorialist doffed his gloves. Noting that Mexican society suffered an "infection of liberalism," he stressed that suicides occurred infrequently when liberalism did not exist. He claimed that although the Anglo-Saxon race had material wealth and progress, their morality was in a state of regression. They might have factories, banks, and commerce, he wrote, but they "hide their profound, innu-merable and smelly ulcers; their cities crowded with criminals, their dissolute homes, their derisory, when not anarchic, marriages, . . . their barbarous cus-toms, like taking revenge into their own hands, . . . their rapacity, . . . their lack of loyalty." Ultimately, the author contended that moral deterioration correlated with material progress and concluded that Mexico ought not to go the way of the United States and Great Britain.[35]

Broadsides printed in the shop of Antonio Vanegas Arroyo, featuring the illustrations of José Guadalupe Posada, shared similar views as conservative, religious newspapers. A 1900 broadside titled "Shocking and Terrible Occurrence in the City of Silao in the First Days of the Twentieth Century: Suicide of a Greedy Rich Man," depicted Bardomiano Urrizalde as a nattily dressed dandy in the center of the frame (see figure 7). Surrounded by menac-ing demons signifying the seven deadly sins of avarice, lust, wrath, sloth, pride, envy, and gluttony, the vicious man looked crazed and evil. The text claimed that mental illness did not cause Bardomiano to end his life but rather that he was driven to suicide by materialism and atheism. The verse below the large image recounted that the sinful man had inherited his wealth without hard work, charged high interest rates on loans, and engaged in unlawful activities. He deceived women and gambled, eventually losing all of his money and end-ing up a pauper, forced to rent a hut from an indigenous Mexican. The verse continued to ridicule Bardomiano, noting that shop owners refused to sell him strychnine, a gun, or ammunition. Having no choice but to take the pauper's method of suicide, Bardomiano boiled match heads in water, con-sumed the lethal concoction, and suffered horrendous stomach pains as demons swirled around and reminded him of his wicked life. Art historian Patrick Frank argued that the broadside image "approaches the iconography of a temptation scene," and in fact, Vanegas Arroyo's shop also produced devo-tional prints in large numbers.[36] The message of the broadside was clear and no doubt resonated with its working class audience: Bardomiano's greed, sloth, and lack of work ethic had propelled him to suicide.

Suicide was a common subject for illustrator Guadalupe Posada and pub-lisher Vanegas Arroyo. The 1906 suicide of a sacristan in the Mexico City Metropolitan Cathedral piqued their interest. Septuagenarian Máximo Silva had cleaned and maintained the church and its interior and exterior spaces for years. The broadside emphasized the horror of the suicide, pointing out that his hanging at the altar of the kings in the west nave of the cathedral profaned sacred space. Máximo left no note and did not give any motive for

## ESPANTOSISIMO
—Y—
# TERRIBLE ACONTECIMIENTO
### EN LA CIUDAD DE SILAO EN LOS PRIMEROS DIAS DEL SIGLO XX
## ¡SUICIDIO DE UN RICO ENVIDIOSO!

En la cuidad de Silao, pertenenciente al Estado de Guanajuato vivía un hombre extremadamente rico, tan rico como muy pocos habrá en el mundo. Se llamaba Bardomiano Urrizalde La exorbitante fortuno de que gozaba se la debía únicamente á la cuantiosa herencia de sus padres y á la desordenada usura que practicó después; ayudado además con todos los medios ilegales y hasta infames que se pusieron á su alcance. Su carácter era digno de censurarse por todos.

Bardomiano no tenía ninguna religión; era materilista y ateó; estas ideas tan fuertemente arraigadas en su alma trajeron como era natural sus funestas consecuencias, y la envidia fué una de las pasiones más dominantes que tuvo; de este vicio resultaron la avaricia, la gula, la soberbia, la lujuria, la ira y por último la pereza.

Así pues los siete vicios rodeaban á este desgraciado sér y no solo le rodeaban sino que formaron profundas raíces en él.

Pero vamos á describir su desdichado y maldecido fin en este mundo.

Por mucho tiempo á Bardomiano no se le negó nada de cuanto deseaba, pues como tenía dinero este le facilitaba todo; el mismo salía en busca de personas á quien prestarles dinero con un exagerado premio dejándoles de cobrar por mucho tiempo y después les cargaba los réditos pretestando que ellos eran los que no le querían pagar y de esta manera les abría juicio y les embargaba sus intereses, quedándose dueño de ellos y dejándolos en la miseria más grande del mundo.

Tenía el vicio de cortejar á las mujeres, engañándolas y después de conseguir sus infernales deseos las abandonaba dejándolas en deplorable estado de pobreza.

La mayor parte de las noches se ocupaba de jugar en su casa, para lo cual tenía ciertos individuos amigos suyos, que le servían de convidadores y paleros, quienes les llevaban jóvenes de buenas familias y allí los desplumaban en un abrir y cerrar de ojos, robándoles á veces lo que podía.

Al rayar al día para celebrar sus triunfos del juego formaba banquetes con sus compañeros de vicio, bebiendo, y brindando con ellos y muchas mugeres de mal vivir que estos mismos le conseguían, con

FIGURE 7. José Guadalupe Posada, *Espantosísimo y terrible acontecimiento en la Ciudad de Silao en los primeros días del siglo XX: ¡Suicidio de un rico envidioso!* (ca. 1900). Type-metal engraving. Amon Carter Museum of American Art, Fort Worth, Texas, 1978.89.

his self-murderous intentions. The broadside's text noted that he was a man of advanced age who had lost his wife the previous year. Friends reported that he talked frequently about joining her in the other life. The broadside noted that all religions, "not just Catholicism, condemned the act of killing oneself." The illustration showed the sacristan hanging, his tongue protruding, in the left plane while priests and authorities milled around a stretcher to the right (see figure 8). The text claimed that morbidity had gripped his mind and that he had thought hard on the best way to commit suicide, even at one point musing with a fellow sacristan about whether either of them would have the courage to throw themselves out the window of the cathedral tower.[37] Demons did not appear in the image of this broadsheet, and the message was one of God's mercy for the sad sacristan. *El Imparcial* reported on the suicide, noting the juxtaposition of the macabre hanged man and the beauty of the cathedral's altar. The sacristan hung himself with the heavy cord that held back the curtains around the altar. He chose the niche that held the "incorrupt body" of martyr saint Teodoro. In the days following the suicide, Archbishop Próspero María de Alarcón, accompanied by members of the city council, walked around the cathedral blessing the church and throwing holy water on the walls and paving stones to cleanse the sin from the holy space.[38] Another Posada illustration, this one undated, accompanied a song verse entitled "La última nota, triste canción" (The final note, sad song). The drawing portrayed a troubled man holding himself up by leaning on a table where a suicide note lies. In his left hand, he grips a small liqueur glass that may be a draft of poison. Dressed in huaraches and loose campesino pants and a shirt, the man is depicted as being on the brink of committing suicide. In the song verse, he laments his loss of hope and fortune, admits his sins, and describes his unanswered pleas of forgiveness. He intones, "I surrender to the dubious death cult in the funereal darkness. I am a corpse that wanders unburied, always looking for happiness."[39] The "death cult" may be a reference to the suicide fad that seemed to plague Mexico City at the turn of the century.

The suicide of María Luisa Noecker, introduced in chapter 2, captured the imagination and headlines of the mainstream and penny press for months in 1909 and 1910. Several broadsheets illustrated by Posada commented on the situation since the young woman allegedly killed herself because she had been deflowered by the famous bullfighter Rodolfo Gaona. According to multiple witnesses, Luisa had been deeply infatuated with Rodolfo and managed to get invited to a party that he was expected to attend. Witnesses disagreed on the

FIGURE 8. José Guadalupe Posada, *La sacristan que se ahorca en la catedral* (Mexico City: A. Vanegas Arroyo, n.d.). Fernando Gamboa Collection of Prints by José Guadalupe Posada, 1888–1944, Center for Southwest Research, University of New Mexico Libraries.

events that occurred between the hours of midnight and sunrise on the night of that party, but the fact remained that Luisa shot herself twice in her bedroom shortly thereafter. Newspapers exploded with articles and calls for the arrest of the bullfighter. Rodolfo had risen to the height of fame from his humble, indigenous beginnings in Guanajuato. At the time, Spanish bullfighters received the most attention and adulation from the Porfirian upper classes. However, Rodolfo fought his way into the spotlight with several spectacular triumphs from 1906 to 1908, and he was granted the recognition of *alternativa* (senior matador status) in Spain the same year. It was rare for Mexican toreros to earn the title of alternativa in Spain. Rodolfo also received notice because he invented a new pass with the cape, termed the *gaonera,* which placed the body of the bullfighter in front rather than behind the cape.

Posada had illustrated broadsheets of Rodolfo before the suicide scandal. For example, he covered Rodolfo's goring by a bull in Puebla in 1908.[40] When news of Luisa's deflowering and death hit the headlines of *El Imparcial,* a broadsheet soon followed. *El Imparcial* quickly condemned the young torero, but in Posada's rendering, Rodolfo received no blame. The broadside placed culpability squarely on the young Luisa, claiming that she had acted indeco-rously and with foolish abandon. The print, "Sufferings, Reflections and Advice from the Suicide," featured two portraits of Luisa. In the top left quadrant was a lovely image of her surrounded by a funeral wreath, and the image in the lower right quadrant depicted her shooting herself in the head in her bedroom while her maid ran from the room crying for help. The verse accompanying the illustration includes the line "I let myself go too far," allud-ing to the fact that she went to a party with strange men and that she drank too much alcohol and lost control.[41] The broadsheet did not moralize the act of suicide itself but warned that excess and gender impropriety could lead to disastrous results, much like the seven deadly sins had led to the self-destruction of Baldomiano. Like those with a religious view, it rested fault on the individual for the act of suicide.

Liberal papers like *El Imparcial* and religious dailies like *El País* sparred frequently in their front-page editorials. Religious papers faulted the corrupt-ing influence of *la nota roja,* which delighted readers with the salacious details of murders and suicides. The religious view posited that only religious skeptics or atheists would kill themselves. *El Imparcial* took that conjecture head-on in a series of editorials published between 1905 and 1906. The writer countered the thesis, noting that most suicides worldwide believed in God and that "suicide was as much a social problem as a religious one." Suicide letters invoking God and asking His forgiveness proved the faith of their authors. He reasoned that suicides knew that their crime would result in divine punishment but that they hoped for God's mercy. Simply put, "believer-suicides trust totally in the mercy of God, in the belief that clem-ency can obfuscate and lessen [divine] justice." [42] *El País* responded with an essay titled "How Barbaric!" The piece accused *El Imparcial* of perpetuating grand lies and proceeded to list high-profile Mexican nonbelievers who had committed suicide, "The poet Manuel Acuña, positivist atheist. The book-seller Fidencio López, positivist atheist. Eduardo Velázquez, Jacobin atheist." It went on to note that in the course of a century, "no suicide has been perpe-trated in any seminary while there have been many youth of atheist instincts" who took their lives in the Escuela Nacional Preparatoria (National Preparatory School).[43] Likewise, there had been no suicides among priests or members of religious organizations, but there had been suicides among known masons and "propagandists of impiety." [44]

Three days later, another editorial appeared in *El Imparcial* to respond to the challenge from *El País*. The writer repeated his thesis that the majority of suicides were, in fact, believers and challenged the implication that suicides lacked religion because they committed the sin of self-murder. The author elaborated the logic of the argument and noted that if suicides and delinquents could not be considered believers then "religions without sinners were the same as religions without proselytes." [45] Not content to let the challenge rest, El País published a front-page response two days later. Holding no punches, the editorial began with the headline "It Is False What Is Said by 'El Imparcial.'" This time, the writer marshaled statistics and the theories of prominent positivist scientists such as Enrique Ferry to prove unequivocally that suicide rates rose with the growing impiety of society. Going further, the writer surmised that nations that adopted liberalism experienced the highest rates of suicide. [46] This sentiment received support in a 1902 editorial in the journal La Ciudad de Dios, which claimed that sociologists worldwide had discovered that suicide among children had moved from sporadic to epidemic levels. Quoting German sociologist Dr. Bar, "The suicide of a child is a product of our modern civilization. Degeneration and insanity on one hand, vicious upbringing on the other hand." The La Ciudad de Dios writer surmised, "The lesson is obvious. Religion cannot be divorced from schooling. Schools without God in the final analysis are abominations, only less monstrous than absolute ignorance." [47]

Almost a year later, in 1906, a writer for El Imparcial took up the theme of atheism and suicide again. Gloating between the lines of text, the editorial bore the subtitle "Only Sextons That Commit Suicide Are Crazy?" The writer challenged the prevailing El País attitude that only atheists killed themselves and that only individuals that embraced religion possessed the moral brakes to hold back fatal despair. The journalist detailed the suicide of the sacristan who worked in the cathedral, recounted above. He had hung himself in a niche near the main altar. El Imparcial lampooned the reporters of the religious press, who insisted that the sacristan suffered insanity and therefore was not responsible for his crime and, furthermore, because he had not had individual will in committing the crime, God would not punish him. Never in the religious reporting of the poor sexton's suicide was the man charged with lacking religious belief. [48] How could El País be so hypocritical, implied the El Imparcial editorial?

Two weeks later, an article in El Imparcial attacked the simplistic view of the religious newspapers that held firm to the belief that atheism led to suicide. The writer countered their claims, "Suicide, like vice and like crime, recognizes multiple causes, varying for each individual; social more than personal causes, in many cases organic and atavistic more than moral, and upbringing in many." Agreeing with the earlier argument that most suicides believed in God, the editorial paraphrased the parting words of María R. Dévora, a twenty-year-old woman who shot herself in the heart. She wrote a goodbye note to her lover on the back of a circus program, soliciting him to place a *milagro* (religious folk charm) in the plate of Santo Niño Atocha and light four candles to the Virgen de Soledad. The author emphasized that this case and other like it proved that religious faith and suicide were not antithetical. In other words, María, just like other devout suicides, hoped that prayers would assist her soul to leave purgatory.[49]

## CONTAGION, LITERATURE, AND SUICIDE

The religious journal *El Amigo de la Verdad* printed an editorial by an author calling herself the "Messenger of the Priesthood" in 1895. It asked, "What child doesn't take delight in listening to the stories of his nurse? The devil takes advantage of this inclination to introduce evil" into the minds of children. Moreover, the article argued, reading novels and dramas "impregnates" the imagination with "iniquitous ideas" that unconsciously develop over a lifetime and "are put into practice, perhaps without thinking, because they mesmerize like the serpent before Eve." The Messenger provided the example of the story *Les Mystères de Paris*, a realistic serial novel by Eugène Sue that was published between 1842 and 1843 in Paris and prohibited by the church. She claimed that the book caused youth to model themselves after the two main characters, Rodolphe and Violetta, a prostitute he saves from a brutal man. The story features all levels of Parisian society and critiques social institutions as well. The editorial also mentioned the opera *La traviata,* which had recently been performed in Mexico City. She charged that the opera influenced young women to dress with "certain negligence" and pale their faces to appear consumptive like the main character, also named Violetta. She continued, "Think about what impact this reading will have on a maiden, a half-open bud, who inhales the poisoned perfume of the passions that drags us back to the corrupt nature of original sin."[50]

*El Imparcial,* usually targeted by the religious press for instigating immorality, also editorialized that poor reading choices could lead to dissolution. However, it claimed that the concern hinged on a "social problem" caused by the dissemination of lewd literature. Pollution was the ready metaphor as the article noted that vendors trolled the streets of Mexico City selling obscene books, stamps, and folios. It called upon the health department to conserve "public decorum" and rid the city of indecent ephemera, noting "evil books often cause major harm to men. The evil book, just like the good ones, will live on after its author has died. The leprous book, although furtively, can enter our libraries, can enter our homes. The vile book is susceptible to transform character . . . . A book is a voice that lives. It is a spirit that flies in the face of the world . . . . Men die, monuments crumble . . . . That which remains and survives is human thought."[51] The mission was to prevent human thought from being corrupted. *El Amigo de la Verdad* and *El Imparcial,* two unlikely bedfellows, agreed that themes and values propagated in fiction and drama could infect the collective psyche of developing minds.

Politician, educator, and avid positivist Agustín Aragon founded the journal *Revista Positiva* in 1901. Published three times a year, the journal served as the "organ of Positivism in Mexico." Aragón expressed the views of many Mexicans when he penned the article "Social and Moral Influence of Reading Novels in Youth." He reasoned that there were two camps of authors: those who write to delight the senses and those who write to convey social and moral aesthetics.[52] Aragón deeply believed that artists had a moral responsibility to create works that "provoke interest in social problems" and "create sympathy for the noble qualities" of their protagonists. He noted that all youth could be altruistic *and* selfish and thus argued that a moral novel could spur "healthy emotions." Unlike critics of naturalist author Émile Zola, Aragón contended that the Frenchman portrayed the real human condition and that he "teaches in his novels that happiness resides in truth, salvation in work . . . [and] God."[53] Aragón named George Eliot and Felix Holt as other examples of moral authors. On the other hand, he warned that Goethe's *The Sorrows of Young Werther* could easily influence youth to commit copycat suicide. This sentiment echoed an earlier article that appeared in the national medical school journal, *La Escuela de Medicina.* Published in 1885, ten years earlier than the warning from the Messenger of the Priesthood, the article cautioned that the dramatic performances of Goethe's novel "make suicide very poetic and spiritual and in that moment produce a thrombosis of intelligence and the poisoning of exalted imaginations." It also argued that the causes of suicide were well known and provided a list of them: "the abuse of pleasures, masturbation, excess of alcoholic beverages, passion for gambling, anger, ambition, envy, jealousy, idleness, tedium, loneliness, nostalgia, domestic troubles, extreme fondness for music that exalts the senses, terror, regrets, desperation, misery, dishonor, and overall all, a hereditary disposition." [54]

Youth most readily succumbed to copycat suicide. *El Diario* revisited an editorial originally published in *El Imparcial* in which Luis G. Urbina ridiculed youngsters who killed themselves so that their death throes would be narrated in full melodramatic splendor in the crime pages of dailies: "What bliss, naively foolish, she that sacrifices life for a press scandal, that brings names and vulgar episodes to tongues." [55] Furthermore, Urbina recognized the problem to be of the bourgeois classes—in other words, he considered the literate classes to be most at risk because they clamored for notoriety and fame and read despicable literature. *El Diario* ended its discussion of Urbina's essay by noting that its rival, *El Imparcial,* reproduced Urbina's editorial and agreed with it in spirit but then also published in the same issue a part of the novel *La hija del asesino* (The daughter of the assassin), by Carolina Invernizo, an author Urbina had pointed out as corrupting to young minds. [56] *El Imparcial* reprinted Urbina's entire editorial. In it, Urbina noted the degeneration of the privileged classes and claimed, "The illiterate *indio* does not know the idea of death. In his embryonic and hazy fetishism he has full confidence that he will live forever. Their lively funerals that seem Egyptian show this well, around the graves each year one places meat and sweets for the dead who never loses his form or his appetites or his desires. The *indio* cannot be Christian: he cannot imagine souls without bodies." [57] Urbina was clearly referring to the Day of the Dead rituals practiced in Mexico on November 1 (All Saints' Day) and November 2 (All Souls' Day). Yet his point was to stress that only the prosperous classes possessed a death instinct. [58]

The press did not fault European authors and dramatists alone. Social commentators believed that Mexican authors also contributed to moral laxity among youths. Spanish American literature employed themes of suicide as well. Vicente Riva Palacio, the father of the Mexican historical novel, was an immensely popular author, so his novels sold out quickly, and subsequent editions were published at short intervals. He published *Monja y casada, virgin y mártir* (Nun and wife, virgin and martyr) in 1868. The protagonist, Blanca de Mejía, jumps off a cliff to escape the lecherous overtures of Guzmán. Rafael Delgado's *La calandria* (The calendar) (1891) narrates the tragic story of Carmen, who loves Gabriel but caves to the charm of rich Alberto. Gabriel then rejects the conflicted woman, and she poisons herself. Delgado's message is that the young heroine lacked parents to educate her and the moral fortitude to forge on and so perished as a result of an incurable illness. Modernist writers especially dabbled in "alienated protagonists" and "psychological introspection."[59] *El Universal* condemned Juan Antonio Mateos's novel *Las olas altas* (The high waves), published in serial form in *El Mundo* in 1899. Mateos was a liberal politician who had been imprisoned for speaking out against Mexico's Emperor Maximilian I in the 1860s, and he also served as secretary of the Supreme Court of Justice under President Benito Juárez. Mateos was both fiercely patriotic and not immune to employing melodrama, and thus his novels communicated nationalistic themes and took on historical events. *Las olas altas* provoked critical comment from rival papers even before it was published. Readers must have been eagerly awaiting and discussing its imminent publication, and reporters stirred interest in it. *El Imparcial* printed a notice that Mateos would give a reading from the book, and *El Mundo* would publish the work over several issues. Both newspapers received government subsidies from the Díaz regime, and Rafael Reyes Spíndola served as editor for both. A front-page advertisement noting that *Las olas altas* could be purchased at a discount with coupons appeared in *El Imparcial* on June 12, 1899.[60] The plot of the novel focused on the decadence of the aristocracy and their lack of authentic morals. No doubt the romantic undertone of the story and its "taste for death, destiny's fate or the vision of woman as angel and demon" scandalized certain commentators. One of its protagonists, Francisco, dies "in conditions of absolute indignity amid drunkenness, vomit, and dirt."[61]

A front-page diatribe against *Las olas altas* in *La Patria* preceded all of the announcements concerning the novel's pending publication. Ireneo Paz directed and edited the independent paper. A fiercely combative journalist, Paz had killed Santiago Sierra, the brother of Porfirian statesman and secretary of public education Justo Sierra, in a duel in 1880. *La Patria* represented pure liberalism, and its writers verbally assaulted journalists and politicians associated with the científicos and the Díaz regime. In fact, Paz spent many days in prison for attacking Díaz in print. *La Patria* published a steady parade of barbs against the government-subsidized newspapers, which included *El Imparcial, El Mundo,* and *El Universal.* An editorial published by the paper under the title "Un novela inmunda é infecciosa" (An unclean and infectious novel), began with biting sarcasm: "Our correct and distinguished colleague *El Mundo,* which has always made note of its exquisite morality, for which it could have entry and sympathy in honorable homes," will begin publishing a novel by Juan A. Mateos. The writer impugned Mateos's untalented writing style and poor grammar and the fact that the "ignorant classes" devoured his stories. Moreover, he concluded, "We consider this man a detestable novelist, ordinary, vulgar, impossible." He noted that the first part of *Las olas altas* possessed "ferments of corruption, mouthfuls of hedonism, flatulence of black pustules." The virulent prose continued. The editorial, which was mostly likely penned by Paz, asked from which brothel did Mateos take his characters, and it also condemned the plot, in which "mothers rejoice loudly at their daughters being disgraced by *camaristas*,[62] in which their daughters pride themselves in their filth with lackeys and demand and get [parents] to follow their orders; in which parents affectionately call by the diminutive first name the thief that raised their daughters. This vile book is recommended by *El Mundo* to families whose homes it penetrates."[63] *El Universal* defended the honor of Mateos, noting, "A newspaper with the moral responsibility to reflect a principled attitude so significant should be cautious in the choice of its subjects so as not to compromise a name that warrants prestige."[64] Clearly, journalists had strong opinions about what types of reading materials should be found in honorable homes, but there is no doubt that reporters brought the issue of Mateo's *Las olas altas* to such a pitched fever so that they could launch attacks on their rivals. Middle-class and elite Mexicans were not the only ones reading novels at the turn of the century. The literacy rate hovered around 50 percent in Mexico City by 1910, even with the large influx of rural migrants.[65] Male artisans made up a large portion of this reading public.[66]

Journalists commented regularly on the infectious impact of novels. When Carlota Rodríguez gulped down mercury cyanide in 1920, a reporter for *El Demócrata* took the opportunity to ridicule young people who sought notoriety through staging their unnatural deaths. He began his article, "Werther's disease is still present in the city, and the tormented spirits of hysterical girls and neurotic boys find certain refuge in death, arriving at the supreme moment with astonishing serenity." He claimed that the old never think of suicide and that suicidal girls forget that they will lie naked on the cold slab of the hospital.[67] Indeed, a lot of the focus on salacious reading material and copycat suicide centered on young women. Most commenters believed the female mind to be most impressionable. A reporter for *La Gran Sedería,* a daily published by Francisco Montes de Oca, agreed that suicides were increasing among men and women in the capital.[68] He noted that 50 percent of women who killed themselves or attempted suicide did it because they had been deceived in love, whereas most men who chose suicide felt world-weary and were bored with life. He pointed out that suicide rates increased each year and argued that the "enlightened classes" made up the bulk of suicides in the city. Certainly, contemporary newspaper coverage reinforced this sentiment. However, the surviving official documents do not. The reporter observed a "profound immorality that extends over the entire social body . . . . The bountiful energies atrophy making them impotent to fight malice, bad faith, meanness, sordid greed, and the frenetic egoism of honorable men, but for weak and nervous spirits that chokes the virtue that is the moral strength to fight against the evil passions of others." He proceeded to lament that this "triumphant immorality" of the elite had spread despair and a "profound skepticism" to the middle classes. He linked rising immorality and suicide to the "despotism of petty kings . . ., the lack of equity in the practice of law, the lack of justice for those who have more rights to it, and the persecution of those who complain." He criticized the lack of press freedom and called the immorality of illustrious men a gangrene that spread to the lower classes, claiming that it led to "jaded youth of the middle class" and girls and young women who became prostitutes because they did not have examples around them of the hard work of being wives of humble workers and honorable mothers.[69]

Post-revolutionary commentators were convinced by the theory that novels could corrupt sensitive minds. The suicide of a young single woman, Sara Maravillas, in 1930 was one persuasive example of youths being led astray by literature. Sara imbibed copious amounts of aguardiente at the wake of her grandmother and then announced to her old friend Eugenia Nieto that she was going to drown herself in the Grand Canal, a flood abatement system heralded as one of the modern feats of engineering of the Porfiriato. Eugenia joked back, "Go on, and me in the arms of the pulque seller on the corner!" Sara exited the wake and made her way to the canal. Two firemen saw her walking along the waterway, sensed something awry, and ran toward her, but it was too late. She jumped into the water and drowned. Journalists learned that neighbors understood Sara to be excessively romantic. She referred to one boyfriend, a painter, as "her artist" and another, who sang songs in the streets, as "her Caruso." She bought novels from the poor booksellers in Tepito plaza, including books by José Vargas Vila, a Colombian author excommunicated by the Catholic Church in 1900.[70] A modernist writer, Vargas Vila claimed in his 1900 novel *Ibis* that suicide was always a virtue. Allegedly, its publication led to seventeen suicides.[71] The novel *María*, by Colombian Jorge Isaacs, was another of Sara's favorites. The plot centered on the tragic love between a racially vague María and her cousin Efraín. The star-crossed lovers faced many obstacles that kept them apart, and the narrative ended with María's untimely death by suicide.[72] *El Universal'*s article about Sara noted that firemen still had not found her body twenty-four hours later but that, ultimately, "the gases of decomposition" would float her corpse to the surface.[73]

What about poorer youth, who lacked resources to purchase novels or newspapers? Certainly, many listened to serial stories read aloud by neighbors or sensational headlines shouted out on the streets by newsboys. A 1901 editorial commented on the number of recent suicides committed because of destitution, citing "a Frenchman who came to this country seeking his fortune, a medical student, a sick and unemployed waiter, a foreign writer, and a married woman." The reporter argued that although suicide because of poverty was common among Europeans, it should not exist in Mexico. Beggars and workers did not kill themselves, he contended; individuals that committed suicide "are always people of other cultures, of other aspirations, another system of life." He claimed that misery was not the sole cause of the suicides in Mexico but rather that other motives combined with a lack of money led to suicide. Ultimately, the writer opined, if people "try to fly without wings, that is to say, rise to levels to which they were not born," they will find themselves restless when they see that they cannot improve their position. Thus, he declared, if people accepted their lot if life, there would be fewer suicides among the impoverished.[74]

Posada's opinion on the issue might have differed, as he created two engravings that blamed poverty for suicide. One depicted a French man stabbing himself in the presence of his family (see figure 9), and the other, entitled "A Woman Who Kills Herself for Lack of Food," showed a woman who sought a fatal departure because of her impoverished situation. A 1902 report on the death of seventeen-year-old Antonio Salazar affirmed the belief that destitution could lead to suicide. Antonio desired to marry Lucrecia Ferrer but lacked a job and the resources to make a life with her. He lived with his father and extended family on Calle Lecumberri. The reporter mentioned his address probably to alert readers that he lived in the working-class neighborhood of Tepito. He implied that residents of that barrio ought not to seek to rise above their birth. Antonio's friends recounted that he spent many hours crying over his situation and said they advised him to find work. He tried for a time and saved some money. Yet the reporter stated that, "in the end, understanding that riches would never rain from the sky and not feeling up to dedicating himself prosaically to a paying job, Antonio resolved to end his

FIGURE 9. José Guadalupe Posada, *Un francés que se mata delante de su familia* (Mexico City: A. Vanegas Arroyo, n.d.). Fernando Gamboa Collection of Prints by José Guadalupe Posada, 1888–1944, Center for Southwest Research, University of New Mexico Libraries.

life." Forced to borrow a pistol because he could not afford his own, he went to his room and shot himself. In his final letter, written to his father, he atoned for his past sins and ironically asked that he not be buried in luxury.[75] Other working-class youth who committed suicide faced the same judgment. María Fuentes and Guadalupe Ortiz, the two best friends who drank poison together in Chapultepec Park in 1909 (introduced in chapter 2 and discussed further in chapter 5), also hailed from Tepito. Journalists mistook them for upper-class girls at first, but when it was discovered that they were in fact from working-class families, the narrative in the papers changed to imply that the two killed themselves because they could not achieve the good life that they desired.[76]

It seemed youth were especially prone to suicide pacts. Cases of youths conspiring to self-destruct in tandem provoked considerable alarm among the public. Despondent lovers or best friends would sometimes pair up to end their emotional agonies together. Suicide pacts worldwide received heightened coverage around the turn of the century. Mexican newspapers commonly reported on multiple suicides in Europe and the United States, and they were especially interested in alleged suicide clubs, which had by-laws requiring that one member commit suicide each year.[77] *El Imparcial* printed two articles on the mysterious suicide of four French seamstresses in Paris on July 27, 1897.[78] Nine days later, the newspaper's sketch artist drew the alleged death scene, showing the four young women and a dead dog on the floor. The sketch featured French authorities entering the room and a brazier still burning. Asphyxiation caused their deaths. The women were all in their twenties, and a family member had found them dead, three on the bed and one on the floor.[79]

A 1909 article in the newspaper of the American expatriate community in Mexico City, the *Mexican Herald,* remarked on the rise of suicide in Mexico, especially suicides by lovers or two friends who, finding their "plans for happiness thwarted," decide to end their lives together. The writer posited that boredom and melancholy as a cause of suicide occurred in the young rather than the aged:

> Few people of middle age realize what moral storms overcome the young who by reason of their years should be full of the joy of life. Possibly there is as much mental suffering among young people as among the aged and dependent. Often, elderly people, having cast away ambition, have come to develop a tranquil personal philosophy; they do not enjoy keenly, but neither do they suffer overmuch. They have arrived at a moderate estimation of life, have experienced its evil and its good, and expect little. Young people brooding despairingly would do well to confide their sorrows, real or imaginary, to the elderly philosophers who could direct them into the paths that lead, if not to happiness, at least to a calm contentment.[80]

The Hotel Viena, located in the center of Mexico City, was the chosen site for one suicide pact. On a spring day in 1899, a couple checked in, signing the register "Vicente Salas and wife." Hotel clients noticed nothing unusual about the pair. They simply kept to themselves. Hotel guests summoned the manager after they heard loud thuds from the quiet couple's room. One guest told police that the thuds sounded like bodies falling off a bed. The reporter who covered the suicides for *El Imparcial* surmised by the quality of the duo's clothing that they hailed from the middle class. Potassium cyanide was their poison of choice. Investigators discovered that the couple had used an alias to rent the room. In reality, they were María Dimas and Domingo Beltrán. Love letters sat on a table in the room together with a note that emphasized that no one was responsible for their deaths.[81] Domingo and María loved each other, but the young woman's parents disapproved of their relationship. Domingo worked for the Ferrocarriles de Distrito Federal de México (Federal District Train Office). Their friends noted his hard-working nature and the fact that he deeply loved María. According to the article, an inspector had noticed that Domingo's paperwork was not in order and removed him from his post at the kiosk at the Zócalo. This act damaged his dignity, and he resolved to kill himself. María tried to dissuade him but eventually agreed to meet him on the street. On the pretext of going out for roasted chicken accompanied by her two little sisters, she ran off with Domingo. The star-crossed couple wandered the streets for six hours while Domingo attempted to convince María to join him in death. Finally, they ended up at the Hotel Viena and sealed their suicide pact.[82]

Reporters judged some suicide pacts as understandable and others as products of insanity. Two young women, Rosa Herrera and Delfina Martínez, unwittingly married the same man, and upon learning in 1911 that they were parties to bigamy, they made a pact to end their shame and misery together through death. Rosa had met Vicente Guadalupe Rosas when they were just children. They fell madly in love, and she married him at the age of seventeen. They lived in harmony for two years until he moved to Morelia, Michoacán, to work as a painter. There, he met Delfina, who was as "good looking as Rosa." Eventually, they married and moved to the capital. Vicente began feeling guilty for abandoning his first wife. He resolved to unite his wives under one roof and to financially provide for both of them. For their part, the deceived wives realized that neither had known of the other and became unlikely friends. They tried to live in polygamy but could not endure the shame. Resolving to commit suicide together, Rosa and Delfina procured strychnine, consumed it, and lay down together to await death. As the women lived in accommodations that lacked privacy, a neighbor saw them convulsing on a bed and called the authorities. Delfina succumbed to the poison, but medical authorities transferred Rosa to the Hospital Juárez, where she was able to recover.[83] An article about the deaths published in *El Imparcial* expressed empathy for the duo, explaining that the women had sought a tragic escape from their husband's subterfuge, but it never discussed the fate of the bigamist husband. Ten days later, Gonzalo de la Parra, who would later edit the anti-Huerta newspaper *El Diablo,* penned a front-page treatise for *Ilustración Popular* on the double suicide without naming the young women. A sketch of the death scene covered two-thirds of the page (see figure 5 in chapter 2, which also contains a discussion of image). De la Parra commented on the number of people who killed themselves because they had been deceived in love, but he claimed that the latest suicide of the two women caught in a bigamist's trap "had shaken the metropolis." He narrated the details of their tragedy. They both fell in love and married the same "cheap Don Juan" but could not morally abide the arrangement. One of the women decided to kill herself, and the other, "elevating herself without knowing it to the stature of a Shakespearean heroine," decided to die with her. De la Parra criticized the police, the judge, and the medical inspectors, claiming that they had all "violated the purity of that tragedy in which two women, through the miracle of love, placed themselves above the vulgarity of humanity." He faulted the egoism of the bigamist and compared the women to Shakespeare's Juliet, who died for love. The two wives represented pure love, and de la Parra exclaimed, "Love is not dead in the land, it lives hidden and asleep in the bottom of the women's hearts." [84] Rather than live with the shame and sin of bigamy, the women chose death as their exit. The love they shared for each other sealed their eternal bond. De la Parra considered this motive for suicide to be honorable.

A sisterly bond propelled others to death. In 1921, *La Demócrata* published an article about two sisters who pledged to die together after one had a "trivial" dispute with her husband. The reporter reasoned that it was the couple's first argument and that the woman believed that her husband had stopped loving her. The sisters ingested strychnine together. The husband then summoned his wife to accompany him on an outing. Not long after they had left the house, the terrifying symptoms manifested, and she died soon afterward. The sister decided to go to the movies with an old friend. Like her sister, she succumbed to the ravages of the poison that evening. In this case, the reporter sneered at the sisters' impulsive and overly emotional decision to end their lives for what he deemed were insignificant reasons.[85] While the two women married to the same man were considered to have chosen an honorable exit from their sin, the sisters were regarded as capricious and foolish.

Men also entered into suicide pacts. Authorities expressed befuddlement upon the discovery of two corpses on the street a couple of blocks from each other in the spring of 1930. They searched the pockets of the victims for identification cards but came up empty. Soon, a friend of both deceased men, Julio Macías, identified them as José Martínez and Jesús González Sánchez and revealed their tragic story. Once authorities recorded their fingerprints and identities, a tale just as incredible as a telenovela was revealed. José and Jesús both loved Mathilde Rodríguez. Jesús was Mathilde's lover for two years, but then he beat her brutally. Police came to their home and arrested him. Medical authorities wanted to take Mathilde to the Hospital Juárez for treatment, and the police intended to prosecute her abuser, but she escaped the ambulance on the way to the hospital. In fact, she never returned to testify against Jesús, and police had to release him. Mathilde then left Jesús and took up with José. The men agreed to fight for her. It was decided that whichever man lost would surrender his claim on Mathilde. José prevailed and the couple lived amiably for a period until she abandoned him for another man and left the capital for Tapuchula, Chiapas. Jesús and José then met to lament the treachery of Mathilde, and they hatched a suicide pact in a cantina on Calle Martínez del Rio in Doctores, an artisan neighborhood south of El Centro. Jesús procured a small vial of mercury cyanide. As they sat at their table, they burned their identification papers and poured the poison into a bottle of tequila. They drank as much as they could, stood up, said their goodbyes, and walked out the door. One made it a few steps before hitting the pavement and expiring. The other stumbled a few blocks before he fell dead. Both cadavers ended up in the morgue of the Hospital Juárez.[86]

Capital residents opened their papers on November 19, 1930, to learn of another suicide pact, this one achieved by two medical school students. Manuel Corona and José Olvera had begun their first year of medical training when, for unknown motives, they traveled to an abandoned mine and shot themselves with the same pistol. Oddly, the young men tried to hide their suicides from their families by sending them letters reporting that they had embarked for France to further their careers and find a better life. However, both families suspected something sinister about these claims. Days later, one of the students' friends told police that he had gone spelunking with them in some deep caves not far from the city. Investigators found their bodies deep in the cave and one gun at the scene.[87] Manuel's father noted that his son suffered from an extremely sensitive nervous system and that his friend José was a taciturn loner. Could these have been code words for homosexuality? Perhaps the young students intended to conceal their deaths to protect the honor of their families.

Unlike articles on suicide pacts during the Porfiriato, postrevolutionary reports did not have an editorializing tone. Journalists simply interviewed friends and witnesses and reported what they learned. Reporters seemed to place blame on the disloyal Mathilde Rodríguez, who left her two lovers bemoaning her treachery over drinks, although that judgment was implied, whereas it likely would have been made explicit had the events occurred during the Porfiriato. When *El Universal* reported on the suicide pact of the two students in the cave in 1930, they simply reported facts without speculating about immoral deeds or poor upbringing. Although reporters continued to sleuth crimes after the revolution, they lacked the urgency of Porfirian newspapermen to act as amateur detectives.

Suicide letters often revealed a person's motives for killing him- or herself. Collected by authorities at death scenes, goodbye letters became part of case files. Investigators used them to help determine whether a death was in fact a suicide—and if so, if the person had been influenced in their drive for self-extinction—or whether the person had died of natural causes or been murdered. Most notes contained a few lines notifying authorities that the suicide alone was responsible for his or her death. This was perhaps intended to save loved ones from a lengthy interrogation during their moments of grief. Sometimes, suicides used their goodbye notes to bequeath their property or to ask that their cadavers not be subjected to autopsy. Others left notes that were intended for parents, friends, or estranged lovers. Yet historian Susan K. Morrissey argues that the "conventionality of notes" allow historians to treat them like texts that might reveal specific patterns of motives for suicide across time and space.[88] Whether they penned simple instructions regarding the fate of their bodies and belongings or gave explicit motives for their deaths, suicides must have contemplated how their words would be received and interpreted. In fact, suicides must have hoped that their notes would help loved ones and authorities make sense of their deaths. Simply put, these notes allowed them to construct themselves in their deaths.[89] Occasionally, suicides used their notes to point to a culprit for their demise, and their despedidas could be seen as an attempt at revenge. Judging from the materials collected in the inquest files for suicide in Mexico City from 1900 to 1930, men were more likely than women to pen suicide letters before 1920. It was not until after 1915 that more women started to leave letters—both goodbye letters and old love notes—at the sites of their suicides. In fact, a 1917 *Excélsior* article expressed surprise that Manuela Domech, a seemingly well-adjusted middle-class woman, did not leave a letter to explain her fatal consumption of mercury salts.[90] Although scripts of suicide could be communicated through a journalist's narration and reading of a death scene, a letter penned by the victim lent additional intimacy and agency to the event. If they read newspapers, prospective suicides knew that their deaths might be recounted for thousands to read.

Coroners and other officials asked straightforward questions of the suicide's loved ones and coworkers, any witnesses to the death, or anyone else who had been at the scene or who was intimate with the deceased. They hoped to get at a suicide's method and motive, and they recorded any details they gleaned from these conversations in their inquest documents. They also logged the age, gender, and civil status of the suicide. Inquests also included reports from medical experts on the cause of death and physical descriptions of any wounds on the body. Authorities questioned conscious suicide victims at the scene. Others were interviewed as they convalesced in their homes or, more commonly, at the Hospital Juárez. Thus, some inquest files contain short testimonies of individuals who died later in the hospital, and others include statements of victims who fully recovered. As noted in chapter 1, women failed more often than men in killing themselves. This is because most women chose poison as their vehicle to death, and individuals who poisoned themselves had a better chance of being saved than those who employed a firearm. Some poisons acted faster and were more lethal than others, but many poisons could be counteracted if time allowed. Some distraught individuals attempted suicide in the hopes that they would be saved, like Soledad Madrigal Lora, a sixteen-year-old girl who tried to kill herself at least four times. On the fourth attempt, she swallowed potassium permanganate and then screamed when the pain grew too unbearable. Her family ran into her bedroom and called an ambulance. Medical intervention saved Soledad.[91] Chapter 1 laid out the main motives for suicides for men and women, and they did not differ by any dramatic measure. Often, the term *disgustos* was used to explain why individuals had been driven to death. Disgustos usually referred to trouble or a falling out with family members, a lover, or a spouse. This could be a marital spat or a fight with one's parents. Love or being deceived in love topped the list of suicide motives as well. Fortunately, letters and testimonies add some nuance to our understanding of why individuals made the decision to end their lives and the meanings they assigned to suicide. The meanings and motives prove a remarkable continuity over time. Motive changed little from the Porfiriato through the revolution.

Love had everything to do with it. Micaela Balcazar ingested strychnine on Christmas Day in 1921. Her family discovered her in a state of intoxication and had her transferred to the hospital for treatment. She survived and returned home within a few days. When investigators arrived at the scene, they collected letters, including a love missive from one Baldomero García. Penned in an elegant and even hand, it read:

My unforgettable Micaela,

The first letter I sent you was very happy, or better said, you made me feel happy because your answer told me that you understood the words found in your heart. Since this date for a thousand diverse circumstances that I cannot explain, we cannot change impressions. Tired of and annoyed by our mutual silence, I break this deathly quiet, causing me to send this second letter in order to show you one more time that my affection and love for you have not suffered at all. I live only to think of you and I desire to know if you have saved my notes that I write. It is useless for me to forget you. I ignore that suggestion, that mysterious force that subjugates me and attracts me to you. I remember one occasion, one afternoon, in the Alameda you talked with some concern about the commitments that bound me, the reasons why the common bonds of our union could be impeded. There is neither reason on my part nor any bulwark or stumbling block to prevent our love. For you, maybe there is. Tell me the truth. I will not persist in my foolishness and leave you be and not bother you or hinder the path of your future well-being.

On hold for your response, I remain the one who loves you. Baldomero García.[92]

Something had gone horribly awry in the relationship of the two young lovers, and it propelled Micaela to take the drastic step of swallowing poison to end her misery. She penned a letter for whoever recovered her corpse that stated that she took her life because she did not want to put up with any more "deceptions or slights." She wrote, "They insult and speak badly of me . . . and condemn me as the most guilty woman in the world . . . . A coward is the cause of all of my [misfortune] . . . . Enrique González robbed me of my happiness. Because of him I lost the man I love. I prefer death. A disgraced woman, M. B."[93] Micaela revealed in the letter that she had been deceived in love, but she went even further to exact revenge by naming the man she deemed responsible for her unhappiness.

Although suicide notes are immensely private and personal, Irena Paperno has argued "that the production of a person's mind that came into being after that moment—the letter—was an equivalent of his dead body. As with the body, the suicide's letter was thought to belong to the public domain because it was evidence of pathology, be it physiological or social pathology."[94] Indeed, officials in Mexico City at the turn of the twentieth century pored over these letters for clues, and dailies printed them verbatim to embellish their stories. The staging of the death and the letter (or letters) left behind allowed suicides to engage the public and, if the story was published in newspapers, to shape the conversation surrounding their demise. For instance, when Micaela Balcazar named Enrique González in her note, she probably hoped that investigators would question him and, ultimately, that her letter would shame him before a large reading public. In 1930, Raquel Arteaga left a note naming her boyfriend, Manuel Enrique González, as the reason she committed suicide. She charged Manuel with slipping a narcotic in a drink he bought her at the market so that he could gain sexual access to her. She also blamed Diamantina M. de Pinedo, who allegedly performed a "surgical intervention to further the cause of the seducer."[95] It is not known if this Enrique González is the same individual named in Micaela's letter of 1921. There weren't any follow-up articles on the fate of the investigation. Plácida Arroyo did not leave a letter behind when she killed herself in 1905, but pictures speak a thousand words. She hung three portraits of her lover in a tree and then slipped a noose around her neck next to them. She did not have to name him in a letter as the act of hanging him like a Judas figure next to her spoke loudly of his role in her suicide.[96]

Love also drove Humberto Ubico to his demise. However, unlike the young Micaela Balcazar, Humberto sought neither revenge nor notoriety. A young soldier from Guatemala, Humberto decided that he hated living after being deceived by a woman. He later confessed to police that he had drunk a large amount of alcohol and consumed mercury dichloride. This compound was taken as a treatment for syphilis before the discovery of antibiotics after World War II and also used in photography labs, so it was readily available for purchase at drugstores. Humberto penned a short letter to a judge, "Señor Judge, Are there pains and motives? Only death knows. I stand before them. Pardon what I have done. No one is responsible for my death."[97]

Carmen Díaz also thought being deceived by her lover was reason enough to commit suicide. Just seventeen years old, Carmen lived in a consensual union with Homero García for six months before he broke the news that he was leaving the city without her. She then procured mercury cyanide from a drugstore on the pretext of killing rats and rented a hotel room, seeking privacy to end her life. However, a porter noticed her with a black glass tube full of pink pills and saw her dissolve some of them in water. She asked Carmen what she planned to do with the solution, and the desperate woman argued that it was to kill rats, although it is not clear why a hotel guest would act as exterminator. Moments later, the porter returned to find Carmen sitting against the wall, visibly in pain and red-faced. She jammed her fingers down the suicidal woman's throat to make her vomit and called authorities. An ambulance transferred the poisoned woman to the hospital. Carmen had scribbled short letters to Homero, a friend, and her mother before she swallowed the deadly concoction. She asked Homero, "Why have you deceived me? You have liked and pretended to love me . . . . My affection for you has made me believe everything you told me . . . . Goodbye Homero. Be happy and don't have too much hate. Carmen."[98] In the letter to her mother, Carmen explained that she killed herself because she loved Homero so much. She died about three weeks later. Mercury cyanide was one of the most deadly chemical compounds in a poisoner's arsenal. It, like its cousin mercury dichloride, was used as a treatment for syphilitic sores and had antiseptic properties as well. Mercury cyanide is highly soluble in water and can poison through the skin, via inhalation, and by ingestion.

Breakups also led to suicides and attempted suicides. Thirty-eight-year-old Alberto Brusco, a single carpenter from the state of Chiapas, convinced a young woman named Alicia to leave her home in 1928. They moved from town to town and finally settled in Mexico City. They lived amiably for some time but then started to fight, and Alicia eventually left him to work in different cabarets around the city. When she fell upon challenging financial times, she asked him to take her back. He told her he could not abide her, and she threatened to send someone to kill him. On a fateful day in 1928, Alberto went for a walk with his friend Alfonso Domínguez. When they arrived at the intersection of Ecuador and Santa María La Redonda, Alberto took out his 9mm Browning pistol and shot himself in the chest. Alberto posed to shoot himself again, but Alfonso grabbed the gun. Alberto testified that he had shot himself accidently, but his friend set the record straight.[99] He had shot himself because of romantic difficulties with Alicia. Fortunately, he recovered from his wounds.

Eliazer Tello was another star-crossed lover who shot herself in 1928. Tello was thirty years old. She had spent thirteen years in a relationship that was essentially a common-law marriage but that lacked the conjugal rights of a civil marriage. Apparently, her lover then became engaged to another woman and abandoned Eliazer.[100] Three months later, suffering from loss of love and facing impending financial hardship, the stricken woman took out a .32-caliber Colt handgun that her partner had gifted her, fired two shots into her body, and replaced the gun in its box. She survived and recuperated from her wounds.

Natalia Solís poisoned herself with strychnine in 1919, survived long enough to murmur a few words to investigators, and then expired. A single woman from Spain, she lived alone in a rooming house. The porter pondered why the good-looking young woman with many admirers had suffered melancholy the last several weeks of her life. Natalia spent hours writing and posting long letters, but she received few in return. Only her mother wrote her from Spain. On the fatal morning, she left the house at 10:00 am and returned thirty minutes later. She walked in and made it only as far as the water fountain before she fell writhing and convulsing to the patio floor. Two letters from the twenty-year-old young woman's mother found their way into investigators' hands and became sensational fodder for an article published in *Excélsior*. Writing in tender prose, Natalia's mother advised her not to waste her health, telling her that she was young and should not lose her soul. The mother wrote, "Don't write me again to say in your letter that this is the last you will write me . . . . God will not permit you to die of the illness you suffer." The reporter concluded that Natalia suffered no other infirmity than "incurable melancholy" as a result of a spoiled love.[101] The tone of the article was matter-of-fact but also acknowledged that disappointment in love and subsequent loneliness conformed to an accepted logic of suicide.

An unrequited love seemed the most serious knock in life for young men and women. Lucrecia Baños Ayala ingested potassium permanganate in an attempt to end her life in 1929. The chemical solution was sometimes sold as Condy's Fluid or Condy's Crystals and could be used as a disinfectant in human and veterinary settings.[102] In fact, it was commonly used in homes as an all-purpose disinfectant. It is extremely caustic, and an overdose can eat through a person's esophagus and stomach lining. Fortunately, alkaline and coating agents like baking soda and milk can alleviate its impact. Lucrecia's aunt Guadalupe Ayala Silva testified that her young niece had an intense but unrequited love for Manuel Pérez. Lucrecia survived her ordeal but refused to testify about her reasons for attempting suicide. Nonetheless, authorities called for the apprehension and detention of Manuel. Letters found in Lucrecia's purse revealed part of the story. One of these letters, addressed to Manuel's father, stated that she had a strong affection for his son but that he was not responsible for her suicide. She penned that she could not live without Manuel and that she was blind and foolish in love. She pleaded, "Therefore I urge you, in the name of God, don't make his life hard, don't scold him, it will be a comfort I will take to my grave with my deepest appreciation . . . . Have mercy that in my depths I am not bad." Another of the letters was written to her mother: "I would not want you to see this tough time, but whom but you could I turn to? For this with all of the pain of my heart I pray that you forgive me and don't condemn me for what I have done. I have already told you that I love Manuel more than my own life . . . . I have already lost the love of Manuel. I lost everything." [103]

Suicides that that also involved murder doubly shocked society. In these cases, an individual turned to suicide in a desperate attempt to escape judicial punishment after committing a murder. A very public murder-suicide occurred in the upscale neighborhood of Colonia Roma in 1921. *El Demócrata*'s subheading read, "Perhaps this tragedy will serve as an example to other flirty girls of this neighborhood so that they keep in mind not to play with men's hearts." [104] The paper lifted the line from a lengthy goodbye letter left by the murderer and suicide, a Spaniard by the name of Antonio Mira. Antonio was a business associate of Wally Engels. He met Wally's daughter, Magdalena, in 1913, when she was twelve years old. He did not give her any further thought and had not heard from the Engels until he traveled to Mexico again in 1920. He landed in Veracruz and succumbed quickly to yellow fever. The Engels had moved from Veracruz to Mexico City, but Mrs. Engels arranged for Antonio's care and convalescence. Once the young man had recovered, Wally invited him to stay in his home in Mexico City. The young Magdalena was nineteen years old at this point, and Manuel fell in love with her. He wrote in his suicide letter that she returned his affection. In his mind, they were betrothed. However, the arrival from Dolores Hidalgo of María Arauza, Magdalena's best friend, upset the idyllic scenario. Antonio wrote that María had poisoned Magdalena's mind. She convinced her friend that she should wait for a millionaire boyfriend with a car, and Magdalena acted increasingly distant from Antonio. She stopped meeting him. Her mother also started to shun him. One morning, he noticed that Magdalena and María had stopped to talk to the woman who sold cigarettes and who also, for a few cents, "sent messages and encouraged vices and love affairs of the youth of the barrio." Antonio entered the shop and told Magdalena that he needed to talk with her. She turned her back to him without responding. He asked again, and she remained mute. Not responding to an individual was a form of disrespect toward that person, but physically turning one's back on someone signaled outright dismissal and a repudiation of the entreaty.[105] Antonio took out his pistol and fired four bullets at his beloved and one at his nemesis and the spoiler of his dreams, María. The spurned lover turned murderer then fled the scene before police officers arrived.

Agustín Iglesias contacted authorities after he read about his close friend's homicidal exploits in the next day's newspaper. He claimed that, on the morning of the double murder, Antonio had told him, "I am tired of the disturbances with my girlfriend, and tonight I am going to kill her." Agustín had brushed off his friend's pronouncement as "meaningless bluster" and had not felt the need to contact the police. Others who had seen Antonio the day of the murder saw nothing amiss in his demeanor. A few days later, authorities received news that an unknown man had committed suicide in the El Volador market. The John Doe was none other than Antonio, and Wally Engels positively identified his body in the morgue of the Hospital Juárez. Antonio had sent a lengthy letter explaining his actions to authorities and the press before he took his life. He claimed that he killed the two young women because they had played with his heart and argued that María should not have meddled in affairs that did not concern her. He wrote that he had fled Mexico City after the murders and had gotten fifty-five kilometers away but then had second thoughts and returned around 8:00 pm to face his destiny. Antonio proclaimed, "I killed the one I most cared for in life, and I must follow her." He added, "I don't care what people say after my death. I have always lived with my opinion and never with others. I make these clarifications in view of the nonsense that is published in the filthy newspapers." [106]

Prostitutes sometimes appeared in the records of suicides, and failing in love fueled their death instincts as well. Journalists referred to these women living the *vida alegre* or *vida galante* (literally "merry life" or "gallant life," connoting prostitution). Many women pursued sex work out of economic necessity, but this did not preclude them from seeking relationships based in love and affection.[107] Heartbreaks hurt sex workers just as deeply as they did other people, and despondency could also lead them to self-murder. In one case, Rosalía Tenorio felt deceived by soldier David M. Aguillón, and so she doused herself in gasoline, lit a match, and ran down the street, falling in flames in front of her estranged lover and a "rival of her class." [108] In reading about the demise of Rosalía, older Mexico City residents might have remembered a famous 1897 case of one prostitute killing another over a common lover. The murderess, María Villa, recounted to criminologist Roumagnac some years later that she had tried to overdose on laudanum when her lover, Salvador Ortigosa, abandoned her. She failed but then sought her revenge by shooting her romantic rival and fellow prostitute La Malagueña.[109]

Carlota Alatorre, a sixteen-year-old Guadalajara native, had worked in a brothel until a businessman took her out in 1910. They lived together for four months, presumably in harmony, until an inebriated man with the last name Hernández, one of Carlota's former clients, showed up at their home asking the porter for entry. Refused twice, he returned and broke the glass on the door by throwing bottles of beer at it. Carlota's boyfriend became incensed and accused her of keeping company with seedy men. She cried all morning, and when he went to the patio to urinate she consumed laudanum with chloroform. She managed to pen a quick letter noting that no one was responsible for her death. She survived.[110] Carmen Flores, a nineteen-year-old prostitute also from Guadalajara, was not so lucky. She consumed two pills of mercury dichloride. Leonor Fernández, the madam of the brothel she lived in, called the authorities. Before she expired, Carmen testified that she had had a mental breakdown when she discovered that her sweetheart was with another woman.[111] Women living the vida alegre lost in love just like their peers who were not sex workers. Prostitutes might have flirted and had sex with men for money, but they wanted to have loyal love relationships too and felt keenly when they experienced loss of love and support. Perhaps many expected that they would be rescued from their brothels, like Carlota Alatorre had been by her lover.

Physical pain and suffering also propelled people to end their lives. In fact, those who suffered from chronic pain or insufferable symptoms sometimes viewed suicide as their only form of relief. Common analgesics of the time included laudanum, which was addictive, and various powders and tonics that did not list ingredients. The twenty-five-year-old widow Dolores "Lola" García suffered from syphilis. She was in more pain each day and reflected these sentiments in a letter to her mother and confidences with friends in 1926. She lived with her lover, General Salvador Sánchez, and he came home from work with a colleague when he learned how badly Lola felt. She told him she sensed that she was going crazy and that she preferred to die. He told her he would get her the common sedative potassium bromide to calm her nerves. Lola swallowed the pills with milk, and he left her alone to rest. Not much time passed before he heard a gunshot and ran to her room to find her dead in their bed. Her friend Dolores Fortiz testified that Lola had suffered from "nerves" for a long time and that the widow had read about suicide in the newspapers and wondered out loud if she would have the "bravery" to shoot herself. Lola's doctor testified that he had been treating her for third-stage syphilis, which damages the brain. There were several treatments for syphilis, many of them containing mercury and/or arsenic, before the advent of penicillin in the 1940s, but many had painful side effects. Presumably, the side effects of the medication and the mental transformations brought on by the disease propelled her to take a tragic exit. Lola left a message to Salvador under her pillow: "My love, pardon me. I suffer horribly. Send this to my children and give notice to my mother." She also wrote a letter to her mother: "Dear Mother, you have no idea how sad I am to be further and further from getting better. . . . The ulcerations will improve, but almost everything else is worse." An earlier letter from her mother that was found in the room confirmed that Lola had experienced serious mental breaks. In the letter, Lola's mother advised her to take injections of "Serum of Query" and also recommended a medicinal wine to reconstitute Lola's strength.[112] The syphilitic woman died of her wounds, and her family buried her in the third-class section of the Dolores cemetery.

Manuel Miranda also suffered an unbearable illness. Driven to desperation, he rented a hotel room in 1912 and shot himself, perishing moments later. His sister told authorities that Manuel was thirty years old, was sick, and had been mistreated by his aunt. He left behind a long letter stating that he had suffered from an unnamed illness for over a year and could not sleep. He lacked the resources to seek medical care because of a "miserable charlatan" who operated a commission shop at San Juan de Letrán 97 and did not pay him for work completed. He also wrote that his aunt did not support him and that his mother lived too far away to launch an investigation after his death. Manuel pleaded, "God and justice prosecute these charlatans."[113] By naming his enemies and providing the address of the businessman who refused to pay him, Manuel hoped for some legal justice after his death.

Agustín Hernández suffered epileptic seizures and decided to drink iodine to end his sorrow. His father lamented that his son suffered regular mental attacks and disturbances, but he wanted to know how a man who had not reached his twenty-second birthday could be so crazy. The young Agustín died later in the hospital.[114] There were few methods of treatment for epilepsy at the time, and there was a stigma attached to having the condition. Victor Padilla, a novice bullfighter, also suffered from the disorder. According to his wife, Antonia Corona Marín, it had gotten bad enough that he talked about wishing he could have a seizure in the bullring and die on the horns of a bull. Unable to achieve that death, however, he decided to swallow poison instead. Fellow passengers on a streetcar had a fright when Victor consumed a packet of strychnine and began convulsing and frothing at the mouth moments later. He could not be cured and died within hours.[115]

Mental suffering could be as excruciating as physical pain. José Baños summoned doctors to the home of his friend Carlos Contreras in 1901.

Medical personnel arrived to find Carlos showing no signs of poisoning but willing to confess. A thirty-eight-year-old soldier, the distressed man admitted to being weakened by his "moral sufferings" and by the fact that his family had to assist him financially. Carlos said he had contemplated suicide for the past four months and had bought three grams of strychnine at a drug store on Calle de Tacuba in El Centro. He stated that he had ingested it that evening. However, doctors found him physically healthy and confiscated the drug.[116] Enrique Minetti, an administrator at the shooting range Tiro Suizo, committed suicide in 1910 and left several notes behind claiming that he had resolved to kill himself because he possessed a "weak character." Apparently, Enrique had stored the receipts of the Tiro Suizo cantina[117] in his wallet instead of in the cash box and had either lost the wallet or had it stolen. Humiliated and at a loss as to how to recover from this mistake, he had decided to end his life. In one of his suicide notes, Enrique asked society to pardon him because "he was crazy and had nothing to live for."[118] Honor also played a role in the suicide of José Díaz in 1911. The owner of a small store, ironically called El Porvenir (the future), summoned police to report that José had entered the establishment trembling and seemed to be very ill. José admitted that he had taken strychnine. The ailing man responded to questions, noting that he was an eighteen-year-old pharmacist and had procured the poison when he worked at a botica. His troubles had begun when he went to a cantina to drink. The owner called José a "petty thief without shame" and asked him how he was going to pay for his drinks. José could not abide the public dishonoring and vowed to seek a deadly exit. He penned a letter to his boss, Francisco Vega Licea, that read, "Finding myself offended by Don José R. Rios, you know the manner in which he treats me, I thought to quickly end my life . . . because I do not have sufficient funds to proceed against Mr. Rios. My honor is finished and my life is also over. Goodbye for always goodbye."[119]

Women also often pinpointed personal weakness or cowardice when explaining their decision to self-destruct. Beatriz Norman, the woman mentioned at the beginning of this chapter, lived with pianist Vicente Montaño, who worked in the Cine Odeon and Café Volga. Cine Odeon contradicted Mexico's image as a backward nation. Featuring modern seating, smoking lounges for men and women, and professional musicians, the theater attracted a modern and aspirational clientele.[120] Beatriz's friends seemed worried that she had purchased strychnine on the pretense of poisoning a dog. The maid also raised suspicion with Vicente, who allegedly hid the poison from Beatriz because she had tried to cut her wrists before. He testified that she suffered horrible jealousy and that they had fought over his friendships with two women, María Carmen Nuñez and a woman known as Lola la Chata.[121] Beatriz argued that she had seen Vicente embrace Carmen and that it was evident to her that they had had sex. Apparently, she returned home at 4:00 am from a night on the town and shot herself. Her roommate's boyfriend, Luis Ibarra, testified that he always took his girlfriend to Cabaret Regis on Saturday nights and left a dress suit in the apartment for those occasions. The night of Beatriz's death, he had also left his .45-caliber pistol on his girl-friend's bed. Beatriz found it and used it to kill herself.[122]

Financial hardship and poverty as impetuses for suicide were actually not as common as one might think. Financial trouble was sometimes one of many factors, such as breakups and unrequited love, that led a person to commit suicide. Nonetheless, men might have felt unemployment and lack of job prospects more keenly than women. Women worked, but they were not expected to hold occupations like men. In other words, in the late nine-teenth and early twentieth centuries, society defined a man by his economic function. Values such as hard work, honesty in business dealings, and provid-ing for a family measured the worth of a man. *El Imparcial* printed a lengthy article on the suicide of the French millionaire Juan Balme, who had lived and worked in Mexico for thirty years. Juan was seventy-two years old and a well-known floriculturist, and it seemed like nothing could possibly drive him to end his life. On the morning of his death, he rose just as he did any other day, took his daily walk, conducted some business, and ate heartily at lunchtime. He then returned to his plants, instructed gardeners in their work, and retired to the greenhouse, presumably to check on the young plants. Sometime later, one of his workers discovered him on the floor of the greenhouse, a pistol at his side, his head bathed in a pool of blood. He had penned two letters, one in Spanish, to authorities, and the other in French, to his wife and children. To Mexican authorities, he wrote that no one was responsible for his death but himself and stated, "Between losing my mind or my life, I prefer to lose the latter." Juan's last words to his family included that he had worked with "true determination and honesty" but that his lawyer and notary in Paris had deceived him."[123] He chose to die rather than face financial dishonor.

Pending financial ruin sent Guillermo Lemus into the abyss of self-destruction as well. On a fall day in 1926, a man living in the room next to Guillermo heard a gunshot and informed the owner of the guesthouse. The two men entered the room and found Guillermo dead with a Colt .45 in his hand and various portraits and letters lying on a desk. One note, addressed to authorities, read, "No one is responsible. It is of my own will and I have my five senses. Sufferings and bad business dealings provoked me." Another letter, to one Manuel, stated which belongings he passed to whom and gave more motives for his death. The letter stated, "Don't believe it was only bad business that pushed me, but I saw a very dark future, and I lack energy and strength to continue struggling. I am truly exhausted body and soul, and besides I have suffered too much." Guillermo also penned a short dispatch to a woman who seemed to be his lover, Aurora "Rosita" Chavez: "My Rosita. I want you to be very happy and to not forget me. Your flowers on my grave will be the best aromas that I will have. Goodbye. Guillermo. Don't marry, remember me." It is not known whether Aurora granted his last wish and remained a spinster. He asked that he be buried with portraits of his wife and Aurora.[124]

Economic ruin propelled lower-class men to seek a final exit as well. Twenty-five-year-old miner Pedro López lost his wife to childbirth eight days before he attempted suicide in 1912. Destitute and living with his mother-in-law and his aunt, he felt distressed thinking of his future raising his two children, one fourteen months old and the other eight days old. Lacking employment and without resources to support his offspring, he mixed potassium permanganate with alcohol and drank it. He later testified that he had bought the chemical at a local botica. His mother-in-law called authorities and had him swallow cooking oil and salt water. Doctors determined that aside from suffering gastritis as a result of ingesting a caustic agent, Pedro would be healthy again in two weeks.[125]

Gabriel Ordóñez, a thirty-seven-year-old married empleado, felt certain that he was on the brink of losing his job. Rather than face being fired, he shot himself with a .38-caliber pistol in 1918. Gabriel died shortly after his deposition.[126] Carpenter Raymundo Luna Ruiz was also driven to attempt suicide by his desperate financial situation. Twenty-five years old and unemployed, Raymundo lived with his mother and sister. His situation in life bothered him considerably, and one day he decided to put an end to his hardships. He stabbed himself with a knife and then tossed it to the street. Desperate and bleeding, he flagged down a car to take him home, where his mother summoned an ambulance. He recovered. His sister and girlfriend of four years testified to his jealous nature.[127] Unemployment and nagging emotions like jealousy had been too much for him to live with.

Suicide is a statistical fact but also a "creative gesture subject to multiple interpretations."[128] Modern journalism meant that news of homicides, robberies, and suicides dominated daily headlines, especially before the end of the Mexican Revolution. Suicide seemed to be on the increase on the cusp of the twentieth century, and the spectacle of each suicide clearly hit a nerve among capitalinos. Residents likely discussed the tragic events in an attempt to understand the mental states and biographical details of the victims but also to debate the effects of social and economic change in Mexico during the Porfirian and revolutionary eras. Motives and meanings assigned to suicide by outside observers and the suicides themselves displayed a remarkable amount of continuity. Motives related to love—such as being deceived by a lover, suffering from unrequited love, or experiencing familial disputes—topped the list for suicide causes across time. Journalists had a penchant and a talent for narrating suicide stories, and when the protagonist was a young woman, they waxed eloquent about her mental state or her life of hard knocks and misery. During the Porfiriato, secular and religious newspapers used the topic of suicide to spar over secularism, public education, popular culture, and one another's positions as outlets of ethical journalism.

The most obvious change in newspaper reporting from the Porfiriato to the revolutionary years was the demise of editorials addressing suicide. Porfirian-era newspapers of all types discussed the perceived epidemic, debating its causes, potential remedies, and its impact on Mexican society. Individual suicides continued to receive coverage in the media, but during the height of the revolution and World War I, they lost their front-page primacy. The papers still intimated that a suicide fever existed, but there was no theorizing about the decline of Western civilization. Likewise, the bitter duel between secular and religious journalists ceased by the end of the revolution. By March 1930, newspapers like *Excélsior* had pledged to end reporting on blood crimes (*la nota roja*) altogether. Supreme Court president José Ortiz Rodríguez lauded the paper: "*Excélsior,* wanting to cooperate with authorities and educational centers of the country oriented toward the popular classes, the prestige of Mexico abroad, and the development of tourism, serves as an example of a national press for its suppression of scandalous reporting, news about passionate tragedies, suicides and information that awakes morbid curiosity."[129]

Even though suicide had moved to the interior sections of newspapers, it still populated the social imaginary of capitalinos. Much concern about youth existed in the aftermath of the revolution. As young men and women entered the workforce and sought leisure activities in public spaces, a new alarm emerged. Women with bobbed hair, makeup, and short dresses shocked traditional society, as did women driving automobiles down the avenues of the city. The modern woman faced off against the traditional rural woman, *la china poblana,* and some Mexicans saw only ruin in the future for the nation's impetuous youth. In fact, it was not uncommon to find so-called unruly young women, who stomped on traditional gender norms by going out with men and disobeying their parents, confined to institutions. Simply put, suicide and the different lifestyles and mindsets that led to that act continued to be filtered through the lenses of gender, class, and age.

# FOUR

## *The Modern Disease*

### MEDICAL MEANINGS AND APPROACHES TO SUICIDE

CONSUELO SOLÍS'S FAMILY MEMBERS PROVIDED several reasons for her suicide. Her brother-in-law, Carlos Cohen Smeke, a twenty-six-year-old businessman originally from Damascus, Syria, told authorities that he had witnessed his brother Victor criticize his wife's cooking. He thought nothing of the fact that she fled to her room after suffering the rebuke. For his part, Victor admitted to sitting down to eat at 4:00 pm and, later, hearing the detonation of a gun. He confessed that he had expressed his displeasure with the meal Consuelo had prepared and that he and Carlos later found her on the bed covered in blood. When asked why his wife might have killed herself, Victor stated that she had an "unusual" character and had suffered from neurasthenia. Carlos told his interrogators that Consuelo was a "fan of certain readings of authors he did not know" and that she had expressed a death wish before. Victor added that Consuelo's father suffered mental illness and had been committed to an insane asylum. Moreover, he said that his wife had an obsession with novels, film, and theater. Consuelo left neither a note nor a testimony, and her family buried her in the third-class section of the Dolores cemetery.[1] The year was 1929, and the possible suicide motives given by Carlos and Victor reflected the prevailing wisdom of why individuals took their own lives. Chapter 3 analyzed media and popular interpretations of suicide; the Smeke brothers communicated that diverse narrative. First, they believed that women possessed weak wills and extreme sensitivity, and therefore Consuelo could not rise above her husband's criticism of her cooking. Second, her husband claimed that she suffered from a nervous disorder, neurasthenia, which he believed to have caused degeneration and a weakening of her natural impulse (or will) for self-preservation. Third, they believed that she might have inherited a predisposition for mental illness from her father.

Finally, they believed that Consuelo had been infected by contemporary popular culture from reading certain novels, falling under the spell of dramatic films, and enjoying the theater too passionately, which caused her to succumb to self-murder at the slightest word from her husband.

Although the Smeke brothers seemed certain about why Consuelo shot herself, the causes of suicide confounded specialists, and they struggled to understand why Mexico experienced rising rates of the malady year after year. Academic journals and popular newspapers published pieces on suicide, and, as chapter 1 discussed, the penchant for collecting statistics propelled many to study and hypothesize about the causes of crime, premature death, illness, and other perceived social ills, including suicide. Defining suicide and crime as social problems drove the impulse to collect moral statistics. Numerical data provided the fodder to nourish authoritative conclusions about the health of the social body. Medical interpretations and approaches to the phenomenon of suicide in Mexico varied from the mid-nineteenth century to 1930. At the crux of the discussion sat several issues, including the status of individual will in the act of suicide, whether suicides suffered mental illness, and fundamentally, whether the causes of suicide originated inside or outside the individual.

The new disciplines of psychology and sociology also informed the debate. Both sciences emerged at the end of the nineteenth century, and their proponents defended them as true sciences. In 1903, the *Revista Positiva* published a thirty-one-page article by positivist intellectual Carlos Pereyra entitled "Abstract Sociology and Its Application to Some Fundamental Problems of Mexico." Pereyra referred to major foreign sociologists such as Émile Durkheim and Franklin H. Giddings and agreed that society ought to be studied like one studies an organism. All parts mattered, and any one of them could infect the others with disease and destroy the health of the whole.[2] Mexican intellectuals read French, and several attended university in Paris, so Durkheim's treatise on suicide would have been accessible to them. Most shared Durkheim's hypothesis that external causes led to suicide in the contemporary age and that suicide was indeed eminently modern. Durkheim's implicit goal in his treatise on suicide was to establish sociology as a science. Social forces rather than individual pathologies interested the French thinker. What is clear from the medical literature is that Mexican specialists labored to understand why Mexicans seemed to exhibit poor health, why they died younger than their European counterparts, and why more and more of them committed suicide each year. Citizenship was a collective affair, and specialists conducted a social autopsy to get to the bottom of social issues.

## FROM FRENCH ALIENISM TO POSITIVIST SOCIOLOGY

Before 1900, French alienists Phillippe Pinel (1745–1826) and his student Jean Étienne Dominique Esquirol (1772–1840) had the most influence on Mexican physicians and their approach to understanding the link between mental illness and suicide. The library at the Escuela Nacional de Medicina contained books by French experts like Esquirol and Alexandre Jacques François Brierre de Boismont (1797–1881), who promoted cold-water baths as a cure for hallucinations and other symptoms of insanity.[3] Esquirol represented a new generation of scholars who debunked humoral theory and posited that mental functions operated in the human nervous system. Humoral theory, which probably predated ancient Greece, proposed that an imbalance of wet, dry, hot, and cold bodily conditions caused illness. Balancing the four humors—yellow and black bile, blood, and phlegm—restored the body's health. Yet it would not be until after 1930 that physicians understood the role of neurotransmitters in the operation of that system. Prior to that discovery, many doctors thought they could find physical markers or aberrations in the brain and spinal cords of mentally ill patients.[4] Indeed, they believed one had to probe and understand the nervous system to uncover the roots of madness. Alienists believed that suicide resulted from mental illness and an inability to control passions. In essence, mental illness negated individual will, rendering a person powerless to resist temptation and restrain explosive emotions. Esquirol defined five types of mental illness: lypemania or melancholy, characterized by despondent passion and an obsession over one or more objects; monomania, also defined by obsession but couple with an "expansive passion"; mania, marked by a focus on a large number of objects and a state of excitement; dementia, characterized by "complete folly"; and imbecility, "in which reason was never present."[5] He argued that suicide was always an act of madness, however briefly the impulse to self-destruct occupied a person's mind. A suicide might be a person who had suffered insanity for years or a seemingly rational individual who lost her mind at the moment she pulled the trigger or swallowed poison.

This notion certainly led to temporary insanity or crimes of passion defenses in court cases.[6] In fact, sectors of the populace acknowledged temporary insanity as a possible cause of violent crime. Nineteenth-century Mexican physicians and legal jurists embraced French alienists like Esquirol because they argued that since suicide was an act of madness, it did not involve individual will. Indeed, the 1871 and 1929 Mexican penal codes named insanity as a mitigating circumstance in establishing fault when one had committed a crime.[7] Moreover, the decriminalization of suicide also rested on the guiding assumption that an individual lacked free will when committing the act. The insane could not be held responsible for any crimes they committed, even a fatal act against their own person. This thinking meshed quite well with the rise of positivism in Mexico and the belief that social laws external to the individual shaped behavior and caused physiological and mental transformations. In contrast, the Christian perspective maintained that individuals possessed full accountability for their actions and the sins or crimes they committed. According to this view, suicides acted from free will, and so did criminals. However, positivist medical experts were still concerned with the notion of the will. They endeavored to understand how a person's will could be weakened by external factors and what measures might be undertaken to bolster the collective will and therefore the fitness of society.[8] Scholars have elaborated on the role of legal-medical experts in criminal trials, where they determined the degree to which a person possessed full faculties at the time he or she committed a criminal act.[9]

How did this cadre of specialists believe that individuals became lypemaniacs or monomaniacs? Esquirol and his fellow alienists argued that the deleterious effects of the struggles of daily life, latent defects of heredity, and modern, secular education could inflame passions. Unrestrained passions weakened the individual and had physiological repercussions on the nervous system. A bankrupt nervous system bred different types of mania. Monomaniacs and lypemaniacs (also known as melancholics) had a strong propensity for suicide. Mexican specialists especially acknowledged the idea that unrealistic and unattainable material aspirations could lead to mental illness and eventually suicide.[10] Such reasons for suicide—giving up on life for not attaining riches—were condemned as dishonorable.

Consensus eluded early thinking on suicide and mental illness. Brierre de Boismont rejected Esquirol's monomania model. He argued that insane and delusional people were not the most likely to commit suicide. He advocated an empirical approach to understanding suicide in the mid-nineteenth century focused on external factors, like climate and living standards. Internal factors, like temperament and gender, were still considered to be important, but the prevailing belief was that "precipitating events" like failed romantic relationships, hedonistic behavior, physical illness, and losses of fortunes could propel people to suicide.[11] Brierre de Boismont's approach foreshadowed that of Émile Durkheim, which would come decades later. He studied juridical inquests and asylum inmates to theorize suicide in his 1856 book, *Du suicide et de la folie* (Suicide and madness). Employing empirical and social-statistical methods, he concluded that advanced, modern life led to despair among individuals, who became crushed by egoism and skepticism and had a tendency to overwork and isolate themselves in modern cities. A conservative Catholic, Brierre de Boismont believed that religion could ameliorate the more alienating aspects of modern life, and he argued strongly against Esquirol, who believed that insanity and suicide were natural bedfellows. However, he also believed that programs to reduce rates of suicide ought to be led by secular experts.[12] Mexican specialists like Luis Vergara y Flores also thought neurosis to be a plague of progress. Modern life transformed the nervous systems of individuals unable to adapt to the paces of modernization.[13]

## GENDER, MENTAL ILLNESS, AND SUICIDE

Gabino Barreda, the intellectual credited with introducing Auguste Comte and the ideology of positivism to Mexico, wrote a long treatise on suicide in the medical school journal *La Escuela de Medicina* in 1883. Having served as a teacher at the Escuela Nacional Preparatoria, Barreda firmly believed in the power of a positivism-driven, liberal education to transform Mexican society. He promoted philosophical positivism, which held that only through scientific method—observation and experiment—could man gain knowledge. When his article on suicide was published, Barreda had already been forced out of the Escuela Nacional Preparatoria by political cronies of Porfirio Díaz. His enemies viewed him as too loyal to the legacies and doctrinaire liberalism of Benito Juárez and Miguel Lerdo de Tejada.[14] Considering his championing of liberal education, it is no wonder that Barreda argued that this structure of education, when institutionalized nationwide, would relegate suicide to the truly insane.[15] He believed that proper secular education would allow individuals to develop "brakes" (*frenos*) that would help them control the passions and selfish instincts that propelled some to self-destruct. However, Barreda also discussed the epidemic of suicide among the British and surmised that Protestantism exalted individual reason, pride, and vanity, leading to a sense of "personal infallibility" that set up the escape route of suicide when goals remained out of reach. A dedicated liberal himself, Barreda nonetheless faulted Protestants for abolishing the worship of images and saints, which, he argued, left hearts weakened because they had nothing to love and venerate.[16] He, like many liberals of his era, felt that religious belief and observation should play a key role in society, just not in political or educational institutions.[17]

The acceptance of the female as a distinct gender emerged in the late eighteenth century, when physicians tossed out the notion that females were imperfect males with their male genitalia inverted upward into their bodies.[18] Sexual difference defined men and women and in the nineteenth century. Jules Michelet, a progressive thinker at the time, scandalized European society by retheorizing female biology and, in effect, "rehabilitating 'woman' so that her potential role as republican mother could be realized." [19] Michelet and other proponents of republican motherhood may have rescued women from "impurity and depravity," but they remained imprisoned by their bodies, especially their wombs.[20] Barreda's contemporaries pondered the enigma of the female reproductive system and placed it at the core of nervous diseases. Porfirian sexual science communicated that the ovary and the uterus propelled action in woman and communicated these impulses to the brain. The inability of women to apply brakes to their passions and emotions seemed to be rooted in the mysteries of their unique biological functions. When a woman acted erratically, her womb was to blame. This sentiment equated to the diagnosis of "moral insanity," coined by English physician James Prichard in 1835. Morally insane individuals recognized right from wrong but lacked the psychological brakes to halt destructive impulses.[21]

An 1884 article in the national medical school journal agreed with French specialists that the causes of progressive locomotor ataxia resided in female sexual parts. The affliction caused an inability to control one's bodily movements, making a walk across a room a meandering and jerky display. The author noted the French case of Francisca R., a forty-eight-year-old woman who lacked the ability to stand and resided in the incurable wing of a hospital. She had been a seamstress, and one day as she was pumping the sewing machine pedal she suffered constant "voluptuous sensations" and, ultimately, repeated orgasms. She left work but soon suffered stomach pains. She refused to operate the machine again but nonetheless endured eight to fifteen days of "violently, erotic sensations." She finally quit her job three years later but continued to experience spontaneous orgasms "without artifice or sexy thoughts."[22]

Physicians judged excessive sexuality and promiscuity to be precursors of mental illness and suicide, especially in women. Francisca R. found herself confined to an incurable ward because her "voluptuous sensations" could not be controlled. Masturbation and spontaneous, unprovoked orgasms certainly alarmed specialists. In fact, profusion in any behavior, including material acquisition, according to these thinkers, led to mental illness and potentially to suicide or criminal activity. An article in *La Escuela de Medicina* listed the following as factors that could lead to suicide: abuse of pleasures, masturbation, excessive drinking of alcoholic beverages, gambling, anger, ambition, envy, jealousy, hatred, boredom, solitude, nostalgia, domestic conflict, extreme affinity for music, fear, regret, desperation, poverty, dishonor, and, "overall, a hereditary disposition."[23]

Another author, quoting French intellectual Germaine de Staël, argued that whereas love was merely an episode in the life of men, it embraced the entire life of women. The text claimed that although there were Mexicans that committed suicide for reasons of love, fewer Mexican women killed themselves than women from other parts of the world, and this was because their upbringing socialized them to stay home, where they could preserve the "virginity of their soul" and not witness very much of the "ordinariness of life" (prosa de la vida).[24] This sentiment gelled with the perspective of Horacio Barreda, who penned an article on the pitfalls of feminism in *Revista Positiva* in 1909. He contended that "liberating" women from the workplace so that they could stay in the home, unperturbed by public life, was a sign that Mexico had moved forward and become more civilized.[25] Certainly, this idea correlated with the gender ideology of the "angel in the home" and other prescriptions of middle-class and elite respectability.[26] Barreda edited the *Revista Positiva*—a journal dedicated to proselytizing positivist ideas—from 1901 to 1913 and communicated many of the beliefs of his famous father, Gabino Barreda. Unlike Gabino, however, Horacio argued in a decidedly unscientific way that women lacked the intellect to think abstractly or to concentrate for long periods of time. He contended that menstruation in particular could bring on mental disturbances in the female brain and provoke criminal activities. In 1894, *La Escuela de Medicina* published an article that referenced Austro-German physician Richard von Krafft-Ebing, who reasoned that a woman ought not to be held responsible for any crime she committed during her menstrual period. In other words, he believed that a menstruating woman could experience a mental transformation akin to temporary insanity, which exonerated her of culpability. Accordingly, he recommended that the temporarily addled woman be isolated and monitored until her condition passed.[27] These same transformations, which attempted suicides sometimes referred to as *trastornos mentales,* caused a psychotic break that destroyed the impulse for self-preservation.

## HYSTERIA AND LYPEMANIA:
## THE FEMALE DISORDERS

Even though theorists and physicians considered suicide to be a social problem in the late nineteenth century, they believed that the deleterious impact of external factors on the physiology and psyche of individuals required intensive study and therapy. Some early therapies to treat mental illness included drinking copious amounts of cold water or being doused with buckets of cold water. Hysteria, like Esquirol's manias, became a common diagnosis for women, some of whom had attempted suicide. Suicidal impulses and mental illness continued to be defined in part by an excess of passions or egoism. Mental illness manifested differently in men and women, according to some specialists. Men more commonly received the diagnosis of neurasthenia, while women were most often diagnosed with hysteria. Up until the late nineteenth century, hysteria in particular had been considered a disorder firmly rooted in the reproductive functions of women. French alienists would rethink hysteria as a condition of the psyche and neurological system, but they never really divorced its symptoms and causes from female biology. Men sometimes received the diagnosis of hysteria, but by and large it was a label placed on women in nineteenth- and early twentieth-century Mexico.

French physician Jean-Martin Charcot (1825–93), a doctor at the Salpêtrière, the infamous Paris insane asylum for women, performed autopsies to understand the connection between clinical symptoms in living inmates and lesions found in their brains and spinal cords after they died.[28] Much to his chagrin, he and his colleagues found no evidence of lesions in hysterics after their deaths, in effect disapproving their hypothesis that mental illness resulted from damaged brains. However, one of his contemporaries, Gustave Le Bon, posited that women possessed inferior intelligence because their brains were closer to the size of those of gorillas than those of men.[29] Considered the founder of neurology, Charcot contributed important knowledge to understanding Parkinson's disease, multiple sclerosis, and neurosyphilis. He attracted a large following of students, including Sigmund Freud. However, scholars now view his teaching methods and public lectures featuring exhibitions of hysterical inmates to be carnivalesque freak shows designed to titillate audiences and enhance his fame. Charcot hypnotized his hysterical muses Augustine, Blanche, and Geneviève to make them manifest the physical and verbal markers of hysteria. Bodily contortions and verbal outbursts abounded during his shows, amusing audiences. Charcot contradicted many of his contemporaries by asserting that hysteria also surfaced in men.[30] Mexican medical student Ernesto Rojas disagreed with Charcot in his 1909 thesis on hysteria, written as part of his studies at the Escuela Nacional de Medicina. The young student claimed that the condition did not arise from female genitalia. Moreover, he argued that doctors erred to think that marriage (a term he used as a euphemism for sexual relations) could cure hysteria, because if sexual activities were a remedy, then there would be no hysterical prostitutes. In other words, hysteria was not a result of ovarian or uterine congestion that could be mitigated by sexual intercourse.[31]

Melancholy, or what Esquirol labeled lypemania (and sometimes hypomania), was another common diagnosis for women. Symptoms included extreme sadness or timidity, a preference for quiet and solitude, misanthropic distrust, hallucinations, and a chronic impulse for suicide. The belief was that venereal disease and masturbation could bring on lypemania and dementia. Agustina P. lived in asylums for thirty-three years. Diagnosed with lypemania in 1910, she died of peritonitis tuberculosis in 1943. Like other patients, she and her family provided a family history. Her mother and sister suffered from "nerves." Agustina had previously survived typhus, but she had tuberculosis, "numbness" in her legs, migraine headaches, and "twinges" in her month and tongue at the time of her intake questionnaire. She neither smoked nor drank, but she attributed her illness to "inheritance" and "moral sufferings" over the past five years. Two years into her residence at the asylum, she explained her evolution into mental illness in almost textbook lypemanic terms. When her beloved aunt died, Agustina experienced trembling all over her body for eight days, pain and heaviness in her head, intense sadness, and a fear of noises that sounded like an electric motor. She refused to eat, cried uncontrollably, failed to sleep, and thought constantly of her dead aunt. Agustina worried that her aunt had died without providing a last confession. Her doctors stated that she suffered from lypemania, but they also wrote in her file that her prognosis was good if she completed treatment. The year was

1912, and to cure her melancholy, she received increasing dosages of intravenous morphine over the course of a day, no injections for eight days, and then a resumption of the therapy. She was also prescribed laxatives of creosote for her tuberculosis. Her medical caretakers erred in their optimistic prognosis. Her sister received notice of her death on May 5, 1943, via telegram. She had not lived outside of the asylum since 1910.[32] Doctors also labeled twenty-five-year-old Imelda J. a melancholic in 1910, and they noted that she failed to obey her mother.[33] Even when girls had reached the age of majority, their parents may still have had considerable control over them, and asylums may have been the convents of the colonial era. They were places to deposit unruly girls and women.[34]

A review of clinical patient files of El Manicomio General de La Castañeda (the general asylum) in Mexico City from 1910 to 1930 found no diagnoses of hysteria for men, only for women. In his 2009 study of La Castañeda, Andrés Ríos Molina found that the majority of female inmates had hysteria listed as at least one of their diagnoses between 1910 and 1913.[35] Indeed, the idea that women suffered weak and sentimental temperaments that rendered them susceptible to moral corruption and drama compelled many observers to label female suicides "neurotics" or "hysterics."[36] Doctors used the label freely, and newspapers picked up on the lingo as well in their reporting of suicides. Scholar Asti Hustvedt contends that hysteria became a catchall label for a host of chaotic symptoms exhibited by women in an era that severely circumscribed their autonomy.[37] The Mexican hysterics at La Castañeda may have suffered the unbearable stresses of the early revolutionary years. Did they lose family members to war? Were they displaced from their homes and forced to move to the capital? Did they simply not conform to expected gender roles? Some specialists at the time questioned gynecological causes of hysteria but still labeled women who deviated from prescribed gender ideology hysterics. Indeed, patient histories at La Castañeda show that doctors often diagnosed hysteria for women who disobeyed parents or went out with men. Asylums housed hysterical and epileptic patients in wards away from the criminally insane, and they often comprised the largest proportion of inmates (*asilados*). Hysteria showed up as one of several diagnoses.

A gender order gone awry disturbed society, especially when it was observed in an asylum. Dr. Romero Rubio, the director of the Hospital del Divino de Salvador, a women-only asylum that predated La Castañeda, felt that he had to defend his professional honor in *El Nacional*. On May 9, 1895, the newspaper published a short article headlined "Hospital for Demented Women" that noted that female inmates were allowed to roam like "night troubadours" unsupervised through the building and grounds of the asylum. Dr. Rubio responded, noting that there were no simple hysterics admitted to the hospital. In other words, inmates suffered from other conditions in addition to hysteria.[38] Perhaps some members of the public had been scandalized by newspaper photographs of Charcot's exhibition of his overexcited muses wrapped in sheets, vocalizing, and contorting their bodies in physical manifestations of hysteria. Herlinda M. first entered the Hospital Canoa for women on July 3, 1909. Doctors released her almost five months later, but she returned in May 1910. That time, she stayed just eight days, although she returned again in July and was eventually transferred to the newly built La Castañeda in September. Twenty years old and born in Cuernavaca, Herlinda worked as a domestic servant but possessed a "violent temper." Doctors discovered that she had been abandoned at La Castañeda by her aunt and that she had been fired from her position after multiple fights with her employer. Nonetheless, physicians did not waste time contemplating her homelessness. They diagnosed her as suffering maniacal psychosis and hysteria. Her symptoms of headaches and stomach distress in combination with her violent temperament convinced them that they were right. Of course, headaches and an upset stomach could be explained by other mundane conditions like dehydration and contaminated food. Herlinda told her doctors that she had wanted to marry a suitor but that her aunt had forbidden it and dropped her off at Canoa. She had no family history of mental illness. Her mother had died of tuberculosis and her father of a heart attack. Doctors found her normal in her physical exam as well. In the final notes of her patient history, doctors found her to be "capricious" and suffering from an "amoral madness."[39] A working-class adolescent who bristled against the dictates of her aunt and employers, Herlinda did not conform to Porfirian ideals of the submissive and obedient worker. Her travails paralleled those of other young women who wished to marry against their mothers' wishes. Some young women eloped with their lovers to force their parents' acceptance. A mother faced with the dishonor of her daughter and the family sometimes acquiesced to let young couples forge independent unions or marriages.[40]

Teresa O. had unruly tendencies, according to her mother and doctor. A frequent inmate of Canoa and finally of La Castañeda, Teresa was diagnosed with hysteria on her first admission to Canoa, when she was fifteen years old. By the time she was twenty-five years old, she had tried to commit suicide twice: first, by piercing her forehead with a spike and, second, by consuming powders of permanganate, a common household disinfectant. Her La Castañeda file described her as a young woman of "bad character" with an "affected walk" who "did not respect or obey anyone." The doctor reasoned that she lacked family history that might point to some atavistic propensity for mental illness or suicide, but he noted that she suffered chronic enteritis, suppurating sores on her neck, and probably syphilis. Teresa grabbed the chance to tell her version of what had happened to her. She noted that her mother had committed her this time to La Castañeda because she did not like Teresa going out in the street. She admitted to leaving the house to get away from her sister, who insisted on pursuing Teresa's boyfriend, a doctor who had cured Teresa of scrofula (tuberculosis of the neck) but also "abused" her. Teresa did not report the abuse because she felt ashamed that she had "done it" with him. She claimed that she had had another relationship with a doctor but said that she now wanted to work. Doctors could not see beyond her hyperexcited state of mind and her entire lack of moral restraint. Her file contained a subsequent entry in 1913 noting that her family had requested her release and a note in 1915 indicating that she had syphilis.[41] Teresa, like Herlinda, may have had bona fide mental disturbances, especially if syphilis had taken its neurological levy on her brain. Yet some women who flouted gender norms or disobeyed their parents and husbands were doubtless inaccurately diagnosed and committed to asylums. La Castañeda also operated as a homeless shelter of sorts, taking in poor women who might otherwise live on the streets. However, long before the advent of modern asylums, gender ideology had dictated that respectable women should remain sequestered in homes when possible and that even working-class women should carry a sense of enclosure with them in the streets.[42]

Even in 1928, many years after Teresa's case, although clinical files might note scientific diagnoses like paranoid schizophrenia, they also remarked on "errors of conduct" related to women transgressing gender-normative behaviors. However, the diagnosis of "moral insanity" had mostly disappeared from asylum records by this point because, as Mexican author Cristina Rivera-Garza argues, revolutionary era specialists saw no credence in this Porfirian pseudo-illness that was used especially to tag disorderly women.[43] Greater exposure to feminism in the years after the revolution may also have provided women the rhetoric to redefine "proper" behaviors. María Carmen M., a twenty-two-year-old student, entered La Castañeda in April 1928. Her intake questionnaire revealed a hereditary disposition to mental illness. One uncle and three cousins suffered from insanity (*locura*). She had endured childhood illnesses of measles, chicken pox, typhus, influenza, and malaria. She admitted that she menstruated irregularly and had become emaciated. In this era, physicians viewed anorexia nervosa as a symptom of other diseases rather than a disease in its own right. Lack of appetite and refusing food were loosely linked to melancholy, and wasting or refusing food signaled that a patient had suicidal impulses.[44] Carmen's parents related that she had seemed to undergo a personality change four years before and that she slept little, talked incoherently, ran away often, and was fixated on marriage. Her mother claimed that Carmen wanted to marry an imaginary suitor. Between 1928 and 1930, Carmen entered residential treatment three times, and doctors noticed that she had "erotic thoughts" and claimed to have consummated sexual relations with a doctor, a lawyer, and an engineer.[45] Diagnoses had a hint of the Freudian forbidden. Erotic thoughts and unrealistic fantasies were seen as sure signs of psychosis, especially in women, who were presumed to naturally possess a passive sexuality. Unbridled erotic thoughts and impulses led to an excess of emotions and, potentially, suicide.

## NEURASTHENIA: THE MALE DISORDER

American physician George Beard delivered a paper on a new nervous disorder to the New York Medical Journal Association in 1868. He coined the illness "neurasthenia," as the condition was characterized by nervous exhaustion, or lack of nerve strength. Beard speculated that the condition was "found in every brain-working household." Moreover, he theorized that it ran in families and was especially common in England, France, and the United States. Mostly, Beard considered neurasthenia to be an "American disease."[46] Both women and men could suffer nervous exhaustion, but in Mexican suicide cases before 1910 it was more commonly diagnosed in men. Beard believed that female neurasthenics had trouble with their reproductive organs such as "irritation, congestion, and imprisonment of the ovaries." An 1895 report on successful operations performed at the Academia Nacional de Medicina included the case of a female patient who received a full hysterectomy because she suffered from hysteria and "painful neurasthenia." The doctor found that her ovaries had been degenerated by chronic inflammation.[47] Testicular issues in men, such as excessive emission of semen, could be considered the result of an exhausted nervous system.[48]

Like the symptoms of hysteria, the indicators of neurasthenia were difficult for doctors to classify. The common list included tenderness of the scalp, headaches, heaviness in the back of the head (signifying brain congestion), protruding eyes, floating specks in the eyes, hearing the pumping of the heart in the ears, inability to concentrate, frequent blushing or twitching of the face, dyspepsia, and sweaty hands, all of which could be symptoms of a host of other ailments. Today, we might link these symptoms to a panic attack or prolonged stress. Chronic neurasthenics also looked younger than their years. They showed fewer wrinkles, possessed soft skin, and had trim physiques. Beard hypothesized that their younger appearance might be due to the fact that neurasthenics hailed from privileged social groups and thus did not perform hard manual labor in the sun.[49] Beard's message was clear: only those from the educated classes suffered nervous exhaustion. It seemed to be a trendy disease that connoted certain class status to the sufferer. A reporter for *El Nacional* mocked neurasthenia as the disease of millionaires, claiming that an excess of money led to mental disturbance.[50] A writer for *El Imparcial* who published under the name Tic Tac ridiculed a preparatory school student who could not perform well in physics class because he was neurasthenic and needed to "recharge his brain." Tic-Tac ended his humorous dialogue with, "everyone suffers and recounts an altered character; some chew their moustache; others pull their hair; some put on a play for whoever will watch; more than a few stay in bed for three days straight; others are incapable of writing a note .... [Neurasthenia,] this mysterious scourge of humanity."[51] Neurasthenia provided a pseudoscientific label that communicated social concerns about modern life and the promises that life held. It was a social problem that could be solved through medicine. It was a modern disease that had a cure but that also provided the words to criticize the pace of modernization and democratization at the turn of the century.[52]

There were as few diagnosed female neurasthenics as there were male hysterics. Charcot "reserved the neurasthenia label for bourgeois male patients with hysteria-like symptoms while placing working-class men into the category of male hysterics."[53] In other words, poor men found themselves feminized by receiving a less manly diagnosis. Medical doctors did their privileged clients a favor by labeling them neurasthenics, thereby distancing them from the feminine category of hysteria. Christopher Forth contends that male neurasthenics could retain their manhood, although Gregory Shaya argues that neurasthenics were considered to be "womanly" men because it was women were most commonly thought to have an "excess of sensibility," which was one of the symptoms of neurasthenia.[54]

Men who toiled outdoors doing physical work did not suffer from nervous exhaustion because the condition was a result of excessive mental labor.[55] An 1892 article in the Catholic daily *Diario del Hogar* poked fun at Charcot and his assertion that all men of talent suffered mental illness. The article told the story of an intrepid French journalist who hunted down the famous alienist in Paris. Charcot had given illustrious men such as William Shakespeare, Lord Byron, and Victor Hugo posthumous diagnoses of neurasthenia. The journalist asked cheekily, if all men of talent suffered the malady, what about celebrity doctors? His query visibly angered Charcot, and the *Diario del Hogar* reporter described the scene, "His black eyes, the terrible black eyes, those suggestive eyes, of supernatural power, that have penetrated to the depths of so many subjects, fixed amazed on the journalist. The professor had not predicted the question." [56]

Neurasthenia was a modern disease of the bourgeois classes. It connoted status rather than shame to the sufferer. In fact, even the national medical school journal advertised tonics such as Neurosine Prunier as remedies for neurasthenia in 1903.[57] Wealthy men who worked too hard developed neurasthenia. Rich housewives did the same and suffered from nervous exhaustion. Beard wrote that even neurasthenic authors "find that in writing they are troubled with pain, aching, heaviness, fatigue, tiredness of the arm, or, in some cases, a stiffness that suggests rheumatism—and they are sometimes so nervous that they cannot write continuously, without suffering from a nervousness which, without pain, compels them to stop." [58] Neurasthenia was an eminently modern disease, and Beard offered cures that ranged from rest to work and prescribed such material treatments as electrotherapy, arsenic solutions, and *cannabis indica,* the last of which Beard found to be "the most trustworthy, most reliable, and valuable of remedies." He also recommended taking a European vacation and horseback riding—leisure activities of the rich that were impractical and unaffordable for many.[59]

A 1908 front-page editorial in *El Imparcial* noted that disillusion in love accounted for most suicides in Mexico. However, the author claimed that in Europe, "hunger throws many bodies in the Seine, dishonor fires some revolvers, and physical illness opens many arteries." He expressed disbelief that neurasthenia could be so widespread in the modern age with its plethora of activities and diversions. He agreed that overwork might paralyze energies and lead to neurasthenia, but he emphasized that the nervous disease did not cause suicide. He consulted with two medical professors, who argued that everyone in the world possessed varying degrees of latent neurasthenia; and relatives of suicidal individuals, who claimed that their kin suffering from neurasthenia were probably hiding a familial legacy of more serious mental illnesses, such as melancholy. In other words, the reporter contended that neurasthenia was sometimes used as a mask to conceal some "secret drama" in the family history of the victim. The doctors theorized that melancholy rather than neurasthenia resulted in suicide. Melancholy ought not be confused with neurasthenia, as the former was closer to insanity, "a sad madness that was very dangerous."[60] Neurasthenia, on the other hand, plagued rich and idle social groups. Those who worked too little and enjoyed themselves too much would develop nervous exhaustion. The doctors said that if people worked hard, they would never become neurasthenics.[61] This message to occupy oneself with work contradicted Beard's advice to relax.

A few months later, a reporter for *El Imparcial* interviewed Dr. Fernando Zárraga, who was at the time director of the Hospital Juárez and would later serve as director of the Escuela Nacional de Medicina, on the looming epidemic of neurasthenia in Mexico. The subtitle signaled alarm: "A Poor Nation Invaded by Neurasthenia!" The reporter began the article, "I, insignificant and invisible hack at *El Imparcial,* I am neurasthenic; my colleague, the theater reviewer, is neurasthenic; the secretary of the editorial staff, that before had muscles of steel, and that today is pensive and whining, also has been attacked by neurasthenia." He went on to note that he saw neurasthenics everywhere and hoped to understand this modern condition. It is difficult to determine how tongue-in-cheek the article was, as journalists and artists were common occupations of neurasthenics. Nevertheless, the article continued with the remarks of the esteemed expert. Dr. Zárraga noted that neurasthenics abounded in present society and that physical, intellectual, and in particular moral overwork could cause the illness. Zárraga also noted neurasthenia's hereditary character and listed its symptoms of headaches, back pain, insomnia, nightmares, vertigo, and extreme fatigue. The reporter asked if a cure existed. Zárraga responded that Molière, the French dramatist who wrote *Le Malade imaginaire* (*The Imaginary Invalid*), whose main character, Argan, is a hypochondriac, might call it an imaginary disease, but he disagreed. Zárraga reasoned that a change of climate often helped victims. He suggested that some patients visit the mountains and told others to take a trip to the beach. Electrotherapy ameliorated the symptoms in some but could contribute to greater insomnia in others. Hypnosis also facilitated relief, but a month of vacation could work wonders for the overtired brain. Zárraga concluded, "Neurasthenia is a social evil, and in Mexico we will be lost if this illness becomes widespread, because a neurasthenic is a person with little energy, incapable of producing in society all that one would hope for in normal circumstances." The reporter ended the article by exclaiming that neurasthenia was an authentic condition after all.[62] One reading it more than a century later wonders how much sarcasm was infused in his reporting.

Santiago Rusiñol, writing for *La Iberia* in 1909, disagreed with the esteemed Dr. Zárraga and refused to consider neurasthenia a real illness. He ridiculed those who thought they suffered from the fashionable ailment and the doctors who perpetuated its diagnosis. He noted that before the advent of this modern ailment, sufferers would have been closed up in an asylum. Now they roamed the streets. Neurasthenics were young and idle, "look at their watches as if in a hurry, and walk through the world as if mourning for themselves." Rusiñol said that if doctors would only change the name to "bestiastenia," the condition would cease to exist. After all, who would want to suffer a condition related to a beast?[63] A couple of months later, an article followed Rusiñol's editorial that announced that neurasthenia was not, in fact, a make-believe disease. The reporter argued that it had become a grave social problem and it struck not just those who might be atavistically predisposed to it but also the most healthy and active members of society. He warned that digestive issues could bring it on. The reporter admonished doctors to treat the ailment as an authentic one and recommended complete repose, massage, and baths. Tepid soaks, electrotherapy, and three weeks in bed without movement ought to cure the patient. A vegetarian diet followed by an agreeable trip would seal the cure.[64]

Antonio Gota de Zaragoza, another doctor, called neurasthenia the disease of the century and concluded that the pressures of modern life led to the ailment. Unprecedented luxury and countless new leisure activities and spectacles, combined with "poisonous media," exhausted nerves and led to the modern disorder. He claimed that it mostly plagued the professions of public functionaries, journalists, soldiers, artists, and musicians. In order for neurasthenia not to establish roots in the young, Gota de Zaragoza recommended exercise, sleep, and fresh air and a balance between work and play.[65] His suggestions targeted the prosperous classes, as working-class children probably had fewer leisure activities and maybe even less access to fresh air, as they lived in the odorous barrios of the city. It is interesting to note that the majority of patients entering La Castañeda fell between the ages of twenty and forty.[66] These ages, theoretically, represented the most productive years of the lifecycle. Whatever their differences, all of these commentators agreed that Mexico's youth faced a potential nervous crisis that would impact the productivity and health of the social body.

DEGENERATION AND THE MORAL
DECLINE OF SOCIETY

Dr. Beard's discourse on neurasthenia did not address degeneration per se, but Mexican medical specialists agreed with French and German experts, who believed that neurasthenia could lead to national decline.[67] Mexican physicians and criminologists looked to Italian Cesare Lombroso to help them understand how societies and individuals could degenerate into barbarity and crime. A positivist, Lombroso placed deep faith in natural science to explain social problems like criminality. He differed from his French colleagues in that he theorized that degeneration not only multiplied in the "dangerous" classes, and would ultimately result in their extinction, but also could be "uncontained . . . scattering forth pathologies" through societies. By the 1890s, Lombroso and his fellow theorists, such as Scipio Sighele, were entertaining the notion of cultural degeneration.[68] They believed that certain behaviors and characteristics could infect mass society. This was what they thought was behind copycat suicides and the epidemic of self-murder among impressionable youth. José Olvera, a founding member of the Medical Association of Pedro Escobedo, foreshadowed the ideas of Lombroso in 1869, however he minimized the theories of the Frenchman Jean Baptiste Lamarck (1774–1829), who believed that acquired characteristics or defects like mental illness or alcoholism could alter a person's genetic material and that these mutations or weaknesses could be passed down to subsequent generations.[69] Olvera had less belief in the notion that acquired characteristics could change genetic material. According to Olvera, mental illness resulted from a crisis of *la moral,* which he defined as encompassing "the soul, psyche or spirit, the mysterious and invisible realm of human experience and motivation that forensic pathology could not adequately capture, explain or describe."[70] Olvera noted the moral decline of Mexican society, noting that young boys had become skilled seducers. He claimed that prostitution, rape, and masturbation had reached rampant proportions in society and that more and more individuals sought excessive levels of material luxuries. Olvera also pointed to the suicide epidemic as a sure sign of the moral decline of Mexican society.[71] He and his contemporaries believed neuroses to be a condition of the privileged classes, as laborers worked too hard to suffer mental illness. They contended that the turmoil of the politically unstable mid-nineteenth century could cause weaker minds to break. Olvera dismissed Lombroso's theory that markers of criminality could be read on a person's body. On the contrary, he believed that only in-depth interviews and probing for invisible signs of criminality or insanity could provide valuable information.[72] Lombrosian ideas had little influence on Mexican psychiatry, especially when it came to racial degeneration. Mexican researchers surmised that the indigenous did not succumb to the influences of modern life and develop mental illness, as their closeness to nature protected them. This fit with the prevailing notion that Mexicans who performed manual labor or lived in the countryside did not commit suicide.[73] It was also thought that indigenous peoples' communal bonds protected them from social alienation.

In research published in 2009, Andrés Ríos Molina found that before the end of the revolution, most Mexican physicians who wrote about mental illness did not work in asylums or hospitals treating the insane.[74] Course offerings in psychiatry at the Escuela Nacional de Medicina were sporadic until 1910. Offering courses in psychology or even considering the field as a viable scientific discipline caused controversy at the Escuela Nacional Preparatoria in the late nineteenth century. There was no place for analyzing mental states in Comtean positivism. Rather, psychology fell under physiology in the venerable French intellectual's theory. However, Porfirio Parra and Justo Sierra claimed that Comte had been wrong, and psychology came to be seen as its own scientific discipline in Mexico's preparatory and medical schools in the late nineteenth century.[75] Psychology was also the bogeyman that was used to attack opponents of President Díaz. Jorge Molina Avilés notes that caricatures of the period labeled the garrote that stifled anti-Díaz actors "psychology."[76] Porfirian specialists interested in mental illness and insanity worked from the legal medicine section of the medical school. Likewise, articles on mental illness appeared in the legal medicine section of the *Gaceta Médica de México*.[77] Establishing a defendant's state of mind was key to court decisions in criminal and civil cases. If it was determined that the perpetrator of a crime lacked reason (sanity), then he or she could not be held responsible for his or her actions. Similarly, a person diagnosed as demented did not possess legal personhood to sign contracts, sell property, leave wills, or contract marriage. Mexican civil and penal codes provided the space for legal-medical experts to testify in court cases to determine a suspect's state of mind and capacity to know right from wrong. The result during the Porfiriato was the professional guild Consejo Médico Legal (Legal Medical Council), founded in 1886. Its members, some of the more illustrious científicos of the Porfiriato, shaped the narrative about which mental states were most dangerous to society and which nullified culpability in crime. As Michel Foucault has so brilliantly stated, the emerging science of psychiatry initially was more about protecting society from dangerous elements than understanding the individual's pathology and finding treatments.[78]

Inheritance and environment, Mexican experts agreed, did play a role in mental illness. Mental disorders could run in families, showing up in the children of alcoholics, syphilitics, epileptics, and the demented. Indeed, families suffered stigma and shame when they had individuals who suffered from these conditions in their family trees. It was thought that mental illness and propensities for vices like alcoholism descended through lineage. Mexicans gave a nod to the genetic acquisition theories of Jean Baptiste Lamarck. The experts also believed that environmental conditions like rapid modernization, urbanization, technology, and the associated faster pace of life could provoke mental illness in those unable to adapt. Clearly, the causes of mental illness were a moving target during the Porfiriato. Empiricists like Porfirio Parra wanted to establish identifiable causes and symptoms.[79] Nonempiricists like Olvera saw mental illness as a disease of the soul or spirit. Parra abhorred the notion that *la moral* should have a place in science, claiming that it ought to be relegated to the questionable realm of unlicensed curanderos and charlatans.[80] However, medical experts found themselves in a quandary when it came to explaining how nervous exhaustion could result from physical causes alone, especially in a rapidly modernizing society. There was also the spectacle of the morally insane prostitute or the alcoholic, both of whom were believed to lack self-control and free will and have no power over their immoral behaviors.[81] The debate over the role of *la moral* in mental illness showed that positivist physicians did not always adhere to the idea that only the physical body and brain could yield the answers to the mysteries of insanity.[82]

In 1887, two decades after Olvera advocated for moral treatments and a greater emphasis on the environmental causes of insanity, Mariano Rivadeneyra foreshadowed some of the theories of Émile Durkheim. He argued that modern changes in the fabric of urban life and work made cities "nurseries of insanity." The pace of life and the struggle to make ends meet could provoke mental illness. Rivadeneyra believed that modernity led to madness in those who could not adapt to its forces of change.[83] His argument for external causes based in the pace of modernization was refuted by 1910 with the "medicalization of madness and physicians' insistence that its origins lay in the diseased and defective brain," at least in theory.[84] A later generation of positivist physicians used hydrotherapy, purgatives, and other forms of physical approaches to treat mental illness, but they did not follow their French and English peers in offering moral treatments. Moral therapies were equated with the religious and metaphysical, and that was something these Mexican doctors could not abide.[85] The asylum intake questionnaire focused on race, gender, family history of illness (mental and physiological), childhood illnesses, venereal diseases, menstrual status, and habits such as drinking and smoking. Theories of degeneration informed the format of the questionnaire and the intake interview. As Stephanie Ballenger points out, asylum entrance documents did not provide room for the patient to explain their thoughts on their mental decline.[86] Doctors did show interest in vices as possible determinants of mental illness, but all treatments and therapies in the Mexico City asylums were medical and physical. They included medicines, purgatives, enemas, hydro- and electrotherapy, and physical restraint. No moral treatments were prescribed. Some patients accepted that their vices drove them crazy. Ramona Muñoz, an inmate at La Castañeda, had been diagnosed with "manic and degenerative excitement." An indigent former domestic servant, Ramona lived in the epileptic ward. She admitted to being a pulque drinker and cigar smoker, which, according to prevailing medical wisdom, undoubtedly contributed to her violent temper.[87] She fought with her employer and her coworkers, and when she was brought to the asylum she had to be immobilized in a straitjacket. The doctor certified her as cured after she had been in the asylum for two years. However, he did note that she angered easily and needed to be watched by her family.[88] The presumption was that her family had to be vigilant in preventing her from engaging in vices like excessive drinking and smoking, which could lead to another bout of mental decline.

As the discussion above reveals, Mexican physicians differed from their counterparts in other countries about what they believed to be the roots of mental illness and the causes of suicide. Early Porfirian specialists considered the pressures of modern life to be mitigating factors that could drive an individual into the abyss of insanity. Their approach was more benign than that of the following generation, and they suggested the victims of modernity might be cured. Later Porfirian specialists read the same Italian, French, and English theories but took a more punitive approach to mental derangement. Degeneration theory dominated thinking in psychiatry during this era, and mentally ill citizens were believed to threaten the progress of the nation. As Rivera-Garza argues, these beliefs were reflected in the clientele of La Castañeda from 1910 to 1930. By and large, the asylum's patients were artisans, day laborers, domestic servants, and prostitutes.[89] For the proponents of degeneration theory, the asylum served to remove dangerous individuals from society and prevent them from transmitting their vices and evils across the nation.

## DISTRUST OF THE MEDICAL ESTABLISHMENT

Mexico City residents had an uneasy relationship with the Manicomio General de La Castañeda. Located in Mixcoac, the asylum embodied the pinnacle of Porfirian progress and modernity. The suburb on the outskirts of the capital had welcomed wealthy Mexicans seeking respite from the bustling and modernizing city. The asylum was built on the grounds of a former hacienda, La Castañeda, from which it took its name. It was made up of twenty-five buildings surrounded by verdant forests and lush gardens. Cristina Rivera-Garza noted that committee members composed of doctors and lawyers convened in 1896 to design the modern Manicomio General and "made recommendations to the authorities that exposed medical strategies to treat insanity, special tactics to prevent contagion, and social concerns with the order and progress of society—all fundamental values of the Porfirian regime."[90] Inaugurated on September 1, 1910, during Mexico's month-long centennial anniversary of independence and in the presence of domestic and foreign dignitaries, La Castañeda showcased the most modern medical treatment available at the time. Students and doctors had a laboratory and test subjects that they could use to understand and develop treatments for mental illness. Chronic underfunding, however, stymied many of its plans.

Investigative reporters and letters written to newspaper editors by concerned citizens often pointed out scandals that had occurred at the asylum. On December 3, 1916, the newspapers *El Demócrata* and *El Universal* broke the news that a husband had wrongly incarcerated a woman from a distinguished family. What could have gone wrong in the marriage? *El Imparcial* had announced the nuptials of Manuela Collantes and Ramón Rivero on September 13, 1903. The archbishop officiated their wedding in the temple of Santa Brigida, and First Lady Carmen Romero Rubio de Díaz attended the ceremony.[91] Clearly, the Collantes family traveled in stylish circles of the Porfirian elite. Manuela Collantes's name had appeared in society pages as early as 1898, when the *Mexican Herald* listed her as one of the patronesses of the bike races in Tlalpam.[92] A decade later, the same paper noted her presence at the "premier social event of the week" at the home of Mrs. Martin Reynolds in Colonia Juárez.[93] After that, however, she seemed to disappear from social life. It is not known what transpired in the seven or eight years between the end of her very public social life and her institutionalization at La Castañeda.

In its December 3 article, *El Demócrata* sensationalized the situation by surmising that Ramón Rivero had barred his wife's relatives from visiting her and that he had colluded with doctors to keep her locked up with lunatics. The paper asked readers to contemplate a man "who possesses a heart of porphyry and a soul of granite, who could not be moved by the bitter tears of a virtuous woman and a model mother?" Reporters managed to gain access to Manuela and her family. Manuela stated that she was in the asylum against her will and that she was neither sick nor taking any medicine. She told reporters that she had pleaded with her husband to remove her and that he had given her false promises that he would as soon as he attended to some matters.[94] Two days later, on December 5, *El Demócrata* published a letter from Ramón, in which he claimed that his wife was mentally ill and had been diagnosed as such by a Dr. Schemonti. Dr. Schemonti, seeing that his reputation was on the line, penned a long missive reproduced in *El Universal* to refute that he had ever treated Manuela. He said he had lived in a home owned by Ramón but claimed that he had never diagnosed or treated the man's wife. The article also noted that the paper had received letters from readers attesting to Manuela's sanity. The grievance and the sensational news coverage provoked action from the director of public welfare, Lorenzo Sepúlveda. He made an unannounced visit to the asylum to assess Manuela's mental state.[95] *El Universal* vowed to stay on the story until the abused wife received justice. A subsequent article, published December 7, noted that two nurses, Marta Boyer and Isidra Estrada, who worked in close proximity to Manuela, said that she always behaved normally. As a *pensionista* (paying inmate), she would have had the luxury of full-time nurses. The reporter wrote that Sepúlveda requested to review her records and noted that asylum personnel had not taken her photograph, "which is a pity, because photography is a tremendous test to prove the abnormal state of a person." The two-page article also recounted the visit of Ramón and his attorney to the newspaper office. The documents brought by Ramón to the newspaper offices included medical diagnoses of Manuela, including one signed by Dr. Schemonti. The editor tracked down Schemonti again for a comment, but the doctor responded that he was never an alienist and had never examined the incarcerated woman. He claimed that someone had falsified his signature.[96]

Manuela's brother Francisco Collantes, also a doctor, told reporters that his sister had suffered nervousness since childhood; he referred to her as neurasthenic but said that she exhibited no symptoms that warranted institutionalization. Apparently, Manuela had been confined in the asylum in 1914, and when her father and brother tried to see her, Ramón used his influence to block them. They eventually managed to get her to her father's home after six months of seclusion in the asylum. When she was there, her family noted no signs of mental illness. However, she missed her two young daughters terribly. They resided with her sister-in-law, Carmen Rivero de Río. When she went to see them, her husband had her recommitted to La Castañeda. Her brother contended that the staff there injected her with morphine to sedate her.[97]

Two days later, on December 9, *El Universal* announced Manuela's impending discharge and gloated over their role in liberating the wronged and virtuous woman: "*El Universal* has done nothing but aim, for the privileges of humanity, to deliver a person to the side of her family, who for a long time, rightly or wrongly, cried in the middle of an environment of insanity." The article included a copy of a letter written by her father, Pedro Collantes, who noted that he had filed divorce papers against Ramón Rivero on behalf of his daughter.[98] *El Universal* claimed the next day on its front page that Ramón had offered to pay the newspaper to have his letters published, much as he had done with *El Demócrata*. Ever the champion of vulnerable women, *El Universal* editors rejected his documents and his money.[99] The newspaper also informed the reading public that two doctors, Manuel Lazo de la Vega and Enrique O. Aragón, had signed paperwork confirming that Manuela suffered mental instability.[100] Aragón had designed the thirteen-page intake form for La Castañeda. Law required two physicians to certify that an individual needed to be committed to an asylum. Suspiciously, however, the document provided no explanation of her condition. Her husband contended that four doctors, including her own brother, had certified her neurosis.[101]

The drama continued to unfold before the eyes of capitalino readers. Agustín Torres, the director of La Castañeda, sent a letter to *El Universal* attesting to Manuela's mental illness. He also defended the reputation of the institution and noted that doctors there would never admit a sane person. He stated that she was not wrongly confined, explaining that he had a certificate signed by three doctors confirming her mental illness, that she displayed mental disturbances while confined at the asylum, and that nowhere in her file was there a certificate of sanity. *El Universal* reprinted the director's letter and chastised him for not questioning the validity of the paperwork. Reminding readers that Dr. Schemonti claimed that his signature had been falsified, the article also noted that one of the other three doctors had previously served as the director of the asylum.[102] Furthermore, *El Universal* tracked down Juan G. Saldaña, a former asylum doctor who had certified Manuela as possessing sanity. Saldaña was an alienist and had been director of the department of women at La Castañeda. He claimed that he had written to Manuela's father on December 7, 1916. He asserted that when he left employment at the asylum he had certified that Manuela was entirely sane and in full control of her mental faculties. He had noted that Manuela did have a mild tremor in her hand, but he observed that it ceased in the presence of family members. *El Universal* delivered copies of the letter to Lorenzo Sepúlveda, who continued to investigate the matter. The subtitle of the article declared directly that Director Torres had lied.[103] *El Universal* laid down the gauntlet with these charges. However, impugning a public figure's honor would not land a newspaperman in prison during the Porfiriato, as it could have during Díaz's reign.

Torres had a difficult job running La Castañeda. One of his main responsibilities as director, besides improving the care and treatment of the inmates, was to raise the prestige of the institution.[104] The asylum had deteriorated shortly after the fanfare of its inauguration in 1910. Experts had miscalculated the number of beds and misunderstood that most patients would suffer from chronic disorders like alcoholism or neurosyphilis that required long-term care. When the revolution broke out, soon after La Castañeda opened, no one would have guessed that Zapatistas would take residence in the asylum in early 1915 and even draft two of its most dangerous inmates in their army.[105] Residents dodged bullets and lacked sufficient clothing and food, and windows and doors hung from their hinges. Investigative newspapers found ample fodder to criticize the government for the suffering of Mexico City's most vulnerable citizens.

Angela Llaca decided that she had to tell what she knew about the case, and so she walked into the newspaper offices of *El Universal*. She was a typist who had worked for Ramón Rivero, and she also delivered clothing to his wife at the asylum. She stated that Manuela possessed her full faculties because, on sifting through the delivered clothes, she remarked on more than one occasion, "My goodness what clothing; I regret that my family guards their social position and Ramón sends me such humble clothes. You tell him that he can send me others or tell my family." Llaca suggested that a crazy woman would not care about her social position or her clothes. Llaca also stated that she had helped Manuela dress on more than one occasion and noticed bruises, products of pinching or blows that she must have received. She informed Ramón, and he replied dryly that his wife had caused the bruising herself. Llaca told the reporter that she saw nurses hold Manuela down with a sheet and administer injections.[106] *El Demócrata* reported these same facts,[107] and then the stories abruptly ceased. It seemed that Manuela would undoubtedly be freed to return to her father's home. The paper trail is quiet until a decade and a half later, when a Manuela Collantes de Rivero shows up in 1932 volume of *Diario Oficial* as renting 182 Londres Street in Colonia Juárez in Mexico City.[108] Presumably, she was estranged from her husband as she is listed as the sole leaseholder.

Reporters would continue to investigate and criticize the treatment of the insane at La Castañeda after the revolution. On July 26, 1919, the top story in *El Demócrata* was a critique of the asylum bearing the headline: "In Mexico, Public Welfare Is not a Work of Charity but a Labor of Inquisition." The subtitle alerted readers, "As grave as the lack of reason in the patients is the lack of humanitarianism in the directors, doctors, and nurses." [109] A front-page article a month later based on the reports of doctors who had worked at the asylum complained that patients died of hunger while Enrique O. Aragón, an administrator, pursued numerous romantic escapades. They faulted Director Torres for feeding patients *atole* (corn milk) and nothing else morning, noon, and night. The reporter contended that autopsies revealed that patients had died of starvation. The exposé continued to pile on damning criticism, noting that inmates never received curative treatments. The 1919 article reprinted a letter signed "Vigilant Nurse of the Asylum." This whistleblower recounted that the director and administrator routinely disappeared with different nurses behind closed doors. The implication was that they were engaging in illicit sexual activity.[110] The article provoked several residents to send letters to *El Demócrata* to relate their own critiques of the asylum. The leadership of the asylum changed, but the criticism continued in the capital's papers. Finally, in September 1920, interim president Adolfo de la Huerta visited La Castañeda with the new director of public welfare, Rafael Alvarez, and reporters. *El Demócrata* noted that director Ruperto Serna and administrator Luis Ochoa were not on hand to meet the party when they arrived. Moreover, they found the storeroom lacking clothes, beds lacking sheets, and the dispensary lacking bromides.[111] To add fuel to the fire and put the final brush strokes on the black legend of the asylum, newspapers related the story of Teresa Durán y Córdoba, another woman who had been wrongly and forcibly trapped in the asylum.[112]

Drug compounders and pharmacies also came under the scrutiny of investigative reporters and the larger public. On occasion, reporters lamented how easy it was for young people to secure mercury or potassium cyanide, which they could use to commit suicide. In 1919, a series of articles highlighted the scandalous operations of some boticas that falsified compounding prescriptions and used dangerous materials. *Excélsior* reported that many pharmacies lacked oversight by a licensed pharmacist. Miguel Torres, a licensed pharmacist, told *Excélsior* that failed students and young women who previously worked as seamstresses or waitresses ran many compounding drugstores in the city. They consulted with the sick and prepared recipes without any training or professional title. Moreover, Torres contended that businessmen rather than pharmacists owned the boticas and ran them like they would run a butcher shop. *Excélsior* reporters decided to investigate. They looked in the help wanted section of their own paper and noticed that boticas were advertising simply for "an employee of a botica." Nowhere did the advertisements list minimum qualifications or training. *Excélsior* called on the government to enact regulations of all laboratories, boticas, drugstores, or pharmacies to protect society from tainted drugs. Moreover, *Excélsior* suggested that all existing employees of these establishments should be trained in free pharmacy technical schools and that all establishments ought to be certified by the public health department.[113] Apparently, the article caused great outcry in the city. The next day, *Excélsior* reported that the public health department had been studying the issue for some time. They discovered that few students in the medical school finished their pharmacy certificate before they took jobs in the industry. They proposed a new health code that would make botica owners responsible for any mistakes in dispensing or formulating remedies and also prevent employees from making substitutions in drug formulas.[114]

The optimism of *Excélsior* faded six months later, in August 1919, when the paper published an article charging drugstores with immorality and unscrupulous pricing. An agent from the Departamento de Trabajo (Department of Labor) ordered the same prescription for an injection from multiple businesses. The recipe included tincture of Van Swieten, cocaine chloride, and pure water. The formula cost fifty-five centavos to produce. The reporter writing the exposé for *Excélsior* noted that the agent found that pharmacies charged dramatically different prices for the prescription. The cost of the drug ranged from one peso at Botica Central to more than three pesos at the private Hospital de Jesús. Sanborn's charged two pesos for the prescription. The agent ordered three other prescriptions from pharmacies and found the same discrepancies in prices charged to the public. The article noted the discrepancy in prices of certain ingredients that made up the recipe's formula. They criticized first-class pharmacies for charging the most for drugs because they had the advantage of buying ingredients in bulk at lower prices while small boticas did not. The state chemical lab of the health department also analyzed the drugs and published the names and addresses of the establishments surveyed along with notes about how accurately each had carried out the recipe. For example, the Botica Popular on Calle Acequia in the barrio of Nezahualcóyotl, a working-class neighborhood east of El Centro, most accurately prepared the formula. The Farmacia de Salud in Colonia Doctores had the most trouble producing the injection with the correct proportions of ingredients. The Department of Labor concluded that boticas, which served the lower- and working-class barrios, were less likely to cheat customers. The department also promised to conduct investigations of other commercial establishments to let residents know which provided the most quality for their money.[115]

The public health department began investigations anew in 1930, after noting chronic irregularities in the dispensing of patented and unpatented medicines in the capital city.[116] *El Universal* displayed its sensationalist bent in publishing an article in 1930 that charged capital doctors with injecting patients with adulterated drugs and even causing the death of the wife of a prominent general. They blamed arsenic-based drug formulas sold by crooked contraband sellers in Europe. Belgium seemed to be at the root of the controversy, and Mexican doctors unfortunately and unknowingly injected the tainted drugs into their patients. The article cautioned society to avoid injections of arsenic compounds altogether.[117]

A few days later, *El Universal* informed readers that even though it had highlighted the danger of arsenic-based drugs, the German pharmaceutical company Bayer-Meister Lucius stood by the purity and safety of the salvarsans they produced. Salvarsans were the most widespread treatment for syphilis until penicillin was popularized after World War II. In fact, the company distributed a film to doctors that demonstrated the safe fabrication of the drugs.[118] *El Universal* stated that the German company could be trusted but warned against charlatans who administered cures to Mexicans in the poor barrios around the city. In 1930, the paper reported[119] on the return to the city of the infamous Pedro V. Fernández Rocha de la Canal de Aguila, who supplanted the "famous Niño Fidencio" in writing bogus prescriptions to be filled in the boticas.[120] Soon, those with incurable diseases were flocking to the charlatan, who held consultations with would-be clients on Ribera de San Cosme Avenue and in the northern neighborhood of Guadalupe Hidalgo. Fernández dispensed prescriptions as if he were a legitimate doctor, and boticas were all too happy to sell the questionable formulas to poor clients who had no chance of being cured. Fernández, who referred to himself as the True Niño Fidencio, advertised himself as a "Psychic, psychometer of the Esoteric School of Chromopathy of Calcutta, India." He claimed to offer the following services: "Diagnostics of psychometry. Radio-psychic cures, magnetic, electro-magnetic, radio-pyrotechnics and radio-vibratory." More scandalous, according to the reporter, was that some of his medical formulas included very high concentrations of mercury cyanide. Public health agents investigated Fernández, but doctors advised the *El Universal* reporter that existing law allowed the government to do very little to prevent the concoction of various "enervating" formulas. Doctors planned to pressure Congress to enact new regulations to prevent such medical scams in the future.[121]

Regardless of reports that charlatans were plying false remedies on street corners, many publications, including the medical school journal, did not shy away from advertising various medicines and tonics that claimed to cure all sorts of ailments. *El Nacional* advertised an injectable solution of iron and strychnine that was said to cure neurasthenia, hysteria, chlorosis, and anemia on its front page in 1897. In 1909, the English-language *Mexican Herald* advertised an elixir called Stomalix that claimed to cure everything from neurasthenia to diarrhea. Panfilo Zendejas y Pandilla, an inventor and proprietor, paid for an advertisement in *El Nacional* in 1918 to market a medicine that he said cured syphilis, menorrhagia (abnormally heavy menstrual bleeding), and scrofula.

Pills, tonics, and injections were not the only remedies for an ailing populace. Modern Mexicans relied on the marvel of electricity not only to light their way but also to cure their weakness. The most ubiquitous advertisement claiming to cure debility in men was for an electric belt that men could wear under their clothes. Women could wear it as well. Ads touted it as the non-drug cure for ailments of the kidneys, back pains, and any sort of nervous condition.[122] Linking sexual dysfunction with nervous conditions, a 1915 advertisement claimed that electricity was the only treatment for incurable diseases such as impotence, spermatorrhea (involuntary excessive ejaculation), and neurasthenia. A 1921 notice advised people experiencing nervous and mental illnesses to call Spanish neurologist Dr. José María Albiñana. Albiñana had been trained in Madrid and was employed at the Academia Nacional de Medicina in Mexico City. The notice advertised a combination of electrical and serum therapy to cure a host of ailments, including neurasthenia, hysteria, mental disturbances, sexual weakness, female problems, insomnia, and anything else related to the nervous system. The doctor kept an office front on Calle Donceles, across from the Chamber of Deputies.[123]

CONCLUSION

Mexican specialists found that the causes and determinants of suicide did not align neatly with theories of mental illness or criminology. In fact, physicians argued over the causes of mental disorders and how to best treat them. Increased levels of mental illness could certainly be a contributing factor to the rising suicide rate, although many theorists believed that suicides lost reason only at the moment of their self-murder. The law did not view suicide or attempted suicide as murder, nor did it hold the perpetrator responsible for the act. Theorizing about "born criminals" did not help experts determine who was most likely to commit suicide. On the other hand, degeneration theory did hold sway with many intellectuals. There was a belief that progressive vices and conditions like alcoholism, syphilis, and gambling and pastimes like film, theater, music, and reading could lead to the weakening and eventually the nullification of the will. Experts feared that an epidemic of weak-willed citizens could bring down the whole of society. Forward, ever forward, was the mantra of state and medical agents, who viewed suicide as a disease of modern, civilized society. They considered it to be an inevitable growing pain that could not be dismissed. They feared the cultural degeneration of an entire nation. Yet physicians disagreed on the causes of suicide. Did physical or environmental variables lead to self-annihilation? The discussions about suicide that occurred in the halls of the Escuela Nacional de Medicina, the pages of medical journals, and the operating room of the morgue paralleled worldwide debates on the topic. Universality, rather than a unique Mexican approach, characterized efforts to curb suicide. However, what may have distinguished the Mexican conversation on suicide from others was the focus on youth, who seemed most susceptible to the stresses and dramas of everyday life. Specialists had just begun to recognize adolescence as a stage of life. Youth were the citizens and parents of tomorrow, and rising rates of suicide among that age group alarmed society. Some, like José Olvera and his students, were ahead of their times. What they promoted in the form of moral treatments of the insane were tantamount to modern therapies. During the revolutionary era, after the major battles had ceased, socializing a new citizenry became of paramount concern. Suicide continued apace, and La Castañeda, Mexico City's general asylum, operated under the scrutinizing eye of the sensationalist press. Modern life and its trials and tribulations continued to be seen as the catalyst for weakening wills and spirits, corrupting minds, and propelling people to take a fatal leap or consume deadly poison. While positivism was no longer in vogue, historical continuity prevailed as post-Porfirian specialists continued to view mental illness and suicide as social rather than individual problems. The state of an individual's mind and personal experiences that might lead to suicide were matters for the future.

# FIVE

# Death in the City

## SUICIDE AND PUBLIC SPACE

HEROIC, PUBLIC SUICIDE HAS A long history, beginning in ancient times. Cato, Lucretius, Socrates, and Brutus were just some of the famous deaths remembered as heroic suicides. Louis Pérez Jr. has also shown that Cubans had a cultural affinity for heroic and martyr suicide, an attraction that is especially evident in the historical memory of great Cubans who killed themselves for *la patria* (homeland).[1] Eddie Chibás is just one example. Chibás shot himself in 1951 during his live radio broadcast to protest fraudulent politics during the reign of Fulgencio Batista (1940–44, 1952–59). Mexico's heroic suicides include the six young cadets who defended Chapultepec Castle against the Yankee invaders in 1847. Rather than surrender to the occupying force, the national myth has it that cadet Juan Escutia leapt from the castle wrapped in a Mexican flag and died moments later, his body crushed on the pavement below. Every September 13, just days before the independence celebration, Mexicans commemorate these fallen boy heroes.[2]

Suicides planned with a sense of purpose and forethought when they selected prominent public buildings or cultural landmarks as the setting of their death. Public suicides garnered notice from bystanders and the press, and it seemed the suicides understood this. Reporters flocked to these scenes to gather details and communicate the most grisly details in the next day's paper. Passersby also stopped, gawked, and discussed the latest tragic deaths in the city. In particular, young women who committed public suicides made self-conscious decisions to script their deaths with careful planning and costuming. In the letters they left behind they asserted tropes of honorable death.[3]

The idea that those individuals who chose to commit suicide in public took careful measures to dramatize their deaths in certain spaces of the city contradicts the idea held by medical experts that suicides had lost reason and individual will. Theorists argued that suicides could not be held responsible for their deaths because they suffered from temporary insanity. Mexico City was undergoing rapid modernization and secularization at the turn of the twentieth century, and public spaces took on new meaning at the same time that intellectuals grappled with the perceived rise in suicide. This chapter focuses on the two most prominent suicide spaces of the era, Chapultepec Park and the cathedral, but also discusses other sites, such as cantinas and the streets. While suicides were quick and fleeting acts, they served as touch-stones for various actors to debate and discuss the trajectory of Mexican society at a point when Mexico was on the cusp of a new century and a social revolution.

### THE URBAN ENVIRONS AND
### THE MEANINGS OF SPACE

Mexico underwent intensive modernization efforts during the Porfiriato. A public building spree transformed the country's built environment into a hodgepodge of architectural styles. Architects designed new spaces, widened streets to form tree-lined boulevards, and erected monuments and statues to visually narrate Mexico's history. Some citizens benefited from development; others suffered and were forced to leave their ancestral villages to seek menial work in the capital. Mexico City teemed with rural migrants who plied goods and offered their services. Many residents felt that these workers represented the underbelly of modernization. Porfirian Mexico City certainly projected a facade of modernity. However, the evolution of the city was not simply a linear progression forward but also a suturing of past and present, which were in constant tension. This suturing could be seen or read as the hub of the modern city shifted away from the historic pre-Columbian and colonial center to newly developed parts of the city to the west and southwest.[4] The Zócalo, the central plaza of Mexico City, had been the heart and soul of Mexican civilization since the Mexica (Aztecs) ruled the valley, from 1428 to 1521. The Spanish built their city literally atop the ruins of the Mexica capital, Tenochtitlán, after their conquest of the Aztec Empire in 1521. For the next three hundred years, the Zócalo confirmed the prominence of the twin pillars of power in Mexican society: church and state. The government palace occupied the full east side of the plaza, and the cathedral rose up from the north side. The cathedral's tower, completed in 1791, provided the best panoramic view of the city and the nearby twin volcanoes, Popocatépetl and Iztaccíhuatl. By the late nineteenth century, the west side of the central plaza was occupied by a long commercial arcade that contained offices, merchant houses, and retail shops.[5]

During the first years of the reign of Porfirio Díaz, the Zócalo embodied the tense intermingling going on in the country of the traditional and the modern, the old and the new, the poor and the rich. Mexicans of all classes and ethnicities packed the central square on national holidays or knelt for mass in the imposing cathedral. Businessmen traversed the plaza, making deals in government offices and then returning to their places of commerce on the western side. Rich and poor citizens stood side by side in the Zócalo watching performances of puppeteers and street musicians.[6] Standing in the center of the Zócalo and scanning its perimeters, one is struck by the architectural symbols of hegemony, or what Henri Lefebvre calls abstract space.[7] Lefebvre argued that abstract spaces like the cathedral, the governmental palace, and the commercial buildings that flanked the plaza represent state power and possess the motive to exclude as well as to dominate. Each of these spaces held particular meanings that came to be commonly acknowledged. Worship was carried out in the cathedral, political activities took place in the government offices, and capitalist exchanges occurred in the commercial houses. A "tacit agreement . . . imposes reciprocity and a communality of use," and this provides an unwritten guide on how to behave in such spaces.[8]

Over time, the elite abandoned their palatial homes in the northern and eastern sections of the city to take up residence in the modern western side. They could leave their homes dressed in the latest Parisian fashions and ride in carriages or hired private cars through the fashionable shopping street of Plateros (now Madero), past the Alameda Park, and along the Paseo de la Reforma, a modern avenue modeled on Paris's Champs-Élysées, to socialize and be seen among the smart set. New middle-class neighborhoods lined Reforma, further shifting attention away from the historic center. The modern city rose up along Reforma, "and this area served the purpose of giving the upper middle classes a place in which to assert their cultural and economic identity apart from the people at large."[9] The stylish streets of Plateros and Corpus Christi sported electric streetlamps by 1880, while other streets in the center still relied on gas and hydrogen carbonate for illumination.[10] Electric trains brought those who could afford the fares from outlying villages to shop and work in the city. Simply put, these sites west of the historical central plaza "represented urbane, civilized, and modern Mexico: in a word, Europe."[11]

The refashioned districts to the west of the Zócalo contrasted sharply with those to the east, which had housed many elite families since early Spanish colonization. When these families moved out, landlords subdivided the mansions they left behind and created tenements, first for poor workers and later for the throng of rural migrants that had come to the city after being displaced from their lands in neighboring states. These spaces took on new meaning as they transformed from elite centers of life and power to crowded, disease-ridden abodes that sheltered the working poor. Social scientists viewed the tenements as their laboratories. In the 1890s, criminologist Julio Guerrero classified residents of Mexico City according to how close they lived to the street. Tenements housed, on average, five occupants in each one-room apartment, and the expansive courtyards of the former mansions served as communal patios where laundry, cooking, and bodily elimination occurred. The lack of privacy in the tenements led to sexual promiscuity and criminal impulses, according to Guerrero.[12] The only connection between the western and eastern halves of the capital was that poor residents living in the working-class barrios of Tepito and La Bolsa provided menial services in elite residences and businesses. They cleaned homes, swept shop floors, shined shoes, nursed babies, and hawked newspapers. A visitor to Mexico City who only toured the colonial buildings of the plaza and stayed and dined in the neighborhoods to the west along Reforma had a distorted view of the capital as eminently modern. Not many blocks away, dirt roadways, with nicknames such as Rat's Alley, Dog's Lane, and Pulque Place, crisscrossed the eastern barrios. In the reaches north of the Zócalo, small factories operated, adding to the malodorous and unhygienic environment of the barrios filled with the working poor. Mexico City suffered an epidemic of typhus in 1884 and an outbreak of cholera a year later.[13] After noting that more than half of all working-class homes in El Centro had cases of typhus in the 1890s and the first decade of the 1900s, the health department routinely sent physicians to these impoverished enclaves to forcibly vaccinate tenement dwellers.[14] Stray dogs were yet another nefarious feature of urban life. Vectors of rabies, murderous when traveling in packs, and spoilers of city sidewalks, "dogs ruled the streets."[15]

Suicides committed in dramatic, public fashion grabbed attention. Most suicides were carefully premeditated, but this was especially true when individuals chose a meaningful site for death and made meticulous preparations to carry out their plans. The city spaces in which a person lived, worked, and loved held special significance for them. They courted in certain places, experienced camaraderie and had drinks with friends in others, and worshipped and celebrated spiritual milestones in the various churches that marked the landscape. In other words, specific places and objects held special meaning, and a person who planned to kill him- or herself took these connotations into account when they chose the place to commit suicide.

## SUICIDE PARKS

Chapultepec Park, like the Zócalo, the Alameda, and other prominent public places, was imbued with social meaning. Some public spaces were open to people of all social classes, yet some sites clearly remained the realm of the privileged classes. In fact, urbanization and public works initiatives acted to reproduce social relations and divide cities between zones of inclusion and exclusion. The poor were not barred from Mexico City's green spaces, but it was clear that the chief function of parks was to provide services to the rich, who could afford leisure activities there. Historian Susie Porter found in her research on female market vendors and the public sphere that public works initiatives like building modern markets or bringing electricity to neighborhoods served the wishes of the elite first and workers second.[16] Creating hygienic and orderly markets improved the shopping experience of honorable housewives. Similarly, elite urban planners hoped that building separate parks for workers would separate them from their social betters.[17] In other words, workers should be invisible. Chapultepec Park certainly held symbolic and political importance to the Porfirian urban planners who carried out an impressive renovation of its historic castle and gardens in 1882. President Díaz made it his summer residence, just as presidents before him had done and presidents after him would do. A tramline connected parts of the city to the park in the 1880s, facilitating access for the elite and middle classes, who picnicked under the grand cypress trees.[18] After the revolution, the state attempted to open up Chapultepec to all Mexicans by holding festivals like Noche Mexicana in the park to attract the popular classes.[19] Young sweethearts kissed on park benches and in the privacy of its gardens.[20]

The young men and women who committed suicide in the green spaces of the city must have chosen these locations in part for the privacy they provided but surely also for the meanings the youths attached to them. How their deaths were interpreted depended upon their age, class, and gender.

Even though late nineteenth-century mores tolerated women in public spaces, gender ideology mediated their entrances into those spaces and how they behaved in them.[21] Breakups and heartaches propelled some to end their lives in the romantic parks of the city. One day during the winter of 1900, Margarita Vivanco had a fight with her boyfriend and felt despondent that he had not returned to make up. She sent him a note asking him to meet her in Chapultepec Park. She hoped to reconcile; she did not know his intentions. The two met in the Jardín de San Fernando, the appointed and sentimental spot, and Margarita's lover terminated their relationship for good. Margarita, according to newspaper reports, had vowed to take her life if she could not convince her boyfriend to take her back. At his refusal, she marched straight into a nearby botica, bought strychnine, a readily available rat poison, went home and ingested the toxic substance in her bedroom. A maid heard her cries of pain and called a doctor.[22] Margarita made the decision to go home to take the poison, but her plan had been sealed in the modern park.

Many couples initiated their romantic relationships in Chapultepec, and courting lovers could be seen flirting in small boats on the lake, picnicking, or stealing kisses on secluded paths. In 1905, five years after Margarita's death, twenty-year-old Federico Biesler, said to be from a good family and to not possess any vices, killed himself in Chapultepec Park. The night before, he attended a dance at the Cotillion Club, socialized with friends, and seemed to be in a pleasant mood, according to all who saw him. Federico stayed until the party ended in the early hours of the morning and then strolled the historic streets of the city. After sunrise, he took one of the first morning trolleys to the park. Witnesses saw him board a boat, cross the lake, and debark to sit on a bridge. Nothing seemed amiss, as many visitors to the park relaxed on benches and bridges, enjoying the verdant scenery or whispering sweet nothings in the ears of their beloveds. Sometime later, Federico's corpse was found resting on the very same bridge. A letter lay nearby, addressed to a Matilde: "In these brief sentences, a passion not reciprocated."[23] Federico appeared to be another young victim of unrequited love who had been vulnerable to the modern plague of suicide.

Ana María Schlonwbits tried but failed to kill herself in the Alameda, several blocks from Mexico City's central plaza in the western, fashionable side of El Centro in 1909. A worker found her slumped over on a park bench near the central kiosk. A twenty-five-year-old native of Germany, Ana had moved to Mexico with her boyfriend, who subsequently abandoned her and left her impoverished. Her ex-boyfriend testified that she had seen him with another woman, and even though they had already broken up by that point, she felt despondent enough to attempt suicide. Ana survived her overdose of morphine, a medicine she apparently ingested from time to time for her "nerves."[24]

At 3:30 am on May 25, 1897, French businessman Armand Mahuizier, who lived on the fashionable shopping street of San Francisco (also known as Plateros), shot himself in the Alameda. A policeman heard the shot and investigated, but he found nothing amiss and thought little more of it until a bicyclist discovered Armand's lifeless body on the ground at 5:00 am. Reporters usually commented on the interior clothing of women only, but *El Imparcial*'s article about the death noted Armand's "fine silk undergarments and silk hat," which attested to his prosperous status. The reporter also surmised that a thief had gotten to the man's corpse first, as the only things in his pockets were letters, cigarettes, and a cigar. His wallet, watch, and the gun he had used to carry out the deed were missing.[25]

The double suicide of two adolescent girls was the most sensational public suicide to occur in Chapultepec Park during the Porfiriato. On November 5, 1909, two best friends, eighteen-year-old María Fuentes and sixteen-year-old Guadalupe Ortiz, crossed the Zócalo, boarded a trolley, and headed for Chapultepec. Each girl was wearing her best dress, cloak, and hat and thus appeared destined for a party or an afternoon with suitors. Three young men, who would later provide testimonies to police, spotted the girls on the trolley and flirted with them on the way to their destination. The five disembarked at Chapultepec, and the three would-be paramours followed the girls at a safe distance until María and Guadalupe shooed them away and turned down a wooded path. The men took an alternate route but circled back to continue their flirtations with the pretty girls. On their return, they discovered a truly horrific sight. Tucked into the verdant greenery just off a footpath in Chapultepec's famous forest, María and Guadalupe tightly clutched each other in death's embrace. A small glass bottle and a bundle of letters and photographs rested several feet from their bodies. The alarmed boys contacted authorities, and the corpses were taken to the Hospital Juárez for autopsies. Reporters flocked to the scene to search for clues and craft a bird's eye reimagination of the double suicide for the next day's papers.[26] The tragic event also drew curious voyeurs to the scene, who likely wanted to visualize the deaths or mourn the calamity of youth suicide, which seemed all too common those days in the capital.[27] The subsequent investigation concluded that María and Guadalupe had died almost instantly after ingesting potassium cyanide, a poison that causes death within fifteen minutes. Physicians found suicide notes tucked neatly under their dresses. One note, addressed to the prefect of police, read: "The motive for taking our own lives is very simple: we do not wish to live this sad life, with its bitterness and torment, even though we are very young. And to not take a wrong turn and live a life to which we cannot aspire, it's death."[28] Only one reporter pondered, "Where did these young girls, who were not of the best education, learn that cyanide of potassium is the most deadly and the quickest acting poison known?"[29]

The fact that María and Guadalupe had wrapped their letters and photographs with ribbon and deposited them at the scene linked them to a long pattern of romantic suicides. Women in particular killed themselves for love, and society sometimes accepted this motive as unfortunate but honorable. Death scenes often were littered with romantic mementos such as love notes and portraits. The two best friends followed this script to a T. Reporting on the double suicide at Chapultepec Park, a writer for *El Imparcial* emphasized the romantic aspect of their deaths. The subheading of the article pointed out that the "the suicides hid to kill themselves on one of the most poetic paths."[30] The reporter also speculated that the girls loved the same man, Elias Rojas, who came to the hospital and identified their bodies just after midnight.[31] A rival paper, *El Diario,* reported on the "two romantics [María and Guadalupe] who sought the solitude of nature, the poetry of the forest, and drank a cup of poison. Tomorrow their white bodies will be in horrible contrast to the black coldness of the Hospital of Blood."[32] The English-language newspaper the *Mexican Herald* continued the theme, noting the careful premeditation of the double suicide and adding a new detail: each girl had worn a locket around her neck with a photo of a soldier in it. The assumption was that love and deception drove the girls to suicide.[33] Indeed, articles noted that women were more likely than men to kill themselves for love.[34] The tone of the reporting suggested that it was honorable, even saintly, to die for love, particularly passionate love. In other words, María and Guadalupe were no different from the romantic heroes of literature (i.e., Goethe's young Werther) who died for the noblest of passions—sublime love. The girls' mental state was never questioned in the early reporting. There was absolutely no speculation of brain lesions or dubious social environments. On the surface, the double suicide at Chapultepec Park conformed to societal values and expectations—two beautiful, prosperous girls, consumed by love and disappointment, sought an exalted and romantic end. Even the girls' morning grooming ritual and the letters penned to authorities followed the expected scheme. They endeavored to leave behind exquisite corpses.

Their construction as honorable and virtuous young women, however, failed within days. María and Guadalupe, who had been cast as two honorable and elegant young women in the flower of life, fell squarely off their pedestal once reporters started being nosy. What the press had initially judged as a tragic but honorable suicide devolved into a dishonorable pact committed by two girls who could not fulfill their lust for the good life. As more details came to light, *El Diario* reversed its course of extolling the girls' virtues and strove to correct the details perpetuated by rival dailies. One reporter interviewed family members and neighbors of María and Guadalupe and detailed the girls' personal histories, which involved single mothers, stepfathers, multiple moves between Puebla and the capital, and increasing deprivation. He noted that the tenement they lived in had only two patios, one surrounded by ten apartments and the other by thirty-one. The implication was that the girls lived in crowded and very public conditions and were therefore prone to immoral and criminal impulses—an allusion to Julio Guerrero's conjecture, mentioned above. The reporter stated that María had had several boyfriends and that the girls did not die for love but because they realized that they could not achieve their desires for wealth and luxury.[35] The underlying tone was that María's salary from her job in the ticket booth of a movie theater could not fund the lifestyle she wanted. Moreover, her presence in public selling film tickets diminished her potential for honor. There was speculation that modern films playing at her cinema had fueled her impossible fantasies. Afflicted with unfulfilled and unreasonable desires for wealth, the best friends chose death. Reporters took their crusade a step further, attending the funeral procession and making special note that the girls had to be buried in the same clothes in which they died, that the family departed for the cemetery in second-class transportation, and that gravediggers interred the girls' bodies in the fifth-class (the cheapest) section of the cemetery.[36] Even *El Imparcial*'s reporter, who gained access to their corpses in the morgue, described them no longer as "white" but as "naked" and with "dark flesh" (carnes morenas).[37] How quickly the narrative changed when reporters learned that María and Guadalupe, although they had looked privileged due to their clothing and modern hairstyles, were in reality working-class girls who lacked honor and had unreasonable desires.

An article in the *Boletín de Policía* impugned the girls' honor even further. María and Guadalupe were transformed from victims of envy into a vengeful older friend and a weak, younger acolyte. The writer referenced Italian intellectual Scipio Sighele, who argued that double suicides usually had an architect and a disciple.[38] The writer noted that María's boyfriend had allegedly spurned her for Guadalupe, and he theorized that María had sought revenge by convincing Guadalupe to agree to a suicide pact. Guadalupe succumbed because she was young, had a weak character, and lacked a father. The reporter argued: "This suicide, like many, is nothing more than revenge, for María deprived her unfaithful lover of Guadalupe, and racked him with misery."[39] The victim was no longer the suicide but the man robbed of his beloved.

The girls may have chosen Chapultepec Park because it provided them the privacy they needed to complete the deed, but it is fruitful to suggest that they made a calculated decision to choose a public and honorable space for their suicide pact.[40] The tree-lined lanes of the park were spaces that Mexico City's youth claimed for courting, socializing, and, in this case, dying. On the way to the park, María and Guadalupe opted to pay the fare for and board the archetypal representation of modern urban life and progress: the electric trolley.[41] Trolleys moved residents from place to place in the city, but they also caused gender disorder, as women traveling alone could attract untoward male attention or exploit the confines of the cars to flirt with strange men. María and Guadalupe boarded a trolley, eschewed the advances of flirtatious men, and traveled from the historic center to the modern city in the west to author their deaths. Although María worked in the ticket booth of a movie theater in the fashionable Juárez neighborhood, she lived with her cousin in Tepito, a working-class neighborhood north of the Zócalo and east of the Paseo. Instead of carrying out their suicide pact at home, in the public baths, or at some site in the historical city center, María and Guadalupe took a trolley excursion to the park and sought a quiet spot off a footpath in the forest. Trolley fares were not cheap. It cost five centavos in 1910 to travel around the city, and an unskilled laborer earned just fifty centavos per day.[42] The girls left notes and personal effects behind to define their motives and selves and the conclusions they hoped the public would draw from their suicides. They also asked that their bodies not be subjected to autopsies, in hopes of controlling the destiny of their cadavers. It was known that autopsies were part and parcel of suicide investigations, and the girls had likely hoped to prevent their bodies from being violated by scientific instruments.

In 1920, more than a decade after the deaths of the two girls, José Amieva planned his suicide in Chapultepec Park with exacting and confounding details. In fact, a journalist for *El Demócrata* questioned his numerous friends over and over again but could not determine a reason for why José shot himself on the Calzada de los Filósofos (Path of the Philosophers) in the famous park. He had not been spurned in love. He had plenty of money and friends. What could have been the cause? José was an orphaned son of Spanish parents and had held a good job working for the city. He had no vices except for dating a series of waitresses who worked in the capital's cabarets. One Sunday, he decided to organize a *gran paseo* (grand excursion) of automobiles with various friends. They spent the day first at the Café Colón and then at the Cafe Inglés, where José picked up one of the waitresses, Isabel González. He told her that he was planning a "long trip into the unknown." Other friends testified after his death that he had talked about suicide but said they had not taken him seriously because of his young age. On Monday morning, he called a tailor to the hotel room where he lodged and ordered a black suit. He arranged to have a car pick up Isabel later that afternoon for a rendezvous in the park. When she arrived, she was surprised to see a large group surrounding a cadaver, that of the young José. The reporter noted that José had not loved just one woman and so was unlikely to have been deceived by a specific love interest and also remarked that he had no debts and that he loved baseball, concluding that whatever drove the young man to death was truly an enigma.[43]

A year after the death of José, a young man chose to end his life on the Paseo de la Reforma in a hired car. Guillermo Barrios Oropeza hired a driver at the intersection of Las Flores and Santa María de la Ribera, located in one of the middle-class neighborhoods of the capital. The driver thought nothing of an elegantly dressed young man who wanted to pay him for the drive to Chapultepec Park. The client appeared to be middle class and seemed to have ample leisure time to frequent the park. Customer and driver arrived at Chapultepec and drove down some of the shady and sunny streets of the park. After riding for half an hour, Guillermo asked the driver to stop at the lake and wait. He got out and sat on one of the benches circling the lake, and the driver observed from a distance that he took out a letter, read it, ran his fingers through his hair, looked perturbed, and tossed the letter to the ground. The driver saw him pick up the letter and light it with a match. The young man then returned to the car, seemingly calm, and told the driver, "Let's go downtown." The chauffeur later told a journalist for *El Demócrata* that he had mused about "these young men of today, given over to romanticisms." Merging onto the Paseo, the driver started to head downtown, but when the car arrived at the intersection with Insurgentes, in the upscale Juárez neighborhood, a loud detonation upset the tranquil journey. The driver glanced back to see his customer with a ghastly wound in his right temple and a gun clutched in his fist. He then panicked, thinking that the police might think that he had robbed and killed his passenger, but a traffic cop had witnessed Guillermo raise the gun to his head and fire. The two men agreed that the chauffeur should drive the victim to the police station right away. After a search of Guillermo's pockets, police officers found his address and informed his shocked family. *El Demócrata*'s article about the death was accompanied by a graphic depiction of the young man, nattily dressed, shooting himself in the back of the hired car. The reporter also prefaced the story with a warning about the suicide epidemic that was infecting society's love-lorn youth.[44] The theme of youthful lovesickness had its antecedents in the nineteenth century, but the tone of reporting had changed from Porfirian times, and by the 1920s, reporters did not exalt suicide for love as they had then.

A few years earlier, in 1916, park-goers steering their boat around Chapultepec Park's lake saw what looked like a dead body near the Calzada de Violetas. On further investigation, they found the corpse of Guadalupe Ponce. She was dressed elegantly in a black suit, her feet were shod in patent leather shoes, and silk stockings showed from under her dress. A velvet hat embellished with feathers covered her head. *El Demócrata*'s article began with a familiar rant:

> Another victim of romanticism! A woman of nineteen years who put an end to her life in a picturesque place! A passage of another timeless and trite tale that would be tragic if it were not disgusting.... The morbid propensity for suicide of many victims already wakes in another case, as much as we want to know the details, it is always the same. A young woman swallows a strong dose of poison, her body falling into the dry leaves of the shady millennial forest. The story is vulgar, the crime repugnant, the sensation it wakes is momentary and only leaves a family mourning, a discordant note in the harmony of life, and the murmur of reprobation in the neighborhood.[45]

Like journalistic voyeurs had done ten years earlier, the paper detailed the personal effects found at the scene, which included a small purse bearing the initials "G. P." and a bottle of perfume labeled "Sweet Pea." Coincidently, a page of *El Demócrata* lay nearby, and wrapped inside it was a white powder, presumably the poison ingested by Guadalupe. Reporters undertook their own forensic investigation by taking traces of the powder in question to a local pharmacy, where a poison a pharmacist subsequently identified it as cyanide.[46] How reporters covered Guadalupe's suicide in comparison to the double suicide in 1909 was revealing. María Fuentes and Guadalupe Ortiz received adulating coverage when reporters thought they hailed from the prosperous class. The girls may have been young and smitten with the same man, but reporters narrated their demise in romantic and even forgiving tones. In 1916, a year when Mexico was still in the throes of revolution, with different factions controlling sections of the nation, reporters and presumably many members of society had less patience and understanding for what they saw as trite deaths.

A reporter for *El Universal* mocked a 1930 suicide attempt by Valeriano Gutiérrez Sáinz, a Spaniard who had escaped the Beneficiencia Española (Spanish Sanitorium) in Mexico City after being diagnosed with partial paralysis. Comparing the events to a comic film, the article narrated Valeriano's haphazard attempt to end his life on the shores of Chapultepec Lake. Despondent, the distressed Spaniard had taken out a Gillette razor, nicked his neck with it, and then jumped into lake. The reporter commented that the cold water must have made him forget his "desires to kill himself" because he quickly struggled up onto the grass and asked a passing woman for help. The article also ridiculed the man for thinking that jumping into the shallow end of the lake would make him drown. The Spaniard suffered nothing more than an "insignificant" wound on his neck, and he returned to the care of doctors at the sanatorium.[47] Humorously, the title of the front-page article read, "A Cut and a Bath in Chapultepec Pond."

OTHER PUBLIC SPACES: THE STREET,
CEMETERIES, AND CANTINAS

A good part of daily life took place in the street. Many men and women walked or rode to their places of employment, shopped in the stores and markets of the city, and, importantly, found places to court and socialize in restaurants, cafes, and parks. Others literally worked in the streets, plying goods as itinerant peddlers, hawking newspapers, or setting up kiosks to sell products to capital residents. Trolleys, cars, and horse-drawn carriages also traversed urban streets and provided the methods and places for public suicides. In 1898, train operator Alfredo Díaz leapt off a train headed for Tizapán when it reached its highest speed. Passengers said that they had noticed him as they crossed at Piedad but that he had then vanished. Officers found him unconscious on the tracks, and he later died at the hospital. All surmised from the circumstances that is was suicide.[48] Concepción González also chose a train as her place and method of suicide, but more was known about her motives, as she did not succeed in killing herself and so the police were able to collect her deposition. Twenty years old and hailing from the middle class, Concepción lived with her husband, Sergeant Enrique Vásquez. She grew suspicious of infidelity, as he had been recently promoted and was presumably more able to spend money on a mistress. She went to the barracks where he worked and demanded that he come out and speak with her. He refused, and she became despondent enough to lie down on the rail lines in the path of a trolley traveling to Atzcapotzalco, hoping to be crushed and relieved of her suffering. Just in time, a police officer and the conductor of the trolley were able to stop the train and save her.[49]

In 1902, Eleanor Bailey, a young American woman who was living in Mexico City with a Mrs. Detwiler on the fashionable Paseo de la Reforma, hoped to join her beloved Luis Garcia Rivero in death. Luis, a Spaniard from Asturias who had lived in Mexico for four or five years, had committed suicide in August that year at the age of twenty-three. A chemist by trade, Luis had lived and worked with his brothers at their liquor manufacturing plant. His brothers were shocked that he had picked up a gun one late afternoon and shot himself. The judicial inquest noted that one of his brothers had found him comatose on his bed at the factory. He told investigators that he suspected that Luis killed himself because of a letter he had received from a woman. Police officers found two letters from Eleanor Bailey on his desk. One read: "Luis of my soul. Just arrived. I have to tell you without fail tonight, when you like. Please answer with the carrier. Your Leonora." [50] The next day, a short notice of his suicide appeared on page four of *El Imparcial*.[51] Police also recovered a .38-caliber Smith and Wesson at the scene. They began taking depositions from those close to him. His colleagues had not noticed anything amiss in his temperament. He had declined to go out to eat with them that day, but he seemed normal. He paid the daily wages to the help and retired to his bedroom. A shot rang out moments later. One friend testified that he was in love with a young woman and kept her portrait tucked in his clothes.[52]

Eleanor pined for her beloved Luis and, according to her guardian, Mrs. Detwiler, had become more and more inconsolable each day since his suicide. One morning, Eleanor announced that she wanted to visit Luis's grave in the Spanish cemetery. Mrs. Detwiler offered to join her, but Eleanor stated that she needed solitude to grieve her lover's death. At the cemetery,

Eleanor pulled out her guardian's gun and attempted to end her own life on her lover's grave. She failed to kill herself and was taken to the hospital. Although *El Imparcial*'s article on the attempt did not mention the analogy, young Werther's beloved, Charlotte, pines for him on his grave after his suicide. Eleanor agreed to an interview with the paper, and she informed the reporter that Luis had been "tall, strong, and handsome. I love him more than my life, and he, me." She claimed that Luis killed himself because one of his brothers had opposed their match due to her inferior social position. The brother, when interviewed by the press, denied this accusation and stated that he had not even known of their relationship. Mrs. Detwiler testified that her gun was missing and presumed that her young charge had taken it. Eleanor surprised the reporter with her frankness, and he wrote that she was unrepentant of her actions and that, since she could not have Luis, she did not want to live. This sentiment also surfaced in a letter she left for a friend named Alicia: "My dearest friend, Oh Alicia! Pardon me if I die and appear ungrateful, but I have a desperate heart and it would be cruel that you or anyone else try to stop me from finding peace and quiet in the cemetery."[53] Ending one's life in a cemetery was common in Cuba as well.[54] And perhaps nothing seems more romantic than ending your life on the gravesite of your departed lover.

Imbibing a few drinks often preceded the decision to commit suicide. Some men even decided to kill themselves in the taverns and cafés where they socialized with friends and coworkers. Other suicides occurred in the streets outside cantinas or popular hangouts. Musician Gastón Moreno shot himself in the Cantina Veracruzano while drinking with fellow musicians in 1929. The proprietor of the cantina testified that, on the night of the event, he had been about to close the establishment but let Gastón and his buddies in for a few drinks. Drinking partners Gustavo Vargas and Salvador Parga testified that, after a few cups, Gastón pulled out a pistol, proclaimed, "This is for me!" and shot himself.[55] He neither left a note nor uttered a reason for his drastic action. Some years earlier, in 1921, chauffeur Efrén Muñoz, twenty-six years old, procured a couple of grams of mercury cyanide and, because he felt "bored with life," went drinking with some friends. After his friends bid their goodbyes, he swallowed the poisonous power with tequila. Thirty minutes later, he felt intense pain and went home and told his girlfriend what he had done. She called a doctor, and he survived his suicide attempt.[56]

In 1911, eighteen-year-old José Díaz stumbled into the *tendajón* (small grocery store) El Porvenir (the future) and fell to the floor trembling. The owner notified a street cop, and José admitted that he had swallowed strychnine. In his testimony, José stated that he was a single pharmacist by training and that he had worked for the cantina La Pura Caña until about a month ago, when he had fallen ill. A few days earlier, he had gone to the cantina to have a drink. The owner, José Rios, had asked him how he intended to pay, calling him a "shameless *ratero*." [57] José Díaz could not support such dishonorable, public insults and opted to kill himself with rat poison. He had procured the poison sometime earlier from his former place of employment, a botica in Mixcoac, south of the city center. The offended young man also penned a letter to Francisco Vega, who was both the owner of El Porvenir and José Díaz's landlord, that read: "Sr. Francisco Vega Licea, I find myself offended by Don José R. Rios, you know how he has treated me, I thought to end my life because I do not have sufficient means to get revenge and proceed against Rios. My honor is finished and so is my life. Goodbye forever, goodbye." [58]

The lovesick, young Salvador Magallón poisoned himself under the balcony of his sweetheart in 1897. Twenty years old and hailing from the middle class, Salvador had courted his girlfriend for almost a year. Every night, he had gone to her house and conversed with her, she standing on her balcony and he in the street, for two or three hours. He had begun talking about marriage, but they had also started fighting. On the fateful night, he stood under her balcony and she came out, asking why he had not visited her the night before. Salvador seemed sad and pensive, and he asked the young woman for a glass of water. She handed it to him, and he took out a blue box from his pocket, poured its contents into his mouth, and swallowed a large gulp of water. A few moments passed, he turned red and grabbed his stomach. He called out for another glass of water, and when his sweetheart returned with it, he convulsed violently and hit the street with a thud. He died soon afterward of arsenic poisoning. [59]

Jumping off the top of buildings or throwing oneself in the path of trolleys or cars were two common methods of committing dramatic, public suicide. Those persons intent on killing themselves by jumping from heights chose sites of three and four stories or more to ensure a likely death. Some suicides chose to leap from buildings that held special individual or societal significance. Others simply jumped out of windows or off roofs of their own homes and workplaces, like Mónica Santillán, who worked as a domestic in a house on the historic Calle de Tacuba in the city center. A reporter and a photographer for *El Independiente* happened to be passing by when they noticed something fall off a roof. As they moved closer, they discovered the body of someone who appeared to be dressed as a servant. The young Mónica had killed herself because her boyfriend had deceived her. A letter from the boyfriend was found on her body. It read, "Mónica, don't blame me, but it is destiny. I cannot continue loving you, because I am promised to Desideria, so don't bother yourself with me any longer." Mónica died instantly, and her body was unceremoniously transferred to the Hospital Juárez for an autopsy.[60] María Guadalupe Servín also tried to leap to her death because she had lost in love, but she survived the ordeal. A reporter for *El Universal* was walking down Calle Soto and Avenida Hombres Ilustres when Guadalupe jumped from a third-floor balcony. She had been courted and deceived by a young man named Escalante. She had attended dances with him, and he had promised to take her to the altar when his financial situation improved. The implication was that he had had sex with her but then reneged on his promise to marry her and therefore repair her honor. She lived with her mother and a young sister of six or seven years. She survived the fall and later told the judge that, even though everyone suspected that he had violated her, he had not. The judge accepted her testimony, and the court did not bring in the suitor for his testimony.[61]

· The *El Demócrata* reporter who wrote about the suicide of Matilde Chazaro in 1924 flexed his literary chops in the article. A drawing accompanied the article showing a young, modern woman falling head first off the top of her mansion. The long title of the article began: "A Morbid Effluvia Populates the City, and the Evil of Suicide Sickens Young People's Spirits." Referencing Lady MacBeth and Nietzsche, the reporter warned, "All kinds of suicides registered in the police annals have captured the daily press headlines with painful regularity. It seems this bad act is highly contagious. Who knows what macabre shadow moves though the city, for not a day goes by when some sick spirit does not make an attempt against their life." What especially upset this writer was that Matilde counted herself among the metropolitan aristocracy; she was a woman of "exquisite upbringing." Her maids said that she had normally been full of joy, but shortly before her death they had noticed a change in her personality. She started to shut herself in her quarters and played "intoxicating ballads" on the piano for hours on end. Her parents tried to seek various therapies for her, but Matilde insisted it was just the heat that was bothering her. On the fateful day, she awakened early, donned black clothing and a veil, and attended mass. When she returned home, she played her "maddening ballads" again. Moments later, at 11:30 am, she opened a window and jumped over the balcony. She died three hours later at the hospital.[62]

Luis Ortega, a twenty-eight-year-old civil servant, was walking across the street at Nuevo México and López around 5:00 pm one day in 1923 when he stopped suddenly after hearing the blast of a gun close by. He moved toward the sound and saw Manuel Castellanos lying injured on the sidewalk. When interrogated, Manuel, a twenty-four-year-old Spaniard, told authorities that he was tired of living and that no one had compelled him to try and take his life. He had planned his suicide with some forethought and penned three notes. One reiterated what he had confessed to police, "I killed myself because I am tired of life." A second note read, "Goodbye, dear brother, goodbye." A third, addressed to authorities, stated, "I advise you that I have a brother in the Carolina Fabric Factory, his name is Santiago Castellanos." Officials transferred the Spanish victim to the Sanitorio de Beneficiencia Española (Sanatorium of Spanish Welfare). Perhaps in hopes of saving face, Manuel later recanted and claimed that he accidently shot himself while cleaning his gun.[63] It is unclear why he would have chosen the street to clean his gun. The fact that he shot himself in the street, whether intentionally or by accident, ensured that he would be discovered by passersby.

Two friends and fellow police officers, Alfonso Domínguez and Alberto Brusco, met each other by chance at the intersection of Calle República de Ecuador and Avenida Santa María La Redonda one day in the summer of 1928. They chatted for some minutes, and then Alfonso turned to leave his friend to go pick up his paycheck. Immediately, Alberto pulled out a 9 mm Browning pistol and shot himself in the chest in the middle of sidewalk. Alfonso ran to him and tried to grab the gun as Alberto lifted it to take another shot. The injured man fell to the street and was carried off for medical attention soon afterwards. Thirty-eight-year-old Alberto hailed from Chiapas and worked as a carpenter and police officer. He stated that he had not tried to kill himself but had accidently shot himself while trying to teach Alfonso a trick with the gun. Alfonso testified to the contrary, stating that Alberto had tried to kill himself and that he had done so over a woman. Apparently, Alberto had taken a young woman named Alicia from her home, moved around the country with her, and finally settled with her in the capital. They fought, and Alicia moved out and took employment in different cabarets around the city. She had asked for a reconciliation because of her dire economic situation, according to Alfonso, but Alberto refused to take her back. She claimed that someone was going to kill her and that he would suffer because he did nothing to protect her. Alfonso claimed that this row had provoked his friend's suicide attempt. Alberto offered nothing more but later asked for police to return his property, which included a watch, five pesos, and a hairpiece (*peluca*).[64]

## THE TOWER OF SUICIDES

In fin-de-siècle Mexico, the tower of the Metropolitan Cathedral became known as the Tower of the Suicides. José Guadalupe Posada illustrated an early twentieth-century broadside that showed a tiny body falling from the top of the majestic church. Some bent on suicide chose religious spaces to commit the deed. Women chose to leap to their death from the church more often than men.[65] In 1899, a journalist for the largest circulating newspaper in Mexico City, *El Imparcial,* recounted the suicide of Sofía Ahumada, a young woman who jumped to her death from the tower of the cathedral. He mocked the twenty to thirty "unemployed" people who loitered around the "stain of blood" left at the site of her tragic plunge.[66] He referred to the spot where she landed: the location of an Aztec sacrificial sunstone altar that was excavated in 1790 during repairs on the church.[67] Whether the reporter was equating suicide to sacrifice or barbarity, his narrative lamented the rise of suicide in the city and warned against the potential for imitation.

One of the most talked about suicides at the tower occurred at the cusp of the 1900s, when capital residents were feeling trepidation for the coming century. When Sofía decided to jump off the cathedral in 1899, she joined an assembly of victims who had succumbed to the infectious mania of self-murder. *El Imparcial's* article about her death was prefaced with the warning: "Suicide spreads, and the number of victims of this imitative mania is already alarming. They employ all forms of destruction known, the knife, the pistol, the rope, the poison; she chose the wrong way to throw herself off when a full trolley passed. This last suicide has produced a terror in society. The method employed is certainly not new."[68]

The article continued with a familiar narrative. Sofía, of middle-class background, had moved to the capital with her three sisters when their parents died. The reporter noted, "She was at the height of her youth, brimming with life; she was, if not beautiful, graceful." The four sisters supported themselves with respectable work. One by one, Sofía's sisters moved out of their shared home for employment outside of the city. Only one sister remained in the capital, but she lived separately with her husband. Sofía eventually moved in with her married sister on Calle Concepción. She met a young man, Bonifacio Martínez, who soon passed by her balcony to initiate a courtship. Bonifacio had learned the watchmaking and clock trade from his father. According to the reporter for *El Imparcial,* he had been in love with Sofía until she unleashed her hysteria and exhibited violent fits of neurotic behavior. The older sister, Tomasa, recounted that Sofía had always been lively and possessed of easy conversational skills but also excessively nervous, known to clench her fists tightly when upset. Two months before Sofía leaped to her death, Tomasa noticed a drastic change in her younger sister. She slept fitfully, rose earlier than usual, ate her meals begrudgingly, and spent long hours lost in her thoughts. Apparently, Bonifacio had broken off their relationship. Sofía told him, "I cannot live without seeing you," and he agreed to meet. They went to the cathedral, where he was working on the clock. They bickered, and as he tinkered with the clock mechanism, she jumped over the balustrade and fell to her death on the pavement below. The reporter noted that the "neurotic" landed with her head to the south, the direction of the plaque that marks the place where the Aztec sunstone was found.[69] Bonifacio peered down in horror and then ran down the steps to the street below, only to run back up the tower because he feared that people would think he had pushed her. Authorities found a letter in her skirt that read, "I was born to suffer! For some time I have thought of suicide as the only remedy for my pain . . . . I do not want the man I have loved to be thought the cause. No. I killed myself because I felt like it. No one is responsible for my death."[70] Her letter went on to inform authorities that no one would claim her body and she would be buried in a pauper's grave.

Police detained potential perpetrators or accomplices in most investigations, and they followed protocol in this case, taking Bonifacio into custody. Since Bonifacio had been atop the tower with Sofía, it was possible he had pushed her or egged her into killing herself. The fact that her shawl was found in the tower and not on her body raised suspicions. Generally, a shawl signified modesty and honorable women did not go into the street without it.[71] The idea that Sofía would have discarded her shawl before jumping seemed unthinkable. Authorities also found an inscribed portrait of Sofía in their search of Bonifacio's home and confiscated it to see if the handwriting matched the letter found in her skirt, as they felt the note looked suspiciously like it had been written in a masculine hand.[72] The next day, the young victim's body continued to rest on the slab at the morgue, just as she had predicted; her family did not claim her body or arrange the burial. Three girlfriends identified her body and told a reporter that they knew she would choose the most extravagant way to kill herself. Coworkers stated that she had procured dynamite in weeks past but said they had managed to get it away from her and discard it in the toilet where they worked.[73]

A common tactic of articles editorializing youth and suicide was to look to the influence of novels. An unsigned editorial published in 1899 in *El Imparcial* agreed with the Italian doctor Luigi Midena, who claimed that novels were the cause of many moral calamities. In fact, it was thought that reading such novels caused liver congestion, which would in turn lead to moral dissipation. The editorial took the Sofía Ahumada case and spun a familiar narrative borrowed from Victor Hugo:

> He was a watchmaker. He knew her from the street. He followed her. Came to love her. There was jealousy .... They arranged to meet at the Cathedral .... This boy was not Quasimodo, but his girlfriend had one of those bizarre temperaments, decadent, novelistic; she took bromide and jumped to her death. While he managed the clock weights, she fixed her eyes on the horizon. While he fine-tuned the needles, she pondered sad things. While he worked his tool, she felt a pessimism that seemed so foreign and deep as to be rare in our country, this bitterness of character .... She decided to kill herself .... [She] made preparations .... [Wearing] new clothes, colorful stockings, letter in her showy interior clothing, she jumped from the tower to eternity.[74]

The reporter continued in this tone of mockery, noting the ten, twenty, or thirty unemployed who contemplated the "tombstone commemorating the calendar of idolatry . . . and the stain of blood" of Sofía's broken body.[75] This reporter had less sympathy for Sofía than the reporter who covered the double suicide of María Fuentes and Guadalupe Ortiz in Chapultepec Park ten years later had had for his subjects. What Sofía Ahumada lacked that the two other girls appeared to have, at least initially, was honor. That she would torture her stolid artisan beau with her hysterics and trifles placed her in the category of young girls corrupted by decadent literature, making her a victim of suicide who lacked virtue. Religious newspapers in particular highlighted the negative influence of popular novels and dramatic plays on a person's will to live. An 1895 editorial signed "The Messenger of the Priesthood" warned readers of the ill effects of novels that only served to "delight the flesh." She continued, "Think about what impact this reading will have on a maiden, a half-open bud, who inhales the poisoned perfume of the passions that drags us back to the corrupt nature of original sin."[76] The message was not yet that madness caused suicide but that popular culture debased those with young impressionable minds who might be "bored with life" or who might be slaves to the latest fashions. A reporter for *El Chisme* expressed shock that Sofía would jump off the tower in full view of passengers enjoying a trolley ride and related that she had worn stockings to the knees so that, when her skirts flew up during the fall, onlookers would not see her nudity.[77]

In 1912, just over a decade after Sofía jumped to her death, a drawing of three figures—two large and one small—falling from the Tower of Suicides appeared on the front page of *El Imparcial*. The victims were two young women and a toddler of almost two years old. The article accompanying the picture introduced one of the victims as Juana López, "of fine presence and a manner of dress that denotes her as a woman of middle-class circumstance from the interior." The reporter was equally impressed with her clothes and, like most reporters covering female suicide, noted her silk blouse and undergarments. Yet, while the *El Chisme* reporter wrote mockingly that Sofía had purchased new undergarments to costume her suicide drama, implying that she could not afford the fine silk, *El Imparcial* stressed the luxurious and expensive silk garments as evidence of Juana's prosperity and good education. Her partner in death, a younger woman named Margarita Pereda, was dressed equally respectably in clothing of silk. The trio had arrived at the cathedral for noon mass, and witnesses had seen them kneeling in prayer at the altar. Witnesses recounted that they asked the doorman for access to the tower to take in the view. According to the reporter, the women removed letters from their pockets, and then Juana threw her son off the tower and jumped immediately afterward. Margarita soon followed. Juana's letter obeyed the formula, stating that no one was responsible for her death. She simply asked to be buried with her son. Margarita diverged from the pattern in her letter, blaming her father for her suffering and her death. In a display of literary license, the reporter speculated erroneously that Juan López, a man who had jumped off the tower six months earlier, was Juana's son and Margarita's beloved. The rift between Margarita and her father, the reporter surmised, was that he had prohibited her marriage to Juan.[78] The mere possibility that star-crossed lovers were involved urged the reporter to paint the suicide in romantic terms, and he scarcely mentioned the murder of the toddler. It was as if a cultural logic existed that made female suicide understandable, and perhaps even condonable, if committed for love. The condition was that a lovelorn woman had to be honorable.

The case of the double suicide and murder took on new twists as it was investigated further. Margarita had not been in love with Juan López.

Instead, reporters revealed that an evil suicide pact had been formed between the more domineering Juana and the impressionable Margarita. A lover had abandoned Juana, and a father had abandoned Margarita. A shared sense of desertion fueled their mutual desire to end their suffering once and for all, and the older friend convinced the younger to succumb to her wicked scheme. The sordid story began with Margarita's mother, Joaquina, and her father, who was not named in the reporting. A love grew between them, and Margarita was born, but the father rose in social status, met a young lady with means, and forsook Joaquina. Nonetheless, he registered as the infant Margarita's father in the civil registry and committed twenty pesos monthly to her education. Joaquina befriended a Frenchman by the name of Bulmé and his wife, who offered to adopt Margarita and raise her as their own. Margarita's benefactor enrolled her in the prestigious high school El Buen Tono, and she excelled academically, learning French in three months. However, her French adoptive father became seriously ill, and he and his wife moved back to France, leaving Margarita in the care of a good friend. At the same time, her biological father stopped paying for her schooling. Margarita encountered him in the street one day, and he ran from her, telling her that she was not his daughter and that he did not know her. Since that day, according to her temporary guardian, Mrs. Prince, Margarita had been despondent and inconsolable. Mrs. Prince recounted that her restaurateur husband had brought home Juana López when he found out she had been abandoned by the father of her child. The problem for Margarita was that her new house-mate talked incessantly of suicide and had already attempted to kill herself a couple times. Once, she had jumped in the path of a trolley; another time, she drank alcohol with matches dissolved in it, but friends intervened and saved her. The Princes alleged that the abandoned single mother had a strong influence on Margarita. Much to the young girl's glee, her adoptive father returned from France and took her shopping for a new dress in an attempt to cheer her up. They shopped happily, but in retrospect he pondered the fateful meaning of her odd question as she glanced up at the cathedral tower: "If you jumped from the first floor, would it kill you?"

On the unfortunate day of the deaths, Mrs. Prince left Margarita and Juana in charge of her young children while she ran errands. She returned hours later to find her children at the neighbors and Margarita, Juana, and Juana's toddler son gone. A note addressed to Bulmé read, "Cher papa Bulmé, I kill myself because I suffer so much. I don't want to suffer anymore. Your daughter, who loves you very much. Margarita Bulmé. All my portraits are for you. Goodbye." The older child of Mrs. Prince told reporters that the young women drank some cups of absinthe before they departed. Reporters concluded that the thirty-two-year-old Juana convinced Margarita to join her in a suicide pact.[79] This was the same dynamic that was used to explain the double suicide at Chapultepec Park. It seemed unfathomable that a young woman would kill herself if she had not been brainwashed by an older accomplice. In this case, the young adopted girl of a French businessman maintained her virtue in death, while the older architect of the suicide, the working-class single mother, won no esteem for her actions.

Angelina Ruiz made sensational news by leaping to her death from the same tower less than a decade later, though her suffering was caused not by loss of love of a father but by shame caused by an unknown lover. *El Demócrata* reported on July 23, 1920, that the young woman, who was of refined education and worked as a ticket seller at the *Salón Rojo*, had jumped from the tower to her death the day before. The subtitle asked whether it was love, desperation, or insanity that drove her to do it. The article recounted her biography, noting that she had lived with her widowed mother and younger siblings.[80] She had worked at the cinema to help the family make ends meet. Her workday began at 3:00 pm. She sold tickets and "gave away smiles" until 10:00 pm, when her mother would meet her each night to escort her home. The reporter wrote that on the walk home, the two would peer in the windows of the cafés and gaze at the elite customers in their fine clothes. He implied that Angelina's mother had saved her from dishonor by accompanying her in the street, even though they both gazed enviably at the rich patrons. He wrote that Angelina had lived the life of most modern youth, one of relative monotony, noting that she had been affected by a "morbid misanthropy" from her experiences working in the ticket booth. One day, she visited the cathedral and asked to take the stairs to the tower. The guard forbade her from ascending because rules dictated that a woman needed a male escort to enjoy the city views from the turret. Undeterred, Angelina boarded a trolley the following day, ran into an acquaintance from work, and asked him to escort her up the tower. He accepted, and they both debarked the trolley at the majestic church. They paid the guard fifty centavos and ascended the stairs. Angelina asked her friend to inscribe their names and the date on the wall: "Angelina Ruiz and Onésimo García . . . 7–22–[1]920." He complied, took out a pencil, and began writing. Moments later, he realized that the young woman he knew just slightly from work had jumped off the tower. The newspaper gave a detailed description of the injuries she sustained from falling so heavily on the stone pavement below, noting her torn clothes, broken leg, and crushed face.[81]

The next day, the focus on Angelina's young, broken body continued, but it was accompanied by a warning to other girls who might be tempted to follow her example. Clearly, the empathy for youths who killed themselves for love had begun to wane by the 1920s. Mexico had just emerged from a decade of revolution. With more than one million dead, lovelorn suicides were no doubt considered frivolous. A reporter for *El Demócrata* wrote, "Read, silly señorita, you think to kill yourself because your boyfriend, an insubstantial youngster, has quarreled with you . . . . On the cold marble slab, . . . completely naked, Angelina's body was already in a state of decomposition."[82] He went on to detail how surgeons approached Angelina's body with the detachment of science, tearing open her flesh and examining her entrails not to look for something spiritual but to seek evidence of lesions that might explain her actions. Another report on a female suicide in 1920 also took a cold view, ridiculing young women who forget that their naked corpses will rest on the cold slabs of the morgue and serve as "fodder for science and men, who justly laugh at them, those who commit that sad madness."[83]

As was the case with most suicide inquests, the judge determined that no crime had been committed and released Onésimo from custody. However, four months later, Angelina's mother appealed the decision after finding various forms of evidence in her daughter's personal effects, in particular a letter that blamed a said Jacobo for her disgrace. Coincidently or not, the owner of the theater where Angelina had worked was named Jacobo Granat. He was a prominent businessmen and proprietor of some of the most modern and toniest hotspots in the city, including the Cine Olimpia and the Salón Rojo.[84] The mother wanted the case reopened because someone stole the watch, rings, and money that Angelina had on her person the day of her suicide.[85] She also alleged that Angelina might have been deflowered by the Jacobo mentioned in the letter and chosen death to end her shameful suffering. Clearly, the mother wanted to understand the reasons behind her daughter's act, and killing oneself to cover up shame was a more or less accepted motive for suicide. Jacobo Granat's lawyer responded to the appeal by noting that his client had had no more relationship to Angelina than that of employer to employee and that there were many men named Jacobo. As for the charge of *estupro* (deflowering), the lawyer contended that the medical experts had not documented a recent loss of virginity during the autopsy and reminded the judge that estupro applied only to girls fourteen years of age and younger.

Angelina Ruiz had been in her early twenties when she jumped off the tower. The mother insisted that she had found a letter from her daughter under a hatbox that said Angelina had had sex with Jacobo and that he had abandoned her. She also revealed to the judge what she considered to be damning evidence of Granat's guilt. According to her, Granat had come to her house after the suicide and offered to pay the funeral and burial expenses. In her mind, these seemingly charitable actions originated in his guilty conscience. The grieving mother failed to have Granat prosecuted, and she did not recover her daughter's personal effects. However, she succeeded in getting the sordid story published in the newspaper, which certainly tarnished Granat's honor and reputation. Although it is impossible to assess, the mother's appeal may have restored some of her daughter's honor in certain readers' minds, at least those who believed that death was preferable to public shame.

Honor was a slippery slope that both journalists and suicide victims attempted to navigate. What was most important was honor's public component—that is, how one was viewed by others. Newspapers purported to offer the most accurate versions of events and victim biographies; yet in reality, they fictionalized crime stories to make them more interesting to readers. The large dailies had investigative reporters who interviewed the family, friends, witnesses, and coworkers of suicides. The victims hoped that their deaths by suicide would be considered rational and honorable. Of course, as the case of María Fuentes and Guadalupe Ortiz shows, reporters had the upper hand when it came to how suicides would be remembered. Although the two young girls attempted to portray themselves as honorable, the newspapers ended up dragging their reputations through the mud, and some went as far as to suggest that the girls had made a diabolical suicide pact. Although reporters by and large no longer signed their names to stories at the turn of the century, the history of rivalries and duels between newspapermen were legendary.[86] Reporters routinely called out rival papers for the errors they printed when covering the same stories. In *El Chisme*'s report on Sofía Ahumada's suicide, the reporter told his readers that the paper was the only one that could correct the erroneous information disseminated about the case by the rest of the dailies in the capital, noting that it had a team of investigative reporters who hunted down the facts.[87] The reporter for the Catholic newspaper *El País* ignored Sofía's relationship with Bonifacio Martínez. He used the spectacle of her suicide to blame the government-sponsored, positivist-liberal newspapers like *El Imparcial* for the increased immorality in society, claiming that such newspapers did not teach capitalinos to read or cultivate themselves but instead induced them to kill themselves by publishing lewd and salacious coverage of crime and immoral acts.[88]

Journalists reported the details of suicides, but enlaced in the litany of biographical details were lessons on honor, proper education, the roots of insanity, and gender ideology. Journalists initially placed María Fuentes and Guadalupe Ortiz on pedestals, extolling their comely and arrogant visages and encouraging readers to sympathize with their suicides, but once they discovered that the girls had lived in a tenement in the working-class barrio Tepito, they condemned their acts. The press disparaged Sofía Ahumada from the outset, although they also employed romantic language to describe the tragedy. Her neurosis stood front and center in the reporting of her death. What seemed most troubling to her chroniclers was the fact that her suicide was *too* public in its pornographic spectacle at the Zócalo. Unlike the best friends María and Guadalupe, who drank poison down a private path, Sofía jumped off the cathedral tower as a trolley arrived, and her fall disheveled her clothes and exposed her body to onlookers. Her friends told reporters that she had desired an extravagant exit, but the press did not play along and romanticize her life and demise. Sofía may have lacked honor in the eyes of the judgmental newspapers, but mourners felt differently, leaving behind flowers as they contemplated the stain of blood and perhaps the fate of youth in modern times.

## CONCLUSION

Few residents of Mexico City committed suicide in the public spaces of the city. Private spaces like the home or a rented hotel room were preferred settings. The most sensational suicides (those covered extensively by newspapers) occurred in the monumental or abstract spaces of the city, including the cathedral, the Alameda, and Chapultepec Park. These spaces were monuments to progress and piety and also represented the dominant spaces of power. When reporters referred to Chapultepec Park as a popular destination for both lovers and suicidal youth, the park transformed from a homogenous abstract space to a counter-space with multiple meanings created by the suicidal bodies that darkened traditional leisure destinations. Ultimately, the young men and women who made self-conscious decisions to realize their suicides in public spaces chose places that were imbued with historical and cultural meaning. In the case of the double suicide at Chapultepec Park, María Fuentes and Guadalupe Ortiz departed their working-class tenement, groomed and dressed at the public baths, and proceeded to the historic center of the city, where they caught a trolley from the central plaza. The girls traveled from the historic center, down the Paseo, and into the modern city to author their deaths. They left notes and personal effects behind to define their motives and selves in hopes of shaping the discourse that would surround their suicides. They drank poison under the cover of the forest and died in a final embrace. A cultural logic pardoned suicides committed by honorable women motivated by love or deception. The manner of their deaths linked them to a long line of romantic deaths. However, María and Guadalupe hailed from the working-class barrio of Tepito. They desired more in life than their social status provided them. The fact that they desired a social mobility that they could not achieve made society condemn their deaths as capricious and unintelligible.

When Sofía Ahumada and the other women leapt off the tower of the cathedral, their bodies hurtling through the air and landing on the paving stones below, they shattered the ideal meaning of the cathedral, especially as newspapers and broadsides began representing the monolithic structure as the Tower of Suicides. When the young women jumped from the tower, their bodies broke on historic ground. The cathedral sat atop the ruins of an Aztec temple, in which sacrifices had been symbolic and commonplace. The female victims of the Tower of Suicides opted for very public and sensational suicides. Reporters maligned the working-class Sofía Ahumada and Juana López, saving their more romantic intonations and empathy for middle-class Angelina Ruiz and Margarita Pereda. All of the young women chronicled in this chapter carefully planned their suicides to construct their selves in their deaths in the meaningful public spaces of the city. They also endeavored to project their honor. A reporter noticed that Sofía wore socks to just below the knees to cover as much flesh as possible. María and Guadalupe followed the most romantic suicide script by carefully wrapping letters and portraits in fine ribbon to leave at the scene of their deaths. Knowing that their bodies would suffer the forensic probing of male eyes and surgical instruments, the women dressed in their finest clothes and coifed their hair. The public narratives that followed public suicides competed for authority, yet in many ways the stains of blood left behind had the most permanence as certain spaces of death, such as the Tower of Suicides and Chapultepec Park, became linked to modern suicide for years to come.[89]

The tone of reporting on suicides from 1900 to 1930 connoted both continuity and change. Surely, the catastrophic loss of life and the violence of the revolutionary years must have dissuaded commentators from romanticizing suicides. Reporters had less patience for impetuous youth in general during and after the revolution, even though they sometimes lamented the suicides of young women who seemed to be on the cusp of a full life yet chose to end it. Reporters on the whole had less empathy for what they considered to be foolish suicides and attempts, like the failed suicide of the Spaniard Valeriano Gutiérrez Sáinz, who nicked himself with a razor blade and jumped into the shallow end of Chapultepec Lake, or the suicide of Angelina Ruiz, who jumped from the cathedral in 1920. There were other suicides that they did not mock, and in those cases they coldly reported the details with little editorializing. When a police officer discovered domestic servant Matilde Cejudo clutching a letter and visibly pained in the Alameda in 1930, for example, the next day's article in *El Universal* simply reported that she drank potassium permanganate because she had been deceived in love. No suppositions followed.[90] Later that year, the same newspaper showed a little more amazement at the suicide of a well-dressed man who rented a room at the Hotel San Pedro. Determined to succeed in his death wish, the man dissolved mercury cyanide in a glass, drank it, and then walked up to a third-floor balcony, swung his legs over the rails, and shot himself in the head. The fatal trinity of poison, a bullet, and a three-story fall ensured that the man perished. The reporter expressed being chilled at the cold-bloodedness of the suicide's actions.[91] Make no mistake about it, the way reporters narrated and understood suicide may have changed from the Porfirian to revolutionary times, going from over-romanticizing to reporting only cold, hard facts, but suicide remained both a vehicle to communicate grief and sorrow and a social problem to be analyzed and curbed. By the 1930s, *Excélsior* pledged to stop reporting *la nota roja* (blood crimes), stating that this type of news only served to stimulate the basest passions and perpetuate immorality in Mexican society. Women and children in particular suffered from the reporting of suicides and violent crimes. Archbishops, leading politicians, and Emilio Rabasa, a writer and the cofounder of the newspaper *El Universal,* praised the paper's decision, claiming that it would further the uplift of the working classes.[92] Most expected that removing the sensational and gruesome details of suicides from the front pages would decrease the occurrence of suicide in society.

# SIX

---

## *Stains of Blood*

### DEATH, VERNACULAR MOURNING, AND SUICIDE

WHEN SOFÍA AHUMADA LEAPT TO her death from the cathedral in 1899, a journalist for *El Imparcial* pointed out the irony that the "stain of blood" she left behind was so close to the former resting place of the Aztec sacrificial altar. He mocked the twenty to thirty "vagrants" who loitered around the bloody spot where her body had hit the ground.[1] A decade later, when María Fuentes and Guadalupe Ortiz sealed their fatal suicide pact in the forest of Chapultepec Park, individuals visited the poetic path where the two girls perished, locked in each other's embrace. Likewise, strangers were drawn to the girls' working-class barrio a few days later for the wake, a spectacle a reporter described as a "true pilgrimage" (verdadera romería).[2] When Rosa Kipp shot her upper-class lover and then turned the gun on herself in front of his home, *La Semana Ilustrada* published a photo of the bloodstain where they fell and of a bloody handprint left behind on the building's wall.[3] Three different papers commented on the 1914 suicide of Sara Ramos and also mentioned the mourners and voyeurs that gathered at the "stain of blood" she left after jumping from a third-story window of the post office.[4] When Fernando Pérez Fernández, a young man from a prominent family, leaped out the window of his rented room and crushed his skull on the patio of the parish church, priests instructed servants to quickly clean up all traces of blood.[5] They abhorred the idea that the blood of a sinful death would stain sacred ground. They may have wanted to forestall the gathering of onlookers and mourners as well.

How do we analyze the presence of gawkers and mourners that contemplated the stains of blood left by the bodies of Sofía Ahumada and Sara Ramos or of capitalinos who left flowers and mementos at scene of the double suicide in Chapultepec Park? How do we as scholars interpret these spontaneous and fleeting occurrences of vernacular mourning? Does this shared sensibility of lament counter stereotypes of the devil-may-care Mexican, allegedly callous to death and suffering? If death was so commonplace in early twentieth-century Mexico, did residents acknowledge tragic death with no feeling or empathy? Anthropologists and historians of emotions provide many insights but also raise questions.[6] Most recognize the existence of emotional communities that arose from both universal and socially or culturally sanctioned sensibilities. As previous chapters have demonstrated, the spectacle of the young suicide provoked myriad responses across time, but it also produced consistent and immense feeling in society. Newspaper reporting instigated popular forms of contemplation and grieving, but the physical manifestations of commemorating tragic deaths probably contradicted the newspapers' goals. When headlines showcased another young worker who had killed herself for love, newspapers expected readers to discuss the case in homes and taverns to legitimize the newsworthiness of the event and the function of the newspaper. The last things journalists expected were pilgrimages or ephemeral memorials set up to commemorate the death in the public spaces of the city. Journalists referred to those who visited these places of remembrance as vagrants or unruly crowds that needed to be controlled by police officers. Attending an officially sanctioned state funeral in the public thoroughfares of the city was acceptable; memorializing a so-called mundane death in the same spaces was not. Strangers brought together in these fleeting moments of collective emotion and grief on the streets of the capital upended the rules. The individual lost himself in the crowd in these cases. Just as suicide was a political act so was the collective response to violence and tragic deaths in the city. Publics or emotional communities were dynamic entities that changed with time.

VIOLENCE AND MODERN SENSIBILITIES

The Enlightenment ushered in a new era of humanitarianism in the West. There was a shift from the everyday brutality of medieval life toward a less violent era. Widespread plagues had mostly ceased by the fourteenth century, and rates of interpersonal violence declined in Western Europe. Infant mortality rates dropped; life expectancy rose. Death was less visible and, when it occurred, was more shocking to human sensibilities.[7] Intellectuals have proposed explanations for why violence exists in human society, ranging from

Sigmund Freud's aggression theory to Michel Foucault's theory of pervasive modern, structural violence. While the former approach is ahistorical and pays no attention to chronological context, the latter explains ubiquitous and invisible structural bases of violence but minimizes human agency and feeling. According to Foucault, although overt manifestations of violence like torture and public executions declined in modern Western society, violence within state apparatuses designed to control and discipline bodies simply became more insidious.[8] In other words, citizens internalized the social mechanisms of violence that repressed certain disorderly behaviors. To understand social responses to tragic deaths like suicide, a history of emotions approach gives credit to how societies developed over time with changing economies, manners, and politics. Where Freud saw psychological roots of aggression and violence as inherent traits of human nature, sociologist Norbert Elias argued in 1939 that these characteristics or sensibilities were historically contingent. Elias reasoned that human manners and emotions were dynamic variables that responded to changing social and political structures. As societies became more complex, with a division of labor and roles, humans became more mutually dependent on one another and thus more "civilized." Elias offered a theory of modernity, positing that as societies developed and became modern, they also controlled affect and manners. For example, the modern man showed disgust at someone who spit on the floor of his home or blew his nose on the tablecloth.[9] Likewise, some behaviors that had been acceptable in earlier times became taboo in the modern era, and many manners and emotions were internalized through years of socialization. Basically, Elias argued that while emotions may emerge from human nature, they are also shaped by social and cultural milieu.[10] A greater sense of social interdependence resulted in a humanitarian spirit that made spectacles of blood, gore, and violence insupportable.

Scholars differ on the character of human emotions. The nature versus culture debate is alive and well. Anthropologists Michelle Z. Rosaldo and Lila Abu-Lughod theorized that emotions arise from an individual's relation to society. They are social constructions created outside of the individual, and they condition a response that is historically and culturally contingent. Simply put, they posit that all emotions are culturally specific and that there are no such things as universal emotions or sensibilities across mankind.[11] If all psychological traits are relative, then what qualities do humans share? Neuroscientist Paul Ekman argued that all humans share six basic emotions: happiness, anger, disgust, fear, sadness, and surprise. Different cultures may have a range of terms for such emotions, but they share common facial expressions to communicate those feelings.[12] Ekman's critics charge that his research lacked empirical proof.[13] More promising research by neuroscientists has suggested that emotions may be biological in some respects but also constitute a response from "historically-formed brains."[14] Social neuroscientists have begun to study the emotion of empathy—that is, how individuals feel the suffering or emotional condition of another person. Historian and anthropologist William Reddy wedded universalism and social constructivism to suggest that emotions are physical gestures and linguistic expressions. Thus, when an individual conveys an emotion, she also desires to encourage the emotion in others. Reddy termed these emotional statements and gestures "emotives" to describe how societies developed their own "emotional regimes." Likewise, states endeavor to shape emotional regimes and control affect and emotion to exercise hegemony.[15] The control of affect is a hallmark of modernity. Historian Barbara Rosenwein reminds us that in the past, individuals lived in multiple emotional communities, including families, labor unions, fraternal societies, and other identity groups.[16] Emotions were and are situational. What emotional communities existed in early twentieth-century Mexico to process and understand tragic deaths by suicide?

## DEATH CULTS AND TOTEMS: THE INTELLECTUAL DEBATE

Ever since artists José Clemente Orozco and Diego Rivera resurrected and praised the talent of engraver José Guadalupe Posada in the 1920s, the skeleton as a motif to parody life and the inevitability of the grave has infused Mexican popular culture. Posada employed the skeleton in his numerous penny press engravings to satirize Mexican politics and society during the Porfiriato. Some say that depicting poor and rich alike as skeletons communicated that class did not matter because we are all bones in the end. Day of the Dead celebrations have further popularized the *calavera* (skeleton) as an iconic feature of Mexican worldview. Postrevolutionary artists like Rivera exalted the calavera as an aesthetic representation of Mexicans' affinity for death. The proliferation of death imagery in advertisements, art, prose, and even language led intellectuals like Octavio Paz and Claudio Lomnitz-Adler to argue that Mexicans have a culturally unique relationship with death. Paz states that Mexicans caress, taunt, and embrace it. Lomnitz-Adler contends that Mexico's unique cultural hybridity—born from Aztecs, who built an empire on blood sacrifice, and Europeans, who carried out genocidal conquests in the New World—produced a particular death cult that crystallized after the revolution to enshrine death as the third national totem, after the Virgin of Guadalupe and Benito Juárez.[17] Most of the suppositions about Mexican attitudes toward death base their evidence in Day of the Dead celebrations, which Mexicans so colorfully celebrate by feasting on sugar skulls and coffins on the gravesites of loved ones on All Saints' Day and All Souls' Day. Some believe the fiesta to have pre-Columbian roots; others argue that it is an "invented tradition."[18] Paul Westheim and Octavio Paz take the former view, noting the cultural *mestizaje* (miscegenation) of the practice, with its pre-Columbian notion of a capricious God and the ghoulish skeleton, which are prevalent in medieval Christian imagery.[19] Literary critic Guillermo Sheridan disagrees, arguing that Day of the Dead is an invented tradition of anthropologists, film directors, and artists such as Frida Kahlo. He claims that tourism reinforced the manufactured custom and the insidious connection between Mexican national character and death.[20] Paz suggested that Mexicans possess anxiety about their mortality but that jocularity and indifference triumph when it comes to how they feel about death.[21] Carlos Monsiváis argued that the archetypal revolutionary who stood stoically before a firing squad, a figure that was well publicized in print media and verse, popularized the idea that Mexicans laughed in the face of death. Monsiváis believed that this particular relationship with death was naturalized by an authoritarian state and was contrary to Mexicans' authentic yearning for universal goals like modernization, human rights, and democracy.[22] Most recently, anthropologist Claudio Lomnitz-Adler tackled Mexico's alleged fascination with death without purporting to enter the debate sparked by Monsiváis and anthropologists Stanley Brandes and Roger Bartra. Lomnitz-Adler's chief accomplishment is a fascinating history of Day of the Dead and the process with which the state consolidated political power by controlling and managing all aspects of death.[23] What modern state has not endeavored to control death? Lomnitz-Adler is less convincing in his claim of a uniquely Mexican response to death. Mexicans, like others, possess multiple reactions to death. It fascinates *and* repels them. Generalizing attitudes and behaviors displayed during Day of the Dead celebrations to speak for all death and mourning attitudes perpetuates an "essentialist image of a macabre Mexican."[24] Likewise, the assertion that there is a stable Mexican national character ignores difference across space and change over time. As Brandes simply states, "attitudes are situational."[25]

Lomnitz-Adler persuasively argues that "death symbolism and revolutionary nationalism" have become twin ideologies of the modern Mexican state.[26] Death was a visible and mundane occurrence in Porfirian and revolutionary Mexico. The Mexican Revolution cost 1.4 million lives.[27] Infant mortality, disease epidemics, chronic malnutrition, and rising murder rates during the Porfiriato made death commonplace. Life expectancy was abysmally low. An average Mexican could expect to live to age thirty-one in 1910.[28] Death was indeed familiar, and preparations for funerals and burial could be seen by the public everyday. However, "familiarity" ought not to be conflated with flippant dismissal or apathy. Historian Matthew Esposito convincingly shows that by the late nineteenth century, Mexicans had a modern approach to death. They did not await it patiently without anguish like their medieval Christian forbearers had. The gradual de-Christianization of society and the exaltation of the individual during the Enlightenment led to new approaches to death. Phillippe Ariès noted that family took a larger role in funerary practice and carrying out the last wishes of their dearly departed. As a result, funerals and mourning practices became highly active and orchestrated events that required the vigorous participation of mourners. Grievers no longer stood passively by but deeply felt the loss of their loved ones and acted out that sorrow in funeral rites that were as extravagant as they could afford.[29] It would seem unlikely that death was anyone's "steadfast love" as men and women sobbed over the coffins of their dead children or spouses.[30]

Mexican history began with death, when Spaniards carried out a "veritable holocaust [on] the native population," but an analysis of popular responses to violent death refutes the presumption that Mexicans did not fear death as a future fact of a life.[31] On the contrary, many viewed life's course in a linear (and presumably modern) fashion, with death as a final and future outcome. Sudden and violent death appeared untimely and unimaginable. Youth suicide, which was considered unexpected and tragic, caused family members of the victims to reconstruct past events to make sense of the deaths in the present. As chapter 2 examined, this narrative was written on the body of the deceased. Collectively, Mexicans also lamented that so many of their youth, the very group they hinged their hopes on, were bent on self-destruction and could not survive the torments of a modernizing and urbanizing nation. Outpourings of grief were both private and public.

Public memorialization has a long history in Mexico that dates back at least to the colonial period.[32] In 1845, the procession of the remains of former president José Joaquín Herrera, followed by his mourning family and colleagues, wound through the streets flanking the capital's central plaza and ended at the cathedral, where they were interred. In 1876, at the beginning of the Porfiriato, shortly after the opening of Dolores cemetery south of the city center, the Rotunda of Illustrious Men was inaugurated by a procession of the remains of famous statesmen from El Centro, down the fashionable streets of San Francisco (now Madero) and Juárez, around the statue of Carlos V, and down Paseo de la Reforma to their final resting place.[33] The procession acted as a performance of nation and state power. Speeches and eulogies preceded the processions, and residents of the capital could take part in state making at its finest. They were able to participate in the ritual of memorializing death. Indeed, Mexico had developed a keen culture of venerating statesmen and heroic martyrs, evidenced in particular in the multiple state funerals held during the rule of President Porfirio Díaz.

Parallel to official acts of commemoration and statecraft, temporary memorials occurred at literal "stains of blood." When someone committed suicide in a public space, such as a church or a popular park, onlookers and grievers would sometimes gather to leave flowers at the scene once officials removed the corpse to the morgue and collected evidence. Mourners who contemplated these stains of blood shared in performative rituals of memorializing death on the streets of Mexico City.[34] Even though flowers wilted and mementos eventually made their way into trash bins, ephemeral memorials were "highly orchestrated and self-conscious acts of mourning aimed at expressing, codifying, and ultimately managing grief."[35] Spontaneous memorials were especially common in the aftermath of shocking deaths, like suicides. While funeral processions could be observed from afar, the performativity of vernacular memorials at stains of blood invited membership.[36] This participation brought strangers together in an emotional community that shared common reactions to youth suicide in turn-of-the-century Mexico.[37] Spontaneous memorials arose in response to unexpected, violent deaths of individuals who were not expected to die and who had compelling personal stories. All of us are familiar with roadside crosses demarcating the locations of fatal car crashes or the teddy bears and flowers left at the site of the 2015 terrorist attacks in Paris. This form of ritual is a private, individualized act of mourning that invades the public. It occurs at sites of tragic death, and, unlike private or state funerals, no one is excluded from contemplating the scene or leaving flowers. Spontaneous memorialization extends beyond the deceased to the "social and cultural implications of their death."[38] In other words, these ephemeral memorials "personalize public and political issues" and prevent individuals from being written off as statistics. Gathering at death sites or joining processions to the cemetery were political and sometimes unruly acts that asserted a social agenda.

Chapter 2 discussed the modernization of death and burial in Porfirian Mexico. During that time, the belief was that mourning rituals ought to be carried out in private homes and modern cemeteries, not in the busy spaces of the city. A series of funeral carriages and trams transported coffins from different corpse deposits around the city, and authorities designed them to move efficiently and cleanly. Mourners sat in curtained coaches on their journey to the cemetery. Only the poor still hoisted their rude coffins on their shoulders and walked solemnly to the cemetery to bury their dearly departed. Ephemeral memorials at death sites presented an alternate narrative to the control of death in modern Mexico. Although it is impossible to know concretely what motivated these forms of vernacular commemoration, their existence provides us a glimpse of popular attitudes toward suicides and, more generally, violent death. Some visited suicide sites to satisfy a morbid voyeurism, while others left behind flowers to memorialize the lost souls. Journalists fancied themselves to be rational arbiters of public opinion, engaging in an exchange of ideas in a Habermasian vision of a public sphere.[39] Could the temporary memorials be an affective exchange amplified by emotion, mourning, and nostalgia? There is no doubt that the memorials were "populist phenomena, ways for people to mark their own history," regardless of the media narrative.[40] Indeed, temporary memorials are performative in character, as Erika Doss suggests; they "mark instances of untimely and especially traumatic deaths, become places of communion between the living and the dead, and invite broad public participation."[41] The affective arena of the memorials and the arrival of onlookers to contemplate the death sites contrasted with the calculated reporting of journalists for the major dailies, which deemed many suicides dishonorable. Newspaper reports of tragic deaths like suicide nevertheless encouraged collective shock and mourning.

Mass media, including print news, radio, film, and television, has emerged as a defining aspect of modernity. Furthermore, media produces modern emotional communities or publics. Newspapers at the turn of the century played a huge role in the production of meaning. Newspaper coverage of sensational events instructed readers in socially appropriate responses to tragic death. Scholars of the history of emotions have thus far paid little attention to sensational media; however, film and media scholars offer some useful insights.[42] Christiane Voss studies viewers of film as spectators who have "sensorial-affective" responses to events and characters in movies. Voss sees emotions as "narrative phenomena" with a cognitive dimension. She believes that emotions develop and unfold with a sequential dramatic structure, much like a story.[43] Reading a sensational newspaper article of a tragic suicide and seeing its accompanying photograph or sketch is akin to viewing a film. According to Voss's formulation, the reader is a spectator who emotionally responds to characters and events in print rather than on screen. Certainly, scholars familiar with William Randolph Hearst's newspapers and their jingoist propaganda leading up to the Spanish American War would agree that sentiments can be provoked and shaped in pursuit of political goals. Sensationalist newspapers like *El Imparcial* or *Excélsior* (pre-1930) and the penny press of Antonio Vanegas Arroyo, so expressively illustrated by José Guadalupe Posada, shaped emotional communities and instructed readers how to respond to tragic events, whether real or imagined.

The press also played on desires and fears already present in society. For example, the year 1899 provoked angst. That year, on the cusp of a new century, in a city undergoing rapid modernization, Posada illustrated several broadsides that foretold and ridiculed the end of days. Engravings such as that depicting a volcano erupting and skeletons gesticulating in the foreground, bearing the title "The End of the World Is Certain. All Will Be Skeletons. Goodbye to the Living," represented the insecurity and uncertainly of a new century. The verse noted, "For our great sins, we will be judged."[44] The broadside had political overtones as well, noting the murder of Arnulfo Arroyo, who was killed in a conspiracy by prominent Porfirian officials. Sensationalism sold newspapers, and shocking and dramatic articles also created communities of readers who shared common emotions to events like suicide. Mainstream newspaper headlines such as "Horrible Suicide on Capuchinas Street," "Love, Insanity, and Blood," "Aboard an Automobile, a

Romantic Youth Ends His Life," and "A Mysterious Form Strangled a Beautiful and Elegant Woman in Toluca" drew readers to newspaper stands and kiosks.[45] In making the choice to report the horrific details of suicides and other violent incidents, editors instructed readers what types of news should make them feel emotion. Suicide should shock and provoke horror and sometimes empathy in the reader. Perhaps communication studies scholars are right to insist that media has an "emotional agenda."[46] Depicting suicide in visual and narrative forms in the style of police news, or *la nota roja*, offered unrestricted possibilities. Journalists delivered speculation under a veil of factual objectivity.[47] Tragic deaths and crimes became fodder for public conversations about morality, urban dangers, and in the case of youth suicide, a commentary on the health of the social whole.

## STAINS OF BLOOD AND VERNACULAR MEMORIALIZATION

Sara Ramos, a young single woman, had been working at the national post office for more than a year when she jumped from a third-story window to her death in January 1914. A monument to Porfirian modernity and progress, the building had been inaugurated just ten years earlier.[48] By all accounts a lovely and friendly young woman, Sara had stellar performance reviews. She had started at the office by working without pay as an intern and was then hired as a typist. She had fallen in love with Manuel Gavidia, one of her coworkers. All newspaper coverage noted that Manuel had spurned Sara and become engaged to the wealthier Esther Medina, the daughter of a general.[49] Sara had learned of the engagement on Christmas Eve and had confronted Manuel the morning of her death near the elevator with tears, pleas, and recriminations for abandoning her. She then sat at her desk, crying, and asked her boss if she could leave early. She collected her shawl, said goodbye to her coworkers, and walked out the door on Calle de Tacuba. Instead of heading home, Sara turned the corner onto Callejón de la Condesa. She reentered the post office and took the stairs to the upper floors. She strode to the window, threw open the sash, and sat on the window ledge. A worker told the reporter that she appeared pale and troubled. He testified that he had approached her to warn her to back away from the window because she might fall, and as he returned to his station he sensed a movement. Sara had wrapped her black shawl around her face and jumped. Hair flowing and rebozo enveloping her head and shoulders, her body plunged head first to the sidewalk. Her coworkers heard the commotion on the street and gathered around her broken and lifeless body. Her former suitor and alleged author of her despair, Manuel Gavidia, quickly fled the building.[50]

Newspapers used Sara's death to disseminate moral lessons or critiques of society. *El Diario* elaborated on her personal biography. Its front-page story presented a collage of events in her life: a sketch of Sara embracing Gavidia, her typing at her desk, and, in the final panel, her body lying on a stretcher (see figure 10). The article's subtitle read, "She was an employee of that office, and the death of her brother, combined with the deep disappointment of forgotten love, put horrible despair in her spirit that led her to search for peace in the blackness of death." Having gained incredible access to family and friends, the reporter seized the opportunity of her death to move beyond the unrequited love narrative to discuss other pressures and problems Sara faced as a single young clerical worker in the city. He wrote, "She was a victim of the social condition of the innocence of an inexperienced girl, humbled and resigned to her poverty." He cited other tragedies in her personal life, including the deaths of two of her brothers, one torn to pieces under a trolley and another killed in battle in the north (presumably fighting the Division of the North, which was led by Francisco "Pancho" Villa). Family members had worried about Sara and the stresses she faced, and they told the reporter that they had removed poison from her purse some days before her suicide.[51]

The Catholic daily *El País* reported the details of the young woman's death and provided gruesome facts as well, describing an "impressive" head wound and "eyes popping, more pieces of brain, mouth twisted." The reporter noted that Sara, the sole provider for her family, left behind a widowed mother and two younger brothers. The article went on, "The corpse of the unfortunate . . . another victim of the godlessness that prevails today . . . lies on the hospital slab, awaiting the scalpel to shred the flesh, while the gallant, perhaps, suffers the impression that it will not be long until the matter vanishes."[52] The paper acknowledged the temporal nature of news. Another suicide or tragic death would consume headlines and public conversation soon enough.

*El Diario* seized on the prevailing cognitive dissonance that existed in society about women in the workplace. Working in offices, factories, or workshops exposed women to seduction and vice. Women were viewed as easily influenced and weak, and it was thought that temptation could lead a woman down a sordid path. Although workingwomen were provided some services during the Porfirian, they comprised a part of the working poor of

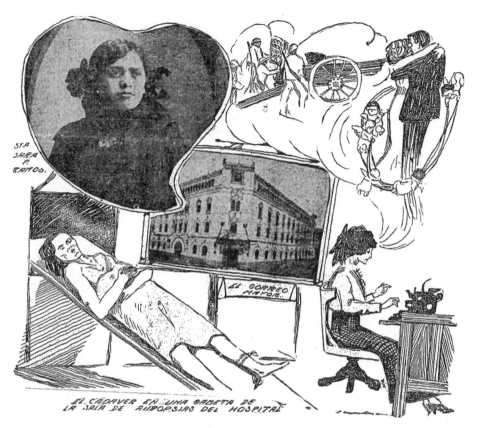

FIGURE 10. Montage of photographs and sketches of Sara Ramos. *El Diario*, January 11, 1914, p. 1.

Mexico City. Labor laws that impacted female workers were not passed until the 1917 Constitution, and they were not enforced until decades later.[53] It was clear that Sara Ramos had to work outside the home to support her widowed mother and young brothers. She had a respectable job as a civil servant. The papers emphasized her work ethic and motivation. Noting her inexperience and humble nature, *El Diario* echoed the common narrative of the poor girl let loose in the big city who either falls into prostitution, becomes a victim of murder, or seeks an end to her suffering through suicide.[54] Papers like *El Diario* and *El Imparcial* fell short of blaming Sara for killing herself for love. They cast her not as godless but as a poor, innocent working girl broken by the pressures of her situation.[55] The Catholic paper *El País* placed blame on the "gallant" who was waiting for the story to fade from public memory and conversation. The images that accompanied the speculative and moralistic narrative also communicated meaning. Readers perusing the front page of *El Independiente* gazed upon the sketch of a respectably dressed Sara hurling herself head first off the post office building. A black shawl modestly covers her face to shield her from the reality of her impending death but also to show the reader that she possessed modesty. Small shoes cover her dainty feet. Honorable women covered their bare arms with shawls or jackets. Office workers wore modern shoes rather than the huaraches of the *indio*. A reader could view this image and the others and empathize with the young clerical worker. *El Diario* presented a collage of images (refer back to figure 10). Besides the photographic studio portrait of Sara and an image of the post office building, there was a sketch of Sara sitting at her desk typing with a thought bubble floating above showing her and her beau in a passionate embrace, encircled by cherubs. A second illustration depicted her brother fighting in the revolution with his squad. A very prominent third sketch shows her corpse prostrate on a slab, awaiting autopsy. In combination, the images illustrated the reporter's biography of the young Sara. They invoked compassion in some and exasperation in others. Another victim of love! *El Independiente* pondered, "Certainly those brief moments before the suicide of the beautiful young woman were the most painful and bloody that you can imagine."[56] Women were always beautiful in their deaths.

*El Imparcial* and *El País* reported on Sara's suicide and printed photographs of people gathered at the spot where her blood had stained the pavement. *El Imparcial* included an inset headshot of her corpse, commenting that her motives were the same that had driven others to leap off the cathedral to their deaths (see figure 11).[57] Recall that the cathedral tower was referred to as the Tower of Suicides (see chapter 5). The subtitle read, "The 'Eternal Male' induced a postal employee to take her life in a moment of agonizing disappointment." Sara worked in one of the busiest sections of the city. Passersby likely witnessed her jump and flocked to the scene to administer aid or satisfy their curiosity. *El Imparcial* gave their story a dramatic and literary opening:

> On a delicious winter morning, the sun set flashes of pale gold on the fronds and flowers of the gardens. In the atmosphere there was a gentle palpitation of atoms. Condesa Alley, on the side of the General Direction of the Post Office, narrow, long, and ordinarily silent, appeared bathed in light and through it ran several employees who went to collect mail. It was the hour that the daily commotion began and at the door of the post office innumerable vehicles of all classes stopped to leave packages sent by businessmen of the metropolis.[58]

EL CADAVER DE LA SUICIDA

SITIO DEL SUCESO Y TRAYECTORIA QUE SIGUIO EL CUERPO DE LA SUICIDA.

FIGURE 11. Crowd at the site of the suicide of Sara Ramos. *El Imparcial,* January 11, 1914, p. 1.

The accompanying images showed onlookers lined up on both sides of the street. Certainly, some hoped to send their packages as forensic experts surveyed the scene and draped Sara's corpse on a stretcher. However, the photograph *El País* published of the scene shows individuals contemplating the stain of blood and bears the caption "People at the site where the suicide fell." A cross section of society, including well-dressed children, men, and women, peer over the curb at the site of Sara's fatal fall. Men in the customary sombreros of the campesinos mingled with men in fedoras.

The individuals that collected at stains of blood were not flâneurs or urban idlers who gazed at the street in an aloof manner. Rather, they were more akin to the French *badaud* (stroller).[59] The *badaud,* unlike the flâneur, immersed himself in the crowd; he did not stand above it. Gregory Shaya writes, "The flâneur observed the city with intelligence and distinction; he turned his overdeveloped sensibilities to dwell upon mysteries and telling details. The *badaud* gawked; he sought out a story that would touch him."[60] The press fueled his curiosity and need to feel something. He lost his individuality and became the public, the audience of mass media. Crowds at scenes of tragic deaths may have been drawn in by a curiosity to see gore and blood, but they also represented the newspapers' audiences and thus were generally depicted as empathetic rather than superficial gawkers.

A young confectioner, María de Jesús Gutiérrez, leaped from the top of a building because she had lost in love just six months after Sara Ramos killed herself. In fact, the reporter for *El Imparcial* began his article, "Even though one has not extinguished the memory of Miss Sara Ramos . . . ." Like Sara, María "could not resist the amorous passions that boiled in her heart" and jumped from a height of twenty-five meters to her death. The twenty-two-year-old had attracted amorous overtures from several coworkers, but she chose Andrés Trejo because she thought him sincere and loved him ardently. Their courtship grew more and more serious, but as they made steps to formalize their relationship, María revealed an obstacle that would prevent them from marrying. The reporter apparently asked Andrés about this hindrance, but he remained mute on the matter. Had María been married to another? Had she had sexual relations with another? They stopped seeing each other for a while, but then friends noticed them strolling together in the romantic parks of the city. Their mutual ardor blossomed once again, but soon coworkers found María weeping at work. Andrés had broken off their relationship when he learned that she attended a dance without him. The reporter waxed eloquently about the abrupt change in María's attitude. Once jovial, the young woman transformed, her "expression fixed on a distant horizon" and a "handkerchief between her lips to stifle her sobs." On the morning of her death, she arrived at her post like any other day but sat down to pen a letter to Andrés. Becoming more and more upset, she left work at 2:00 pm and made her way up to the roof of the building. She lowered herself to one of the cornices overlooking Calle Capuchinas and jumped into oblivion, hitting a marquee and shattering its glass. The fall opened up a gash in her skull and fractured her arms. Her body was removed to the Hospital Juárez for the obligatory autopsy, and forensic specialists found a letter under her clothes that read: "No one is guilty of this. Only I am responsible. The motive is I cannot endure family matters. I ask that you not tell my mother." María also left a letter for Andrés at work: "You are and you will live in my imagination. But perhaps my remorse made me do this. But for you I write nothing. Yours." [61] *El Imparcial* noted that she leapt from the building at one of the busiest times of day. The central avenue bustled with traffic. Indescribable panic gripped passersby, who quickly grouped to contemplate her stain of blood. Several probably searched headlines the next day to learn her tragic story.

Mónica Santillán jumped from the third floor of a building on Calle de Tacuba, just five blocks from where Sara Ramos met her death more than a year later. By chance, a reporter and a photographer happened to be walking down the street at the moment that the young woman jumped from the roof. They approached the "shapeless mass" on the pavement, and the reporter judged from Mónica's clothing that she probably served in the house. After summoning police, the reporter returned to the tragic scene and saw, clutched in her right hand, a letter that read, "Mónica: Don't blame me, but destiny. I cannot continue loving you because I am promised to Desideria. So do not worry yourself with me any longer." It was signed, "You know who." Since a photographer was on site at the time of the death, *El Independiente* was able to publish a photograph of the building and a cluster of onlookers surrounding Mónica's "shapeless mass." [62] Her corpse lay still, undisturbed by investigators, as journalists were first on the scene. The headline named the location of the suicide, the fifth block of Calle de Tacuba. *El Diario* also published a front-page photograph of the site of Mónica's death, although her corpse had been whisked away to the hospital by the time it was taken. The photograph included an arrow showing the trajectory of her fall from the third-floor window. [63] Hers was a familiar story of deception in love that resonated with capitalinos. Tragic deaths in public spaces drew the curious. This is an ahistorical phenomenon. Rubberneckers, gawkers, and morbid curiosity seekers are all labels used to denigrate this behavior. However, the fact that capitalinos rushed to death scenes to gaze upon disfigured corpses does not mean that collective emotion was absent. Newspapers fueled curiosity, and the articles provided human narratives that provoked feeling and created publics or emotional communities united by a common sentiment.

Murder-suicides drew intense notice from reporters and the reading public. Adrián Fournier broke off his relationship with Rosa Kipp in 1910. A week later, she arrived at his home on Avenida Balderas with a purpose. He walked out his front door, they exchanged a few words, and she pumped four bullets into his body. She then raised the gun to her temple and pulled the trigger. They had met in the workplace, and their relationship had proceeded peaceably for some time. Friends reported that they had spent many afternoons walking in Alameda Park in animated conversation. No one knew what had torn their love asunder. Reporters flocked to the scene and saw Fournier's corpse lying on the sidewalk and Kipp's body slumped in a sitting position against the building wall with her head resting forward on her chest. She appeared to be sleeping. *La Semana Ilustrada* published a short article under the section "Tragic News of the Week," printing a portrait of Fournier in better times and two photos of the crime scene that included stains of blood, one of a wall marked by a cross where, presumably, a bloody hand had rested, and one of the sidewalk where Fournier had perished (see figures 12 and 13).[64] Such articles and photographs in *La Semana Ilustrada* memorialized sites of tragic death. An earlier piece printed photographs of María Luisa Noecker and the bullfighter Rodolfo Gaona, as well as of María's home, at the corner of Balderas and New Mexico, where she had killed herself (see figure 14). Such photographs and their captions provided readers with addresses so that they could visit the sites of the tragic deaths to pay their respects or simply walk or drive by out of curiosity. Another photographic memorial in *La Semana Ilustrada* showed a portrait of young medical student Manuel Moreno and the neat and tidy room where he had killed himself in 1910 (see figure 15). The collective message was that Mexico's youth possessed an unnatural death wish. They could not survive life's disappointments. Newspapers did not provide solutions to the problem but rather waxed nostalgic for gentler times or provided a veiled criticism of urban youth culture.

Strangers joined funeral processions of untimely and tragic deaths. The 1909 double suicide of Guadalupe Ortiz and María Fuentes resulted in much commentary. The press first extolled the elegance of the girls and then denigrated them, claiming that their motive for suicide was that they could not live a luxurious life. When their family departed the working-class barrio of Tepito with the corpses, mourners stood outside their home. *El Imparcial* called the steady stream of mourners a "true pilgrimage."[65]

When Joaquín Suárez shot and stabbed his cousin Margarita Suárez in front of Santo Domingo Church in 1910, society took notice. While not a suicide but a homicide, the tragic and untimely death of the sixteen-year-old

LA NOTA TRÁGICA DE LA SEMANA

FIGURE 12 *(Top)*. Photograph of the site of Rosa Kipp and Adrián Fournier murder-suicide. *La Semana Ilustrada*, June 24, 1910.

FIGURE 13 *(Bottom)*. Homicide victim Adrián Fournier and stain of blood on wall. *La Semana Ilustrada*, June 24, 1910.

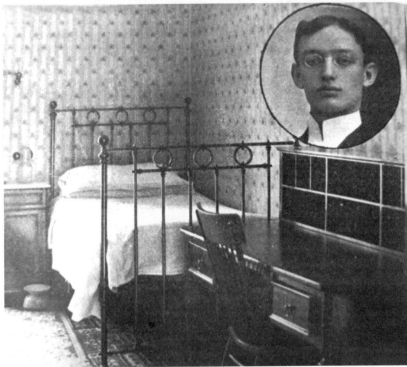

FIGURE 14 *(Top)*. Home of the Noecker family. *La Semana Ilustrada,* December 17, 1909.

FIGURE 15 *(Bottom)*. Site of the suicide of medical student Manuel Moreno. *La Semana Ilustrada,* May 6, 1910.

girl at the hands of a family member who had fallen in love with her shocked residents. Margarita and her sister worked for the Ericksson Telephone Company, and they had told their boss and coworkers that they feared the wrath of their cousin. In fact, they had noticed him skulking around outside their workplace. Journalists described forensic investigators who reenacted the scene of the murderer standing over the twice-shot victim and stabbing her several times in the back. It repelled and fascinated capitalinos. The story dominated headlines for a few days as reporters speculated on the mental state of the murderous cousin and whether he and the victim had had amorous relations, as he attested. *El Diario* reported that anger boiled in society and that many wanted to take justice in their own hands, invade the police station, and lynch Joaquín.[66] The young woman's reputation was at stake. Her sister argued that Margarita had maintained her honor and refused to commit incest with her cousin. *El Imparcial* noted that she had signed her letters to her cousin with the familiar *tu,* which connoted intimacy.[67] Morning newspapers reported that the family would bury Margarita's body at 9:00 am. Urban residents stood on balconies, in doorways, and on roofs to watch the first-class funeral procession. Thousands more, according to *El Imparcial,* clogged the streets to follow the procession to the cemetery. The paper printed a photograph of the crowd that showed that there were more people in sombreros than fedoras, suggesting that most of the mourners hailed from the working or migrant classes of the city. The commotion delayed the family from leaving their home with Margarita's coffin until 10:00 am. Police officers had to direct traffic and manage the throngs of mourners and curious who contemplated the homicide of a promising daughter of the city. Four young men hoisted her coffin on their shoulders and carried it to the corner to meet the funeral coach. They covered the coffin with floral wreaths and set off for Dolores cemetery. The crowd followed.[68]

Although reporters sometimes derided those who flocked to stains of blood left behind by the damaged bodies of suicide victims, the ephemeral memorials present an intriguing narrative. When *El Imparcial* mocked the ten, twenty, or thirty people that gathered at Sofía Ahumada's stain of blood near the former resting place of the Aztec stone altar, they also noted the enormous curiosity that her suicide awakened in society. "An immense multitude" visited the cathedral to see the scene of her death the day after her jump. Presumably, word of the suicide had traveled by mouth, and many had read the front-page reports. The reporter ended his commentary by noting that mourners had painted a cross on the site.[69]

Although it is impossible to know definitively what motivated these forms of vernacular commemoration, their existence provides us a glimpse of popular attitudes toward the suicides of young Mexicans, and tragic death more generally. These manifestations of mourning largely occurred when young workingwomen with aspirations for love and social mobility committed suicide in public. Reporters detailed their lives of hard work and deprivation. Some, like Sofía Ahumada, were recent migrants to the city. Margarita Suárez and her sister were orphans and had moved to Mexico City from Oaxaca to live with their uncle. Others, like Sara Ramos, worked hard to support their families. They also had much in common with their wealthier peers—they were victims of unrequited love and deception, and heartbreak and dishonor drove them to self-destruction.

The mourners who honored the spaces of death of these young women forged a relationship between the dead and the living, but more importantly, they produced an arena of affect and emotion where they could lament the tragedy of lost youth in a turbulent time. Sofía leapt to her death from the cathedral in 1899, when many in Mexico felt deep anxiety about the future. Sara jumped to her death in 1914, when Mexico was in the midst of revolution and President Huerta had tenuous control of Mexico City.

Although statistics are rife with problems, an analysis of the *expedientes* (case files) housed in the Archivo General de la Nación (the Mexican national archive) and a review of the newspaper coverage suggests that suicide was indeed a social problem of youth. Perhaps the phenomenon of vernacular mourning rituals at these stains of blood attempted not only to honor the dead and lament the rising tide of suicide in Mexico but also to show how media coverage of the suicides assigned monikers to public spaces—suicide park, tower of suicides, stains of blood—and converted them into social spaces of death and mourning. In this respect, dying and mourning were public rather than private events.

CONCLUSION

Visitors to sites of shocking deaths included curious voyeurs *and* mourners who left flowers, notes, and other small tokens to express their grief. This outpouring of sorrow could be directed to a specific victim, or it could be a more abstract nostalgia for lost youth or a bygone era, or an expression of anxiety about an uncertain future. Just as people today lay flowers at the sites of tragic deaths, Mexicans a century ago came together in a collective sigh of empathy to contemplate and mourn untimely and violent death. Death imagery may have permeated all levels of Mexican society and politics during the twentieth century, especially after the revolution, but social and cultural responses to youth suicide contradict theorists that suggest that Mexicans possessed a particular indifferent and flippant attitude toward death.[70] Certainly, death was a constant presence in the lives of Mexicans during the early 1900s, especially as typhus and cholera epidemics swept through crowded tenements and bodies filled the morgues. However, urbanizing cities on all continents experienced the same death rates in this period. Indeed, death permeated all aspects of modern urban life. The death toll exacted by a decade of revolution also familiarized Mexican citizens with the transience of life. Some might argue that the daily reality of death desensitized people to suffering and loss, making them unmoved by the demise of fellow humans. Anthropologist Nancy Scheper-Hughes has made this argument about mothers facing the death of children in twentieth-century Brazil, when infant mortality rates were high.[71] Although documentary evidence is thin, travelers' accounts and early twentieth-century ethnographies describe elaborate and emotional grieving and burial rituals for children and adults in Mexico.[72] The fact that Mexicans mourned and memorialized suicides suggests that they were familiar with death because of its commonplace nature and also nostalgic when thinking of their departed, but it also indicates that a collective jocularity and taunting of death existed only in "poetic hyperbole."[73] On the contrary, death as illustrated by one of its causes—suicide— puts to rest the supposition that Mexicans felt and approached death differently than their contemporaries in other countries. Suicide epidemics, it was thought, wreaked havoc on modern nations. Mexicans responded like Americans, Frenchmen, and Russians; they believed that a death grip seized the most vulnerable in the population and that suicide, like crime, had to be analyzed, studied, and reduced to ensure the future of the nation.

# Conclusion

SUICIDE OPENS A WINDOW INTO the vivid social imaginaries of Porfirian and revolutionary Mexico City. The capital underwent significant modernization during these years. A massive drainage system alleviated seasonal flooding issues. Eclectic housing developments sprung up in western sections of the city. Trolley lines crisscrossed large expanses of the city and connected the rural with the urban. More homes boasted electricity and modern appliances. Programs of public hygiene improved the quality of life of the city's inhabitants and curbed epidemic diseases. Mexico City was modern on the cusp of the twentieth century, but this modernity was a hybrid that knitted the new with the old.[1] Markers of modernity were parks replete with fountains, avenues lined with trees, department stores stocked with imported goods, and paradoxically, suicide. A universal human act like suicide was a modern disease to be contemplated, lamented, and by all means studied. To scholars a century later, the act itself matters less than how and why social groups imbued it with meaning. When journalists reported on a young woman who jumped head first off the cathedral or a man who shot himself because he was bored with life, they communicated universal anxieties that hounded their social worlds. When physicians peered into the craniums of cadavers to seek the causes of mental illness, they did so with an arsenal of preconceptions about human behavior. Prevailing gender, class, and racial norms shaped their judgments. It is exactly these notable peculiarities that situate suicide in its historical context. These were universal themes and trepidations that plagued modern societies.

Continuity over the eras rather than difference characterized popular and official attitudes toward suicide in Mexico City. Porfirian- and revolutionary-era scientists yearned to understand the circumstances that led some to self-destruct. Society reacted with various responses, and printed discourse supported and shaped those collective emotions. In fact, newspapers cultivated modern communities of affect and feeling. The suicides sometimes asserted a narrative that countered public discussion. In their final act, they attempted to contour how others would reflect on their deaths. Young people killed themselves at greater rates than people from other age groups, a phenomenon that troubled society because the belief was that the youth of the nation ought to be full of promise and optimism as they looked forward to enjoying the fruits of twentieth-century modernity. They were Mexico's future workers and leaders. After all, Mexico had survived a protracted revolution, and national leaders ushered in an era of peace and stability as they rebuilt the nation. These were invigorating times. Mexico emerged from revolution with a renewed purpose and identity. Youth and female suicide seemed unfathomable.

The Mexican Revolution continues to be a touchstone when discussing the nation's progress or criticizing current politics. New leaders swept in with a bevy of promises that elevated the hopes of a people who had fought the hemisphere's first social revolution against political and economic tyranny. Tragic deaths and disease devastated families; citizens pined for relief. Auspicious times lay ahead to build an independent and revitalized society. It is no wonder that a cadre of postrevolutionary scholars, socialized in that heady milieu, came to shape an idea of *mexicanidad* or *lo mexicano* (Mexicaness). They hungered for a unique Mexican character, a national identity that was based on Mexico's cultural strengths and potential. Porfirians had looked to Europe; revolutionary intellectuals looked inward. Porfirians had denied their indigenous past; revolutionaries embraced it. Thinkers like José Vasconcelos, Samuel Ramos, Leopoldo Zea, and Octavio Paz insisted that Mexico possessed a singular essence that set it apart from its European and Anglo peers. Vasconcelos theorized a "cosmic race" and the rejection of Darwinist ideologies that stratified race in 1929. He argued that Latin Americans epitomized the cosmic race in that their miscegenation gave them the best attributes of all races.[2] Ramos, however, wrote the seminal work on Mexicaness in his essay *El perfil del hombre y la cultura en México* (*Profile of Man and Culture in Mexico*) in 1938. Employing the inferiority complex theory of Alfred Adler,[3] Ramos postulated that Mexicans were failing because they were attempting to imitate or strive for artificial goals that could never be attained. Frustrated, they blamed the object of their failed imitations rather than themselves. As a result, he claimed that Mexicans lacked confidence, acted defensively and belligerently, mistrusted others, needed victims to feel superior to, and felt indifferent to those around him.[4] Octavio Paz echoed these sentiments a decade later, when he penned *El laberinto de la soledad* (*The Labyrinth of Solitude*) in 1949.[5] Paz almost single-handedly propagated the notion that the birth of the nation out of the violence of conquest formed the cavalier and indifferent Mexican archetype. Ramos wrote of Mexican indifference to others, yet Paz took it two steps further. He contended that Mexicans do not fear death because both life *and* death lack meaning to them.[6] These theorists have been criticized for essentializing Mexicans and arguing that the entire society suffers a collective case of post-traumatic stress disorder as a result of the Spanish conquest and the rape of the first mother, La Malinche, by a European conqueror. Paz likens the Mexican experience to being ensnared in a labyrinth of solitude. He suggests that the founding of the mestizo nation by violent conquest nurtured a national morbid melancholy. Roger Bartra prefers the metaphor of a cage of melancholy rather than a labyrinth of solitude. Bartra further states that devoting intellectual energies to delineating a Mexican essence is an intellectual exercise connected decidedly with modernity.[7]

Mexican physicians tackled diseases and perceived maladies related to social problems with a vengeance. Many embraced the theories of French specialists like Esquirol and Durkheim, but they also argued about the most efficacious approaches to understanding mental and physical disturbances in the body that could lead to criminality, insanity, and suicide. Although some late Porfirian medical specialists prescribed cold-water baths, purgatives, and physical restraint to cure mental disorders, others advocated for what they called moral treatments. These specialists believed that writing down life histories and having patients reflect on their own odysseys into psychological despair could yield valuable information to effect a cure. Although revolutionary intellectuals blamed Porfirians for imitating trends in Europe, physicians and medical students did not accept the latest theories and medical approaches from across the Atlantic without scrutiny. Brilliant minds populated the medical schools, asylums, and hospitals. These experts read medical studies, labored over determining the appropriate medical curriculum, collaborated with scientists from Europe and the United States, and dabbled in new sciences like sociology and psychology to understand the mental and physical well-being of society. They viewed society as a superorganism and strove to cure its sick parts. The impetus to understand suicide in Mexico began early.

Death imagery in the public sphere was never a uniquely Mexican phenomenon. Many nations, including the United States, attempted to sanitize public spaces and relegate reminders of death to the fringes of urban life; still, the morbid persisted in all aspects of life. Funeral processions, war, and bodies left breathless by vehicle accidents, violent crimes, and lynchings reminded urban residents of their own mortality. The same conditions confronted individuals in Mexico. Mexicans suffered and mourned death no less profoundly than their contemporaries in England and France. Claudio Lomnitz-Adler argues that death as metaphor in Mexican political discourse arises from the fact that "political control over dying, the dead, and the representation of the dead and the afterlife has been key to the formation of the modern state, images of popular culture, and a properly national modernity."[8] Could this not be argued for any modern state? Most secular states, the very ones Ramos criticized Mexico for emulating, underwent similar programs of controlling public spaces and rituals of death and dying. Rural cemetery movements pushed death outside the city. Anthony Giddens theorizes that modern nation-states have a monopoly on violence.[9] I would argue that nation-states have a monopoly on death as well. Lomnitz-Adler is most persuasive in showing how the Mexican state co-opted and expanded Day of the Dead celebrations for political and economic reasons, but this festivity does not equate to a unique death cult, as Paz and others have boldly asserted. Likewise, the engraver Posada may have papered Mexico City with images and verse foretelling the end of days and showcasing the latest murder or suicide, but have scholars given as much weight to penny dreadfuls in Victorian England and concluded that death defined that society?[10] This study of suicide on the cusp of the twentieth century suggests that Mexicans approached death like any world citizens, with an immense sense of concern, humanity, and sensitivity.

# NOTES

## INTRODUCTION

1. Susan Morrissey's formulation of power versus subjectivity is instructive here. See Morrissey, *Suicide and the Body Politic in Imperial Russia* (New York: Cambridge University Press, 2006). For an analysis of the construction of oneself in self-destruction, see Elisabeth Bronfen, *Over Her Dead Body: Death, Femininity and the Aesthetic* (New York: Routledge, 1992).

2. Marshall Berman, *All That Is Solid Melts into Air: The Experience of Modernity* (New York: Verso, 1982).

3. Ann S. Blum, *Domestic Economies: Family, Work, and Welfare in Mexico City, 1884–1943* (Lincoln: University of Nebraska Press, 2009), 179.

4. Rate of population increase is from Joanne Hershfield, *Imagining la Chica Moderna: Women, Nation, and Visual Culture* (Durham, NC: Duke University Press, 2008), 24. Total population of city in 1910 is from Robert M. Buffington, *A Sentimental Education for the Working Man: The Mexico City Penny Press, 1900–1910* (Durham, NC: Duke University Press, 2015), 7.

5. Pablo Piccato, "Urbanistas, Ambulantes, and Mendigos: The Dispute for Urban Space in Mexico City, 1890–30," in *Reconstructing Criminality in Latin America,* ed. Carlos A. Aguirre and Robert Buffington (Wilmington, DE: Rowman and Littlefield, 2000), 119.

6. Pablo Piccato, *The Tyranny of Opinion: Honor in the Construction of the Mexican Public Sphere* (Durham, NC: Duke University Press, 2009), 64–66, 81–82, 88–90.

7. Matthew D. Esposito, *Funerals, Festivals, and Cultural Politics in Porfirian Mexico* (Albuquerque: University of New Mexico Press, 2010); Claudio Lomnitz-Adler, *Death and the Idea of Mexico* (New York: Zone Books, 2005).

8. Lomnitz-Adler, *Death and the Idea of Mexico,* 377.

9. Ibid., 23–27.

10. Buffington, *Sentimental Education,* 11.

11. Ana M. López, "Early Cinema and Modernity in Latin America," *Cinema Journal* 40, no. 1 (Fall 2000): 49.

12. James Scott coined the phrase "civilizing missions" to mean internal colonization efforts on the part of a state. See James C. Scott, *Seeing Like a State: How Certain Schemes to Improve the Human Condition Have Failed* (New Haven, CT: Yale University Press, 1999).

13. Michael MacDonald and Terence R. Murphy, *Sleepless Souls: Suicide in Early Modern England* (New York: Oxford University Press, 1990).

14. What is less understood is the popular reaction to suicide. Incidences abound of communities desecrating the gravesites of suicides long into the early modern period. See Donna T. Andrew, "Debate: The Secularization of Suicide in England, 1660–1800," *Past and Present* 119 (1988): 158–165.

15. Alexander Murray, *Suicide in the Middle Ages,* vol. 2, *The Curse on Self-Murder* (New York: Oxford University Press, 2000), 398–405. Murray also found that medieval thinkers were less concerned with attempted suicides than with suicides. He argues that the immorality of the action was less important than the loss of the human life.

16. Zeb Tortorici, "Reading the (Dead) Body: Histories of Suicide in New Spain," in *Death and Dying in Colonial Spanish America,* ed. Martina Will de Chaparro and Miruna Achim (Tucson: University of Arizona Press, 2011), 58.

17. Louis A. Pérez, *To Die in Cuba: Suicide and Society* (Chapel Hill: University of North Carolina Press, 2005); Tortorici, "Reading the (Dead) Body," 53–77; Ignacio Maldonado y Morón, *Estudio del suicidio en México: Fundado en Datos Estadísticos* (Mexico City: Ignacio Escalante, 1876); Francisco Javier Beltrán Abarca, "El suicidio en México: Problema social, individuo y poder institucional (1830–1875)" (PhD diss., Universidad Nacional Autónoma de México, 2011); Jesús Moran, *Ligeras consideraciones sobre el suicidio* (Mexico City: Escuela Correccional, 1891); Paulo Drinot, "Madness, Neurasthenia, and 'Modernity': Medico-Legal and Popular Interpretations of Suicide in Early Twentieth-Century Lima," *Latin American Research Review* 39, no. 2 (June 2004): 89–113; Alberto del Castillo Troncoso, "Notas sobre la moral dominante a finales del siglo XIX en la Ciudad de México: Las mujeres suicidas como protagonistas de la nota roja," in *Modernidad, tradición y alteridad: La ciudad de México en el cambio de siglo (XIX-XX),* ed. Claudia Agostoni and Elisa Speckman (Mexico City: Universidad Nacional Autónoma de México, 2001), 319–338. More recently, an entire journal issue was devoted to the subject of suicide in Chile. See *Revista Historia y Justicia,* no. 5 (October 2015–April 2016), www.revista.historiayjusticia.org/edicion/numero-05.

18. Morrissey, *Suicide and the Body Politic;* David Silkenat, *Moments of Despair: Suicide, Divorce, and Debt in Civil War Era North Carolina* (Chapel Hill: University of North Carolina Press, 2011); Victor Bailey, *This Rash Act: Suicide across the Life Cycle in the Victorian City* (Stanford, CA: Stanford University Press, 1998); James Maxwell Anderson, *Daily Life during the Spanish Inquisition* (Westport, CT: Greenwood Publishing Group, 2002); Ty Geltmaker, *Tired of Living: Suicide in Italy from National Unification to World War I, 1860–1915* (New York: Peter Lang, 2002); Irina Paperno, *Suicide as a Cultural Institution in Dostoevsky's Russia* (Ithaca, NY: Cornell University Press, 1997); Pérez, *To Die in Cuba.*

19. Mary Kay Vaughan, "Modernizing Patriarchy: State Policies, Rural Households, and Women in Mexico, 1930–40," in *Hidden Histories of Gender and the State in Latin America,* ed. Elizabeth Dore and Maxine Molyneaux (Durham, NC: Duke University Press, 2000), 194–214. Ageeth Sluis argues that the 1920s and '30s were a small window when post-revolutionary women had greater access to public and political roles. See Ageeth Sluis, *Deco Body, Deco City: Female Spectacle and Modernity in Mexico City, 1900–1939* (Lincoln: University of Nebraska Press, 2015), 14–15.

20. Howard I. Kushner, "Suicide, Gender, and the Fear of Modernity," in *Histories of Suicide: International Perspectives on Self-Destruction in the Modern World,* ed. John Weaver and David Wright (Toronto: University of Toronto Press, 2009), 29.

21. Pérez, *To Die in Cuba,* 5.

22. Kristin Ruggiero, *Modernity in the Flesh: Medicine, Law, and Society in Turn-of-the-Century Argentina* (Stanford, CA: Stanford University Press, 2004), 158–160.

23. George Minois, *History of Suicide: Voluntary Death in Western Culture,* trans. Lydia G. Cochrane (Baltimore, MD: Johns Hopkins University Press, 1999).

24. Morrissey, *Suicide and the Body Politic.*

25. Ibid., 5–6.

26. Pamela Voekel, *Alone before God: The Religious Origins of Modernity in Mexico* (Durham, NC: Duke University Press, 2002).

27. In Mexico and elsewhere, it could be argued that a cultural logic existed to explain female suicide. Killing oneself to cover shame or deception in love was understandable. In fact, when a young, single woman killed herself, it was assumed she had been deceived. Gayatri Spivak analyzes the cultural logic of *sati* (the immolation of widows) in Indian culture. See Gayatri Spivak, "Can the Subaltern Speak?" in *Colonial Discourse and Post-Colonial Theory: A Reader* ed. Patrick Williams and Laura Chrisman (New York: Columbia University Press, 1994), 66–111.

## ONE. A SOCIAL HISTORY OF SUICIDE IN MEXICO CITY, 1900–1930

1. Dirección General de la Estadística, "Estadística General de la República Mexicana," *Periódico Oficial,* no. 5 (Mexico City: Secretaría de Fomento, 1890), iii.

2. Mauricio Tenorio-Trillo, *Mexico at the World's Fairs: Crafting a Modern Nation* (Berkeley: University of California Press, 1996), 128–130.

3. Dirección General de la Estadística, *Boletín demográfico de la República Mexicana,* no. 2 (Mexico City: Secretaría de Fomento 1898), 7–9.

4. Francisco Barrera Lavalle, *Apuntes para la historia de la estadística en México, 1821 a 1910* (Mexico City: Tip. de la vda. de F. Díaz de León, sucs., 1911).

5. Barrera Lavalle, "Historia de la estadística," 20–21.

6. For 1900 statistic, see Claudia Agostoni, *Monuments of Progress: Modernization and Public Health in Mexico City, 1876–1910* (Boulder: University Press of Colorado, 2003), 26; for 1910, see Paul Garner, *Porfirio Díaz: Profiles in Power*

(New York: Routledge, 2001), 174; and for 1930, see Francisco Alba, *The Population of Mexico: Trends, Issues, and Policies,* trans. Marjory Mattingly Urquidi (New Brunswick, NJ: Transaction Books, 1982), 37.

7. Agostoni, *Monuments of Progress,* 26–29.

8. Charles Adams Hale, *The Transformation of Liberalism in Late Nineteenth Century Mexico* (New Haven, CT: Princeton University Press, 1989), 27.

9. Ibid., 29.

10. Ibid., 33.

11. Ibid.

12. Pablo Piccato, *City of Suspects: Crime in Mexico City, 1900–1931* (Durham, NC: Duke University Press, 2001), 221.

13. Kenneth Martin Pinnow, *Lost to the Collective: Suicide and the Promise of Soviet Socialism, 1921–1929* (Ithaca, NY: Cornell University Press, 2010), 143.

14. Jack D. Douglas, *Social Meanings of Suicide* (Princeton, NJ: Princeton University Press, 1967), 172.

15. Lambert Adolphe Quetelet and Enrico Morselli agreed on the regularity of suicides and denied the role of individual agency in the act. See Paperno, *Suicide as a Cultural Institution,* 23.

16. Douglas, *Social Meanings of Suicide,* 9.

17. Morrissey, *Suicide and the Body Politic,* 181.

18. Agostoni, *Monuments of Progress,* 29–30.

19. Laura Cházaro, "Reproducción y muerte de la población mexicana: Cálculos estadísticos y preceptos higiénicos a fines del siglo diecinueve," in *De normas y transgresiones: Enfermedad y crimen en América Latina (1850–1950),* ed. Claudia Agostoni and Elisa Speckman (Mexico City: Universidad Nacional Autónoma de México, 2005), 57.

20. Douglas, *Social Meanings of Suicide,* 8.

21. Henry Morselli, *Suicide: An Essay on Comparative Moral Statistics* (New York: Appleton Press, 1882), 367.

22. F. S. Bridges, P. S. Yip, and K. C. Yang, "Seasonal Changes in Suicide in the United States, 1971 to 2000," *Perceptual and Motor Skills* 100, no. 3 (June 2005): 920–924.

23. George Howe Colt, *November of the Soul: The Enigma of Suicide* (New York: Scribner, 2006), 183–184. Morselli also posited that male suicide rates in Italy correlated with height because he observed that the number of suicides increased from south, where men were on average shorter, to north, where men were on average taller.

24. Brian Palmer, "The Season of Renewal and Suicide," *Slate,* December 7, 2012, www.slate.com/articles/news_and_politics/explainer/2012/12/suicide_rate_season_there_more_suicides_in_spring_and_not_during_the_holidays.html. The medical articles cited in Palmer's article include E. Petridou, F. C. Papadopoulos, C. E. Frangakis, A. Skalkidou, and D. Trichopoulos "A Role of Sunshine in the Triggering of Suicide," *Epidemiology* 13, no. 1 (January 2002): 106–109; and K. S. Chew and R. McCleary, "The Spring Peak in Suicides: A Cross-National Analysis," *Social Science Medicine* 40, no. 2 (January 1995): 223–230.

25. María Luisa Rodríguez Sala de Gómezgil, "Suicidios y suicidas en la sociedad Mexicana" (Mexico City: Universidad Nacional Autónoma de México, Instituto de Investigaciones Sociales, 1974), 75.

26. Lombroso believed that meteorological and climatic conditions combined with additional factors led to crime and rebellion. He noted that more crimes occurred in the southern regions of Italy and France than in the northern parts. See Cesare Lombroso, *Crime, Its Causes and Remedies* (Boston: Little, Brown, 1911), 13.

27. Julio Guerrero, *La génesis del crimen en México: Estudio de psiquiatría social* (Mexico City: Vda de C. Bouret, 1901), 98.

28. Luis Fuentes Aguilar and Consuelo Soto Mora, "Influencia de los frentes meteorológicos en la incidencia de suicidios en México," *Anuario de geografía* 17 (1977): 225.

29. Alfonso Quiroz Cuarón, *Tendencia y ritmo de la criminalidad en México* (Mexico City: Instituto de Investigaciones Estadísticas, 1939), 94–96.

30. Mariano Ruiz-Funes García, *Endocrinología y criminalidad* (Madrid: Javier Morata, 1929), 152.

31. Rodríguez Sala de Gómezgil, "Suicidios y suicidas," 71.

32. Howard I. Kushner, *American Suicide* (New Brunswick, NJ: Rutgers University Press), 111. Miller published two sermons on the topic of youth suicides in the early nineteenth century. A century earlier, Puritan minister Cotton Mather had sounded the alarm about suicides by adolescents and blamed them on bad parenting.

33. William Bowman, "Despair unto Death? Attempted Suicide in Early 1930s Vienna," *Austrian History Yearbook* 39 (2008): 144.

34. Pérez, *To Die in Cuba,* 138.

35. "Aristocratic revolver" was mentioned in "Teórica del mal, las novelas," *El Amigo de la Verdad,* August 17, 1895, p. 2.

36. "Averiguación del suicidio de Olivia Rosenthal," caja 1575, exp. 282011, December 4, 1919, Tribunal Superior de Justicia de Distrito Federal, Archivo General de la Nación, Mexico City (hereafter cited as TSJDF).

37. "Averiguación del suicidio de Elvira Quintanar," caja 1791, exp. 322756, December 28, 1923, TSJDF.

38. Deborah Blum, *The Poisoner's Handbook: Murder and the Birth of Forensic Medicine in Jazz Age New York* (New York: Penguin, 2011), 2.

39. John Parascandola, *King of Poisons: A History of Arsenic* (Washington, DC: Potomac Books, 2012), 162–164.

40. Ibid., 156.

41. "Suicidio de María Dolores Priego," caja 492, exp. 87541, November 30, 1906, TSJDF.

42. Deborah Blum, *Poisoner's Handbook,* 96.

43. Ibid., 105.

44. "Pseudosuicidio de González Castro, Santa," caja 2310, exp. 424631, September 7, 1929, TSJDF.

45. "Suicidio frustrado de Flores, Carmen," caja 1253, exp. 218716, November 28, 1914, TSJDF. A death notice is included in the file.

46. Martin I. Wilbert, "The Sale of Bichloride Tablets," *Public Health Reports* 28, no. 46 (November 14, 1913): 2399–2405.

47. Deborah Blum, *Poisoner's Handbook,* 57.

48. Ibid.

49. "Denuncia de hechos pos las lesiones e intento de suicidio de Díaz, Carmen," caja 1936, exp. 350863, March 28, 1925, TSJDF.

50. "Suicidio de Alfonso D. Vallejo," caja 1469, exp. 260465, October 18, 1918, TSJDF.

51. "Suicidio frustrado de Carlota Alatorre," caja 1290, exp. 230015, October 20, 1914, TSJDF.

52. "Averiguación del suicidio de Berlín, Luz María," caja 2107, exp. 384411, April 4, 1927, TSJDF.

53. United States Congress House Committee on Ways and Means, *White Phosphorus Matches: Hearings before the Committee on Ways and Means of the House of Representatives, Sixty-Second Congress, Second Session on H.R. 2896, January 10, 1912* (Washington, DC: U.S. Government Printing Office, 1912).

54. "Suicidio frustrado de María Concepción Avendaño," caja 1107, exp. 196167, July 19, 1911, TSJDF.

55. Mid-nineteenth-century commentators explained the differing rates of suicide among men and women by the divergence in motivations. Women committed suicide because they had loss honor. However, their protection in home and marriage guarded them from opportunities or situations where they could lose honor. Therefore, the conclusion was that men killed themselves at greater rates because they had greater social roles and larger responsibilities. It was thought that financial hardship or physical illness propelled men to commit suicide. See Kushner, *American Suicide*, 97–101.

56. "Suicidio de José Díaz," caja 1055, exp. 175785, March 25, 1911, TSJDF.

57. Timothy J. Henderson, *The Worm in the Wheat: Rosalie Evans and the Agrarian Struggle in Puebla-Tlaxcala Valley of Mexico, 1906–1927* (Durham, NC: Duke University Press, 1998), 46.

58. Steven B. Bunker and Victor M. Macías-González, "Consumption and Material Culture in the Twentieth Century," in *A Companion to Mexican History and Culture,* ed. William H. Beezley (Malden, MA: Wiley-Blackwell Publishing, 2011), 88–89.

TWO. FROM CORPSE TO CADAVER

1. Modernity as defined by sociologist Anthony Giddens seems the most appropriate term to describe this era in Mexican history. According to Giddens, modernity connotes a society characterized by an ideology that views the world as open to change through human action, an economy oriented to industrial production and a free market, and political institutions formed to provide some semblance of democracy. See Anthony Giddens and Christopher Pierson, *Conversations with Anthony*

*Giddens: Making Sense of Modernity* (Stanford, CA: Stanford University Press, 1998), 94.

2. Chris Shilling, *The Body and Social Theory* (Los Angeles: Sage, 2012), 191–192; Anthony Giddens, *Modernity and Self-Identity: Self and Society in the Late Modern Age* (Cambridge, UK: Polity Press in association with Basil Blackwell, 1991).

3. Giddens, *Modernity and Self-Identity.*

4. Michel Foucault, *The Birth of the Clinic: An Archaeology of Medical Perception,* trans. A. M. Sheridan (New York: Routledge, 2012).

5. Elizabeth Hallam, Jenny Hockey, and Glennys Howarth, *Beyond the Body: Death and Social Identity* (New York: Routledge, 2005), 8.

6. Philippe Ariès, *The Hour of Our Death,* trans. Helen Weaver (New York: Knopf Doubleday, 2013).

7. Bronfen, *Over Her Dead Body.*

8. Margaret Higonnet, "Speaking Silences: Women's Suicide," in *The Female Body in Western Culture: Contemporary Perspectives,* ed. Susan Rubin Suleiman (Cambridge, MA: Harvard University Press, 1986), 69.

9. Gabino Barreda, "Algunas consideraciones sobre el suicidio," *La Escuela de Medicina,* no. 14 (January 15, 1883): 114.

10. Jean Franco, *Plotting Women: Gender and Representation in Mexico* (New York: Columbia University Press, 1989), 96. For an excellent analysis of the murder trial and Gamboa's contemplation of the corpse of Esperanza Gutiérrez, see Robert Buffington and Pablo Piccato, "Tales of Two Women: The Narrative Construal of Porfirian Reality," *Americas* 55, no. 3 (January 1999): 391–424.

11. Franco, *Plotting Women,* 97.

12. Bronfen, *Over Her Dead Body,* x–xi.

13. Ibid., 142–143.

14. Pérez, *To Die in Cuba.* Pérez makes a compelling case for Cuban society's acceptance of suicide, as well as for the political nature of suicide in Cuba.

15. Mario Alva-Rodríguez and Rolando Neri-Vela, "The Practice of Forensic Science in Mexico," in *The Global Practice of Forensic Science,* ed. Douglas H. Ubelaker (Hoboken, NJ: John Wiley and Sons, 2015), 201–202.

16. Ibid., 202–203.

17. Ibid., 204–205. Some of the subjects of these theses are the use of the microscope in forensic investigations, identifying persons, determining whether wounds were caused pre- or post-mortem, the criminal responsibility of epileptics, and the management of corpses.

18. Ibid., 205.

19. *Código Penal para el Distrito Federal y Territorio de la Baja California sobre delitos del fuero común y para toda la República sobre delitos contra la Federación* (Mexico City: Imprenta de Flores y Monsalve, 1874). The code went into effect in 1871.

20. Luis Hidalgo y Carpio and Gustavo Ruiz y Sandoval, *Compendio de medicina legal: Arreglado a la legislación del Distrito Federal* (Mexico City: Imprenta de Ignacio Escalante, 1877), 634–638.

21. Alfonso Quiroz Cuarón, *Medicina Forense* (Mexico City: Editorial Porrúa, 1977), 384.

22. Hidalgo y Carpio and Ruiz y Sandoval, *Compendio de medicina legal,* 645–650.

23. Ibid., 634–638.

24. Jonathan Michael Weber, "Hustling the Old Mexico Aside: Creating a Modern Mexico City through Medicine, Public Health, and Technology in the Porfiriato, 1887–1913" (PhD diss., Florida State University, 2013), 88.

25. Hidalgo y Carpio and Ruiz y Sandoval, *Compendio de medicina legal,* 612–613.

26. Ibid., 613–622.

27. Ibid., 90–93.

28. Ibid., 93–104.

29. Ibid., 105.

30. Ibid., 106–109.

31. Ibid., 111–116.

32. Foucault, *Birth of the Clinic.*

33. "El 'chic' en el suicidio," *El Imparcial,* February 24, 1898.

34. Ibid.

35. Sonya Lipsett-Rivera, *Gender and the Negotiation of Daily Life in Mexico, 1750–1856* (Lincoln: University of Nebraska Press, 2012), 138.

36. "Se causaron la muerte por no resistir el deseo de lujo," *El Diario,* November 7, 1909, p. 1; "Eranse dos vidas, que un día descubrieron su drama," *El Imparcial,* November 8, 1909, p. 2. See chapter 5 for a fuller discussion of this public suicide drama.

37. French journalists also reported tailor's tags from the clothes worn by murder victims in Paris in 1869. See Gregory K. Shaya, "Mayhem of Moderns: The Culture of Sensationalism in France, c. 1900" (PhD diss., University of Michigan, 2000), 130.

38. "Suicidio en el bosque de Chapultepec," *El Demócrata,* March 3, 1916, pp. 1, 6, 8.

39. "Suicidio de una señorita," *El Univeral,* September 4, 1930, pp. 1, 6.

40. "Suicidio en el bosque de Chapultepec," *El Demócrata,* March 3, 1916, p. 1.

41. Ibid., p. 6.

42. Ibid., p. 8.

43. "Suicidio en el bosque de Chapultepec," *El Demócrata.*

44. "Un sangriento drama entre gentes de nuestro pueblo," *Excélsior,* March 3, 1919, p. 1.

45. Ibid.

46. Ibid.

47. Ibid., p. 5.

48. Ibid., pp. 1, 5.

49. "El drama conyugal de la Calle de Rosas Moreno se hace cada día más misterioso," *El Demócrata,* November 13, 1920, p. 1.

50. "El cadaver encontrado en el fondo de una zanja," *El Universal,* September 20, 1930, sec. 2, p. 1.

51. Ibid.

52. Edgar Allan Poe quotation from "The Philosophy of Composition," quoted in Bronfen, *Over Her Dead Body,* 59.

53. Bronfen, *Over Her Dead Body,* 69.

54. José Guadalupe Posada, *Corrido dedicado al 16 de Septiembre de 1897* (Mexico City: Vanegas Arroyo, 1897) depicts the deceased Velázquez on an operating table, surrounded by military men and others dressed in suits and top hats. The cover page shows sketches of four men involved in the conspiracy that led to the inspector's death: Velázquez, the murdered Arnulfo Arroyo, Miguel Cabrera, and Antonio Villavicencio.

55. James Alex Garza, *The Imagined Underworld: Sex, Crime, and Vice in Porfirian Mexico City* (Lincoln: University of Nebraska Press, 2008), 163–171. Garza suggests that many believed that the ex-inspector was actually murdered in his cell.

56. Etching of double suicide, *Ilustración Popular,* April 30, 1911, p. 1.

57. Shaya, "Mayhem of Moderns," 274.

58. Elizabeth Hallam, Jenny Hockey, and Glennys Howarth, *Beyond the Body: Death and Social Identity* (New York: Routledge, 2005), 90.

59. Patrick Frank, *Posada's Broadsheets: Mexican Popular Imagery 1890–1910* (Albuquerque: University of New Mexico Press, 1998), 153.

60. See, for example, Epigmenio Velasco, "Inconsequencias de la prensa de información: El suicidio de la Srita. Noecker," *El Abogado Cristiano,* December 16, 1909, p. 4; and "El 'rapto' Gaona-Noecker: Consideraciones legales," *La Iberia,* 17 December, 1909, p. 1.

61. Castillo Troncoso, "Notas sobre la moral dominante," 332.

62. A *coleta* is the ponytail worn by a matador. *Mafia de coleta* means the "mafia of the bullring," which includes matadors, promoters, managers, etc.

63. José Guadalupe Posada, *Sufrimientos, reflexiones y consejos de la suicida de María Luisa Noeker: En la otra vida,* (Mexico City: A. Vanegas Arroyo, 1909).

64. "Gaona Fails and Weeps in Ring," *Mexican Herald,* January 17, 1910, p. 1.

65. "Noecker Asks Court for Time Extension," *Mexican Herald,* January 28, 1910, p. 4.

66. "Gaona sale para Europa el miercoles," *El Diario,* 4 March, 1910, p. 1.

67. "Rapto y suicidio de María Luisa Nocker," caja 0912, exp. 159578, December 5, 1909, TSJDF.

68. Frank, *Posada's Broadsheets,* 165. When a rival drunk bullfighter boarded a train in Toluca and verbally dishonored Gaona's reputation, the "Gaonista" conductor shut the man up with punches to the face, and when they pulled into Mexico City, the inebriated man was taken to the police station. See "El Diestro 'Corrillo' es aporreado." *La Democracia* (Toluca), January 2, 1910, p. 3.

69. Phyllis Lynn Smith, "Contentious Voices amid the Order: The Porfirian Press in Mexico City, 1876–1911" (PhD diss., University of Arizona, 1996), 53–54.

70. Robert M. Buffington, *Criminal and Citizen in Modern Mexico* (Lincoln, NE: University of Nebraska Press, 2000), 33.

71. "Numerosos crímenes se cometieron el sábado," *Excélsior,* February 24, 1919, pp. 1, 7.

72. Jonathan Michael Weber, "Hustling the Old Mexico Aside: Creating a Modern Mexico City through Medicine, Public Health, and Technology in the Porfiriato, 1887–1913" (PhD diss., Florida State University, 2013), 170–171.

73. *Reglamento de Hospital Juárez de la Ciudad de México: Diario Oficial,* 78, no. 42 (June 17, 1905): 935. The 1905 regulation also set out the hospital's mission to cooperate in the education of students at the Escuela Nacional de Medicina.

74. "En el Hospital Juárez se hace negocio con los cadáveres?" *Universal Gráfico,* July 23, 1929, p. 1.

75. "Monstruosa plaga de ratas en el Juárez," *El Univeral,* June 25, 1930, sec. 2, p. 1.

76. "Autorización para que varios practicantes hagan dissecciones al cadáveres no reclamados," legajo 44, exp. 2, September 6, 1920, Manicomio General, Beneficencia Pública, Establecimientos Hospitalarios, Mexico City (hereafter cited as BP, EH).

77. "Relativo a la Junta Médica Citada por el Director, y donde concurrieron los Dres. Rosendo Amor, Diodoro Espinoza y Ernesto Urlich, para tratar sobre la mejor distribución y tramitación de los cadáveres del Establecimiento," legajo 22, exp. 31, April 5, 1919, Hospital General, BP, EH.

78. "Petición por depósito de cadáveres," legajo 15, exp. 16, August 2, 1929, Hospital Juárez, BP, EH.

79. Amanda M. López, "The Cadaverous City: The Everyday Life of the Dead in Mexico City, 1875–1930" (PhD diss., University of Arizona, 2010), 48. This dissertation also includes an excellent discussion of the relationship between class and space in the cemetery.

80. Phillipe Ariès, *Images of Man and Death,* trans. Janet Lloyd (Cambridge, MA: Harvard University Press, 1985), 238.

81. Amanda M. López, "Cadaverous City," 34.

82. Lomnitz-Adler, *Death and the Idea of Mexico,* 265. See also Esposito, *Funerals, Festivals, and Cultural Politics,* 45–46.

83. Voekel, *Alone before God.*

84. Amanda M. López, "Cadaverous City," 48–49.

85. Thomas W. Laqueur, "Cemeteries, Religion and the Culture of Capitalism," in *Revival and Religion since 1700: Essays for John Walsh,* ed. Jane Garnett and Colin Matthew (London: Hambledon Press, 1993), 184–186.

86. Ibid.

87. Amanda M. López, "Cadaverous City," 41.

88. Ibid., 52–53.

89. Mary Ashley Townsend, *Here and There in Mexico: The Travel Writings of Mary Ashley Townsend,* ed. Ralph Lee Woodard Jr. (Tuscaloosa: University of Alabama Press, 2001), 215.

90. Amanda M. López, "Cadaverous City," 69–70.

91. Weber, "Hustling the Old Mexico Aside," 53–57.

92. Ibid., 58–59.

93. Ibid., 82.

94. Lyman L. Johnson, ed., *Death, Dismemberment, and Memory: Body Politics in Latin America* (Albuquerque: University of New Mexico Press, 2004).

95. Will Fowler, *Santa Anna of Mexico* (Lincoln: University of Nebraska Press, 2007), 224.

96. Alan Knight, "The Several Legs of Santa Anna: A Saga of Secular Relics," in *Relics and Remains*, ed. Alexandra Walsham (New York: Oxford University Press, 2010), 227–255.

97. Samuel Brunk, "The Mortal Remains of Emiliano Zapata," in *Death, Dismemberment, and Memory: Body Politics in Latin America,* ed. Lyman L. Johnson (Albuquerque: University of New Mexico Press, 2004), 141–178.

98. Manuel Acuña wrote the poem "Canto a Rosario." Years later, Ildefonso Estrada y Zenéa wrote *Las Víctimas del Amor: Análisis del Canto de Manuel Acuña a Rosario* (Mexico City: Imprenta de Ildefonso Estrada y Zenéa, 1906) and read aloud his analysis of Acuña's canto in the Mexican Arcade. The author was also one of Acuña's pallbearers.

99. "Los Funerales de Manuel Acuña," *El Eco de Ambos Mundos,* December 12, 1873.

100. Ibid.

101. "La Exhumación de los Restos de M. Acuña," *Excélsior,* October 29, 1917, pp. 1, 7.

THREE. MEDIA, MORAL PANIC, AND YOUTH SUICIDE

1. "Averiguación del suicidio de Beatriz Norman," caja 2106, exp. 384232, July 4, 1927, TSJDF.

2. Susan Morrissey uses the phrase "arbiters of the self" as the title of one of the chapters of her book *Suicide and the Body Politic in Imperial Russia.* She analyzes suicide notes in imperial Russia and argues that the suicides penned notes to explain their reasons for killing themselves or to condemn their foes and thereby shape the public discussion that followed in newspapers or the familial processing of grief in the aftermath of the death. See Morrissey, *Suicide and the Body Politic,* 149–173.

3. See Pablo Piccato, *The Tyranny of Opinion: Honor in the Construction of the Mexican Public Sphere* (Durham, NC: Duke University Press, 2010) for a discussion of pre-Porfirian journalism as key to the construction of Mexican public culture.

4. John C. Weaver, *A Sadly Troubled History: The Meanings of Suicide in the Modern Age* (Montreal: McGill-Queen's Press, 2009), 22.

5. Beltrán Abarca, "El Suicidio en México," 81–82.

6. Morrissey, *Suicide and the Body Politic,* 5–6.

7. Laureana Wright de Kleinhans, "El Suicidio," pt. 1, *Violetas del Anáhuac,* December 2, 1888, p. 583.

8. Ibid., p. 584.

9. Laureana Wright de Kleinhans, "El Suicidio," pt. 2, *Violetas del Anáhuac,* December 9, 1888, p. 596.

10. Ibid., pp. 596–597.

11. Cristina Devereaux Ramírez, *Occupying Our Space: The Mestiza Rhetorics of Mexican Women Journalists and Activists, 1875–1942* (Tucson: University of Arizona Press, 2015), 74–75.

12. Lucía G. Herrera J., "El suicidio," *Las Hijas de Anáhuac,* January 22, 1888, p. 95. The author byline noted that the poem was written in 1880.

13. Shaya, "Mayhem of Moderns," 3.

14. Ibid., 256. Shaya's study centers on Paris, France, during the late nineteenth century. There are strong parallels between French and Mexican sensationalism and the reading public in those countries. Robert Buffington argues that the penny and workers' press in early twentieth-century Mexico City fostered a popular liberalism and class consciousness among laborers. More significantly, however, he points out that penny press editors gained access to the public sphere of ideas and discourse to assert citizenship rights for workers. See Buffington, *Sentimental Education,* 14–15.

15. "La epidemia negra: Suicidios y suicidas," *El Imparcial,* March 23, 1898, p. 1.

16. Ramón L. Alva, "Boletín del 'Monitor,'" *El Monitor Republicano,* July 4, 1895, p. 1.

17. Brothers Ramón L. Alva and Luis Alva edited *El Monitor Republicano* until it ceased publication in 1896. Loyal to the liberal constitution of 1857, the Alvas constantly criticized científicos like Justo Sierra and the style of Porfirian liberalism that did not heed the no-reelection stipulations of the constitution. For a fuller discussion of the conflict between the Alvas and Porfirian liberalism, see Charles A. Hale, *The Transformation of Liberalism in Late Nineteenth-Century Mexico* (Princeton, NJ: Princeton University Press, 1989), 114–115.

18. "El suicidio: Medios de combatirlo en la prensa," *El Imparcial,* June 16, 1899, p. 1.

19. "Los progresos del suicidio en México," *El Nacional,* July 11, 1900, p. 1.

20. Luis Lara y Pardo, *La prostitución en México* (Mexico City: Librería de Ch. Bouret, 1908); Julio Guerrero, *La génesis del crimen en México: Estudio de psiquiatría social* (Mexico City: Viuda de C. Bouret, 1901); Carlos Roumagnac, *La estadística criminal en México* (Mexico City: Imp. de Arturo García Cubas Sucesores Hermanos, 1907); Roumagnac, *Los Criminales en México: Ensayo de Psicología Criminal* (Mexico City: Tipografía "El Fenix," 1904).

21. "Homicidios y suicidios," *La Convención Radical Obrera,* March 14, 1897, p. 1.

22. M. B. Carillo, "El suicidio y la embriaguez," *El Hijo del Trabajo,* April 24, 1881, p. 2.

23. "Cancer Social," *La Caridad,* June 27, 1890, p. 1.

24. Ibid.

25. "Los órganos del liberalismo," *La Caridad,* July 10, 1890, p. 1.

26. "La inmoralidad," *La Caridad,* September 12, 1890, p. 1.

27. Silvio [pseud.], "El Suicidio," *El Hijo del Trabajo,* April 11, 1880, p. 2.

28. "Condenación del suicidio," *El Diario,* October 25, 1906, p. 1.

29. "El suicidio: Plaga de modo," *El Popular,* January 2, 1897, p. 1. Hydrotherapy was a common method utilized in asylums to treat any number of mental illnesses.

30. "El suicidio," *El Nacional,* June 21, 1897, p. 1.

31. "Los suicidios de ayer," *El País,* July 11, 1900, p. 1.

32. "Suicidio, regicidio y barbarie," *El País,* August 4, 1900, p. 1.

33. "Tres suicidios en un día," *El País,* August 23, 1900, p. 1.

34. "El filosofismo moderno en política," *El País,* October 4, 1900, p. 1.

35. "Los que avanzamos y lo que retrocedemos," *El País,* November 4, 1900, p. 1.

36. Frank, *Posada's Broadsheets,* 175–176.

37. The tower of the cathedral that Silva refers to was known as the Tower of Suicides. See chapter 5 for further discussion.

38. "Ahorcado ante el altar: Suicidio típico y sensacional," *El Imparcial,* May 29, 1906, pp. 1, 5.

39. "La última nota, triste canción," illustrated by José Guadalupe Posada, undated, Swann Collection, Library of Congress, Washington, DC.

40. José Guadalupe Posasa, *Cogida de Rodolfo Gaona en la plaza de toros de Puebla, el 13 de Diciembre de 1908* (Mexico City: Antonio Vanegas Arroyo, 1908–09).

41. Frank, *Posada's Broadsheets,* 158–159. See also Kathryn A. Sloan, *Runaway Daughters: Seduction, Elopement, and Honor in Modern Mexico* (Albuquerque: University of New Mexico Press), 77–78.

42. "El suicidio y la fe religiosa," *El Imparcial,* September 4, 1905, p. 1.

43. "Qué Bárbaro!" *El País,* September 5, 1905, p. 1. Founded in 1868 by Gabino Barreda and José Díaz Covarrubias, the Escuela Nacional Preparatoria prepared future political leaders and inculcated the ideals and values of positivism through its curriculum. For more information about the institution, see Piccato, *Tyranny of Opinion,* 135; and Hale, *Transformation of Liberalism,* 154–155. The school and some of its more reported suicides are discussed in chapter 3.

44. "Qué Bárbaro!" *El País.*

45. "Pecadores y creyentes: Todavía el suicidio y la fe religiosa," *El Imparcial,* September 7, 1905, p. 1.

46. "Es falso lo dicho por 'El Imparcial,'" *El País,* September 9, 1905, p. 1.

47. "El suicidio," *La Ciudad de Dios,* April 13, 1902, p. 8.

48. "Suicidio de un sacristán: Relaciones entre el ateísmo y el suicidio," *El Imparcial,* June 1, 1906, p. 1.

49. "Otro Fanático Suicida: El suicidio y la fe," *El Imparcial,* June 15, 1906, p. 1.

50. "Teórica del mal, las novelas," *El Amigo de la Verdad,* August 17, 1895, p. 2.

51. "Un pernicioso contagio en la moral social: La venta de libros obscenos," *El Imparcial,* October 20, 1900, p. 1.

52. Agustín Aragón, "Influencia social y moral de la lectura de novelas en la juventud," *Revista Positiva* 3 (1903): 263.

53. Ibid., 270.

54. "Contribución a la estadística del suicidio en la republicana mexicana," *La Escuela de Medicina* 7, no. 6 (November 15, 1885): 78.

55. Luis G. Urbina quoted and paraphrased in "Condenación del suicidio," *El Diario,* October 25, 1906, p. 1.

56. "Condenación del suicidio," *El Diario.*

57. Luis G. Urbina, "¡El pueblo se mata!" *El Imparcial,* October 23, 1906, p. 1.

58. Ibid.

59. Kessel Schwartz, "The Theme of Suicide in Representative Spanish American Novels," *Hispania* 58, no. 3 (September 1975): 446.

60. *Las olas altas* was the first of four novelettes that made up one story. The other installments, also published in *El Mundo,* were *La baja marea, El vendedor de periódicos,* and *Las olas muertes* (1899). Cynthia K. Duncan, "Juan Mateos (1831–1913)," in *Dictionary of Mexican Literature,* ed. Eladio Cortés (Westport, CT: Greenwood Press, 1992), 411–413; María Teresa Solórzano Ponce, "Juan Antonio Mateos (1831–1913)," *La República de las letras: Asomos a la cultura escrita del México decimonónico,* vol. 3, *Galería de escritores,* ed. Belem Clark de Lara and Elisa Speckman Guerra (Mexico City: Universidad Nacional Autónoma de México, 2005), 337.

61. Solórzano Ponce, "Juan Antonio Mateos," 337.

62. *Camarista* was a double entendre. It could mean maid of the bedchamber (male in this case) or a member of the congress, the Cámara de Diputados.

63. "Una novela inmunda é infecciosa," *La Patria,* May 26, 1899, p. 1.

64. "Una novela inmoral," *El Universal,* June 1, 1899, p. 2.

65. Buffington, *Sentimental Education,* 8.

66. For a discussion of working-class reading choices, see ibid.

67. "Se suicidó apurando una fuerte dosis de cianuro de mercurio: El mal de Werther," *El Demócrata,* August 24, 1920, p. 1.

68. Francisco Montes de Oca directed two other liberal penny press papers, *Gil Blas* and *El Popular.* In 1897, he accused Rafael Reyes Spíndola of receiving government subsidies for *El Imparcial.* They faced each other in a duel that same year. Neither was killed. Mexican law prohibited dueling, but the elite classes condoned it, and journalists in the 1800s routinely challenged each other to spar on the "field of honor." See Piccato, *Tyranny of Opinion,* 245–251.

69. "Los suicidios y las muertes misteriosas: La influencia de la inmoralidad," *La Gran Sedería,* July 22, 1897, p. 1. Despotism in the government and in families was believed to be a common motivation for suicide in imperial Russia. See Morrissey, *Suicide and the Body Politic in Imperial Russia,* 242–256.

70. "Una doliente resolvió así arrancarse la existencia," *El Universal,* April 3, 1930, sec. 2, p. 1. José Vargas Vila possessed deeply anti-U.S. sentiments and radical liberal views. Steeped in the *modernismo* movement, Vargas Vila's novels titillated and offended readers. He presented scandalous scenarios and taboo sexual practices that resulted in his being excommunicated and his books being banned by schools and bookshops. See Raymond Leslie Williams, *The Colombian Novel, 1844–1987* (Austin: University of Texas Press, 1991), 39.

71. Schwartz, "Theme of Suicide," 446.

72. Jorge Isaacs wrote just one novel, *María,* which was reputed to be the most popular nineteenth-century Latin American novel. The book tackled such themes as impossible love, María's Jewish ancestry, and a crumbling aristocracy, and Isaacs wrote in the purely Romantic style of his era. See Doris Sommer, *Foundational*

*Fictions: The National Romances of Latin America* (Berkeley: University of California Press, 1991), 78, 188–189.

73. "Una doliente resolvió así arrancarse la existencia," *El Universal,* April 3, 1930, sec. 2, p. 1.

74. "El suicidio por miseria: No tiene razón de ser en México," *El Imparcial,* October 16, 1901, p. 1.

75. "El suicida de ayer," *El Imparcial,* August 29, 1902, p. 1.

76. "Se causaron la muerte por no resistir el deseo de lujo," *El Diario,* November 7, 1909, p. 1.

77. A secret suicide club in Bridgeport, Connecticut, was one such group that newspapers covered over the years. For other examples, see "Suicide Clubs," *Deseret Weekly* 45 (1892): 552.

78. "Los modas parisienses: Suicidio de cuatro mujeres," *El Imparcial,* July 27, 1897, p. 2; "Los dramas de París: Suicidio de cuatro mujeres," *El Imparcial,* August 5, 1897, p. 1. In her study of suicide in Edwardian and Victorian London, Olive Anderson found that the suicides of children and hardworking seamstresses merited great sympathy in English society. See Olive Anderson, *Suicide in Victorian and Edwardian England* (New York: Oxford University Press, 1987).

79. "Los dramas de París: Suicidio de cuatro mujeres," *El Imparcial,* August 5, 1897, p. 1.

80. "Suicide Increasing," *Mexican Herald,* November 27, 1909, p. 1.

81. "La tragedia de ayer en Hotel Viena," *El Imparcial,* April 14, 1899, p. 1.

82. "La tragedia en el Hotel Viena: Los suicidas," *El Universal,* April 15, 1899, p. 1.

83. "Dramático suicidio de dos mujeres," *El Imparcial,* April 20, 1911, pp. 1, 8.

84. Gonzalo de la Parra, "La Eterna Tragedia del Amor," *Ilustración Popular,* April 30, 1911, p. 1.

85. "Un suicidio a duo, es la última palabra de la locura trágica," *La Demócrata,* November 30, 1921, pp. 1, 2.

86. "Suicidio de dos rivales desdeñados por la amada," *El Universal,* May 22, 1930, pp. 1, 3.

87. "Empujados al suicidio por causas que se ignoran," *El Universal,* November 19, 1930, sec. 2, pp. 1, 8.

88. Morrissey, *Suicide and the Body Politic,* 149.

89. Bronfen, *Over Her Dead Body,* 65.

90. "Un suicidio que da mucho de que hablar: Una señorita que no revelaba pena alguna, se suicidó sin que dejara explicación de su proceder," *Excélsior,* November 7, 1917, pp. 1, 4.

91. "Casi un record de suicidios y no puede morir," *Excélsior,* January 9, 1930, p. 1.

92. "Suicidio de Micaela Balcazar," caja 1671, exp. 299596, December 26, 1921, TSJDF.

93. Ibid.

94. Paperno, *Suicide as a Cultural Institution,* 106.

95. "El Castigo a un burlador," *El Universal,* April 3, 1930, sec. 2, p. 1.

96. "Suicidio de una loca," *El Imparcial,* December 21, 1905, p. 1.

97. "Suicidio frustrado de Humberto Ubico," caja 1752, exp. 314843, March 1, 1922, TSJDF.

98. "Denuncio de hechos por las lesiones e intento de suicidio de Carmen Díaz," caja 1936, exp. 350863, March 28, 1925, TSJDF.

99. "Intento de suicidio (Alberto Brusco)," caja 2219, exp. 406009, August 18, 1928, TSJDF.

100. "Intento de suicidio de Eliazer Tello," caja 2154, exp. 392339, December 22, 1928, TSJDF.

101. "Sin que se sepa la causa, una joven se mata con estricnina," *Excélsior,* March 23, 1919, pp. 1, 5.

102. Michael D. Jackson, *The Palm at the End of the Mind: Relatedness, Religiosity, and the Real* (Durham, NC: Duke University Press, 2009), 87n21.

103. "Intento de suicidio de Baños Ayala, Lucrecia," caja 2289, exp. 419937, July 11, 1929, TSJDF.

104. "El suicidio de Antonio Mira, ha puesto sangriento epílogo a la tragedia de la suntuosa Colonia Roma," *El Demócrata,* September 13, 1921, pp. 1, 6.

105. For an interesting discussion of bodily comportment and status, see Sonya Lipsett-Rivera, *Gender and the Negotiation of Daily Life in Mexico, 1750–1856* (Lincoln: University of Nebraska Press, 2012).

106. "El suicidio de Antonio Mira, ha puesto sangriento epílogo a la tragedia de la suntuosa Colonia Roma," *El Demócrata,* September 13, 1921, pp. 1, 6.

107. Katherine Elaine Bliss, *Compromised Positions: Prostitution, Public Health, and Gender Politics in Revolutionary Mexico City* (University Park: Pennsylvania State University Press, 2001), 44.

108. "Suicidio espantoso," *El Imparcial,* March 18, 1905, p. 1.

109. Bliss, *Compromised Positions,* 44.

110. "Suicidio frustrado (Carlota Alatorre)," caja 1290, exp. 230015, October 20, 1914, TSJDF.

111. "Suicidio frustrado de Carmen Flores," caja 1352, exp. 237261, March 10, 1916, TSJDF.

112. "Averiguación sobre el suicidio de Dolores García Vda. de Córdoba," caja 1977, exp. 358618, August 24, 1926, TSJDF. A medical publication doubted the efficacy of serum of Query, even though it had seemed to cure syphilis in a laboratory rabbit. See "La pretendida sueroterapia de la sífilis," *Gaceta Médica de México* 1, no. 5 (February/March 1920): 151–152.

113. "Diligencias sobre el suicidio de Miranda, Manuel," caja 1174, exp. 209116, November 19, 1912, TSJDF.

114. "Conato de suicidio de Hernández, Agustín," caja 2170, exp. 395518, January 6, 1928, TSJDF.

115. "Joven novillero se suicidó en un tranvía," *El Univeral,* November 13, 1930, sec. 2, p. 1.

116. "Averiguación de intento de suicidio," caja 0094, exp. 016887, June 25, 1901, TSJDF.

117. It seems that Tiro Suiza may have been a gun club with a cantina.

118. "Averiguación del suicidio de Enrique Minetti," caja 1013, exp. 180283, September 19, 1910, TSJDF.

119. "Suicidio de José Díaz," caja 1055, exp. 175785, March 25, 1911, TSJDF.

120. Laura Isabel Serna, *Making Cinelandia: American Films and Mexican Film Culture before the Golden Age* (Durham, NC: Duke University Press, 2014), 64–65.

121. Lola la Chata may be the infamous Lola of later tabloid coverage. Lola la Chata, or María Dolores Estévez Zuleta (1906–1959), was an infamous drug trafficker who became well known in Mexico City in the 1930s. In the 1920s, she sold marijuana, morphine, and heroin, along with chicharrones, in La Merced. See Elaine Carey, "Selling Is More of a Habit Than Using: Narcotraficante Lola la Chata and Her Threat to Civilization, 1930–1960," *Journal of Women's History* 21, no. 2 (Summer 2009): 62–89. It is said that Lola la Chata was one of the inspirations for William Burrough's writings. Presumably, she was his source for heroin during his Mexico days.

122. "Averiguación del suicidio de Beatriz Norman," TSJDF.

123. "¿Por qué se privó de la vida el millonario D. Juan Balme?" *El Imparcial,* August 6, 1908, pp. 1, 8.

124. "Averiguación sobre el suicidio de Guillermo Lemus," caja 1977, exp. 358652, September 2, 1926, TSJDF.

125. "Suicidio frustrado por Pedro López," caja 1117, exp. 197964, October 17, 1912, TSJDF.

126. "Lesiones e intento de suicidio," caja 1511, exp. 269830, July 9, 1918, TSJDF.

127. "Averiguación de intento de suicidio de Raymundo Luna Ruiz," caja 1911, exp. 341961, June 4, 1925, TSJDF.

128. Lisa Lieberman, "Romanticism and the Culture of Suicide in Nineteenth-Century France," *Comparative Studies in Society and History* 33, no. 3 (July 1991): 628.

129. "Mujeres y niños han de ser ajenos a la crónicas del crimen," *Excélsior,* March 26, 1930, pp. 1, 4.

FOUR. THE MODERN DISEASE

1. "Averiguación del suicidio de Solís, M. Consuelo," caja 2290, exp. 420118, April 14, 1929, TSJDF.

2. Carlos Pereyra, "La sociología abstracta y su aplicación á algunos problemas fundamentales de México," *Revista Positiva,* no. 3 (August 13, 1903): 351–386. *Revista Positiva* began publication in 1901. The phrase "order and progress," appeared on its masthead. The journal was the mouthpiece of the scientific political elite, who endeavored to solve Mexico's social problems with scientific methods and solutions.

3. Diego Pulido Esteva, "Imágenes de la locura en el discurso de la modernidad, salud mental y orden social a través de las visiones médicas, criminológico, legal, y literaria (Ciudad de México, 1881–1910)" (PhD diss., Universidad Nacional Autónoma de México, 2004), 17; Claudia Agostoni, "Médicos científicos y médicos

ilícitos en la Ciudad de México durante el Porfiriato," *Estudios de Historia Moderna y Contemporánea* 19 (January–July 2000): 13–31. Irena Paperno found that alienist ideas about the external causes of suicide prevailed in nineteenth-century Russia as well. Positivists held sway in this same era. Paperno notes, "The transition from the medical to social model of man was achieved by transferring notions that traditionally described the individual body to the collective body of society." See Paperno, *Suicide as a Cultural Institution*, 26.

4. Epilepsy does lead to scarring of the frontal lobe. However, epilepsy is not classified as a mental illness today.

5. Weaver, *Sadly Troubled History*, 35; Beltrán Abarca, "El suicidio en México," 79–80.

6. For a discussion of some relevant court cases, see Pablo Piccato, "The Girl Who Killed a Senator: Femininity and the Public Sphere in Postrevolutionary Mexico," in *True Stories of Crime in Modern Mexico*, ed. Robert Buffington and Pablo Piccato, 128–153 (Albuquerque: University of New Mexico Press, 2009); and Victor M. Macías-González, "The Case of the Murdering Beauty: Narrative Construction, Beauty Pageants, and Postrevolutionary Mexican National Myth," in Buffington and Piccato, *True Stories of Crime in Modern Mexico*, 215–247.

7. *Código penal para el Distrito Federal y Territorio de la Baja California sobre delitos del fuero común y para toda la República sobre delitos contra la Federación* (Mexico City: Tipografía de Flores y Monslave, 1874), art. 34; *Código penal para el Distrito y territories federales* (Mexico City: Talleres Gráficos de la Nación, 1929).

8. Susan K. Morrissey argues that this was also true of positivist thinkers in imperial Russia. See Morrissey, *Suicide and the Body Politic*, 198.

9. For example, see Robert Buffington and Pablo Piccato, "The Narrative Construction of Porfirian Reality," in Buffington and Piccato, *True Stories of Crime in Modern Mexico*, 25–51; and Piccato, *City of Suspects*.

10. Historian Francisco Javier Beltrán Abarca noted that an 1870 article in *El Monitor Republicano* hypothesized that suicide occurred in individuals with a "terrible and insatiable hunger for riches." See Beltrán Abarca, "El suicidio en México," 79–80. This judgment surfaced again in 1909, when a reporter for *El Diario* covering a double suicide in Chapultepec Park argued that the young Tepito residents killed themselves because they could not fulfill their desires for luxury and social mobility. "Se causaron la muerte por no resistir el deseo de lujo," *El Diario*, November 7, 1909, p. 1. See chapter 5 for a discussion of the Chapultepec case.

11. Weaver, *Sadly Troubled History*, 36–37.

12. Ibid., 38–39.

13. Luis Vergara y Flores, "Neuropatía y aberración intelectual," *Medicina Científica* 6, no. 13 (1893): 200–204.

14. Hale, *Transformation of Liberalism*, 142. Barreda would also reject Darwin's ideas of evolution, or *transformismo*, and debate his two most prominent students, Porfirio Parra and Manuel Flores, on the rigor of the scientific method that informed his views on evolution and its applicability as a social theory. See Hale, *Transformation of Liberalism*, 207–209.

15. Gabino Barreda, "Algunas consideraciones sobre el suicidio," *La Escuela de Medicina,* no. 14 (January 15, 1883): 161.

16. Ibid., 162.

17. Voekel, *Alone before God.*

18. Thomas Walter Laqueur, *Making Sex: Body and Gender from the Greeks to Freud* (Cambridge, MA: Harvard University Press, 1990).

19. Ann-Louise Shapiro, "Disordered Bodies/Disorderly Acts: Medical Discourse and the Female Criminal in Nineteenth-Century Paris," in *Gendered Domains: Rethinking Public and Private in Women's History,* ed. Dorothy O. Helly and Susan M. Reverby (Ithaca, NY: Cornell University Press, 1992), 96.

20. Ibid.

21. Cristina Rivera-Garza, "She Neither Respected nor Obeyed Anyone: Inmates and Psychiatrists Debate Gender and Class at the General Insane Asylum La Castañeda, Mexico, 1910–20," *Hispanic American Historical Review* 81, nos. 3–4 (August and November 2001): 657.

22. "Las crises clitoridianas al principio o en el curso de la ataxia locomotriz progresiva," *La Escuela de Medicina,* no. 10 (November 15, 1884): 131–132.

23. José de J. Castañeda, Máximo Silva, and Carlos Aguilera, "Contribución a la estadística del suicidio en la República Mexicana," pt. 1, *La Escuela de Medicina,* no. 6 (November 15, 1885): 78.

24. Ibid., pt. 2, *La Escuela de Medicina,* no. 8 (December 15, 1885): 103.

25. Horacio Barreda, "Estudio sobre 'El Feminismo,'" pts. 1–4, *Revista Positiva,* no. 103 (January 1, 1909): 1–10; no. 104 (January 29, 1909): 45–60; no. 105 (February 20, 1909): 77–86; no. 106 (March 26, 1909): 109–126.

26. William French, "Prostitutes and Guardian Angels: Women, Work, and the Family in Porfirian Mexico," *Hispanic American Historical Review* 72 (1992): 529–555.

27. Richard von Krafft Ebing, "La menstruación como causa de irresponsabilidad mental en la mujer," *La Escuela de Medicina,* no. 45 (November 15, 1894): 935–936.

28. Asti Hustvedt, *Medical Muses: Hysteria in Nineteenth-Century Paris* (New York: W. W. Norton, 2012), 12–13. See also Elaine Showalter, *The Female Malady: Women, Madness, and English Culture, 1830–1980* (New York: Penguin, 1987); and Shapiro, "Disordered Bodies."

29. Stephen Jay Gould, *The Panda's Thumb: More Reflections in Natural History* (New York: W. W. Norton, 2010), 152–159.

30. Hustvedt, *Medical Muses,* 26.

31. Ernesto Rojas, "La hysteria psiquica: Tesis para sustentar examen de especialista en Psiguiatria" (master's thesis, Escuela Nacional de Medicina, 1909).

32. Clinical file, "Augustina P.," caja 2, exp. 20, September 10, 1910, Archivo Histórico de Salubridad y Asistencia, Beneficiencia Pública, Establecimientos Hospitalarios, Manicomio General, Expedientes Clinicos, Mexico City (hereafter cited as AHSA).

33. Clinical file, "Imelda J.," caja 2, exp. 56, June 2, 1910, AHSA.

34. During the Porfiriato, women who transgressed the feminine ideal were more likely to be categorized as suffering from mental maladies provoked by immorality. Mental diseases were believed to have physical and/or mental causes. See Martha Lilia Mancilla Villa, *Locura y mujer durante el porfiriato* (Mexico City: Editorial Círculo Psicoanalítico Mexicano, 2001); and Andrés Ríos Molina, "La locura durante la Revolución Mexicana: Los primeros años del Manicomio General La Castañeda, 1910–1920" (PhD diss., El Colegio de México, 2009), 122–140.

35. Ríos Molina, "La locura durante la Revolución," 93.

36. Like hysteria, tuberculosis was considered a female disease and linked to poor working-class women. See Diego Armus, *The Ailing City: Health, Tuberculosis, and Culture in Buenos Aires, 1870–1950* (Durham, NC: Duke University Press, 2011).

37. Hustvedt, *Medical Muses*, 22.

38. "Hospital para mujeres demente," *El Nacional*, May 11, 1895.

39. Clinical file, "Herlinda M.," caja 2, exp. 2, July 3, 1909, AHSA.

40. Sloan, *Runaway Daughters.*

41. Clinical file, "Teresa O.," caja 2, exp. 13, July 26, 1905, AHSA. Teresa O. is also discussed in Rivera-Garza, "She Neither Respected nor Obeyed Anyone," 677.

42. Nancy E. van Deusen, "Determining the Boundaries of Virtue: The Discourse of *Recogimiento* among Women in Seventeenth-Century Lima," *Journal of Family History* 22, no. 2 (1997). Also see the case of a girl named María discussed in Sloan, *Runaway Daughters*, 165–166. María refused to engage a man named Francisco when he tried to talk with her on the street, and she ended up pelting him with rocks to force him to move away. When brought in front of a judge, she defended her actions as honorable. Honorable women did not talk to strange men, as it called into question their reputations.

43. Rivera-Garza, "She Neither Respected nor Obeyed Anyone," 674–675.

44. Joan Jacobs Brumberg, *Fasting Girls: The History of Anorexia Nervosa* (Vintage Books, 2000), 102–104.

45. Clinical file, "María Carmen M. H.," caja 224, exp. 21, April 12, 1928, AHSA.

46. George Miller Beard, *A Practical Treatise on Nervous Exhaustion (Neurasthenia): Its Symptoms, Nature, Sequences, Treatment* (New York: E. B. Treat, 1888), 24–31.

47. "Clausura de las sesiones de la Academia Nacional de Medicina," *El Nacional*, August 7, 1895, p. 1.

48. Beard, *Practical Treatise*, 127, 100.

49. Ibid., 38–104.

50. "La locura del dinero," *El Nacional*, August 30, 1900, p. 2.

51. Tic-Tac [pseud.], "Semana alegre," *El Imparcial*, September 10, 1899, p. 1.

52. Shaya, "Mayhem of Moderns," 46–47.

53. Christopher E. Forth, "Neurasthenia and Manhood in Fin-de-Siècle France," in *Cultures of Neurasthenia: From Beard to the First World War*, ed. Marijke Gijsqwijt-Hofstra and Roy Porter (New York: Rodopi, 2001), 329.

54. Shaya, "Mayhem of Moderns," 53.

55. Forth, "Neurasthenia," 332–333.

56. "Extranjero: Una consulta médica; Charcot y Mottet; Locos neurasténicos," *Diario del Hogar,* June 22, 1892, p. 1.

57. Advertisements for these products started to appear in *La Escuela de la Medicina* in 1887. The advertisement for Neurosine Prunier appeared in *La Escuela de la Medicina,* no. 1 (February 15, 1903). Another ad in the same issued noted the endorsement of Dr. Demetrio Mejia, a faculty member at the medical school, for the efficacy of Preparatión de Wampole (Wampole's Preparation) in treating anemia, exhaustion, and nervous weakness.

58. Beard, *Practical Treatise,* 171.

59. Ibid., 192–243.

60. "¿Por qué se suicidan? Contra la neurastenia: El trabajo," *El Imparcial,* June 1, 1908, p. 1.

61. Ibid.

62. "La neurastenia se está apoderando de nosotros y no es enfermedad utópica: Entrevista con el Sr. Dr. Zárraga," *El Imparcial,* November 25, 1908, pp. 1, 2.

63. Santiago Rustiñol, "La neurastenia," *La Iberia,* March 4, 1909, p. 2.

64. "La Neurastenia: ¿Es una enfermedad imaginaria? Desgraciadamente no," *La Iberia,* May 1, 1909, p. 2.

65. Antonio Gota de Zaragoza, "El neurismo creciente de nuestro tiempo," *La Escuela de Medicina,* no. 19 (October 15, 1909): 488–445.

66. Cristina Rivera-Garza, "Por la salud mental de la nación: Vida cotidiana y estado en el Manicomio General de la Castañeda, México 1910–1930," *Secuencia,* no. 51 (September–December 2001): 73–74.

67. Marijke Gijswijt-Hofstra and Roy Porter, eds., *Cultures of Neurasthenia: From Beard to the First World War* (New York: Rodopi, 2001), 21.

68. Daniel Pick, *Faces of Degeneration: A European Disorder, c. 1848–1918* (New York: Cambridge University Press, 1993), 135–136.

69. Nancy Leys Stepan, *"The Hour of Eugenics": Race, Gender, and Nation in Latin America* (Ithaca, NY: Cornell University Press, 1991), 24–25, 67–68.

70. Stephanie Sharon Ballenger, "Modernizing Madness: Doctors, Patients and Asylums in Nineteenth-Century Mexico City" (PhD diss., University of California, Berkeley, 2009), 259.

71. José Olvera, "Discursos sobre causas de las neurosis en México," *El Observador Médico: Revista Científica de la Asociación Médica de Pedro Escobeda* 1, no. 4 (February 1870): 52–53.

72. Ballenger, "Modernizing Madness," 266.

73. Ríos Molina, "La locura durante la Revolución," 65–67. Ríos Molina cites Dr. Rafael Caraza, who theorized that indigenous Mexicans did not suffer from mental illness because their closeness to nature protected them from modern influences that might stimulate the passions. See Rafael Caraza, "Informe que el médico cirujano del Hospital de San Hipólito que suscribe, rinde sobre el estado mental de Marcelino Domingo," *El Observador Médico,* no. 5 (1879): 34–39.

74. Ríos Molina, "La locura durante la Revolución," 70–72.

75. Hale, *Transformation of Liberalism,* 185–186.

76. Jorge Molina Avilés, "Psicología y positivismo: La enseñanza de la psicología durante el porfiriato; 1896–1910," in *100 años de la psicología en México 1896–1996*, ed. Juan José Sánchez Sosa (Mexico City: Universidad Nacional Autónoma de México, 1997), 23.

77. Ríos Molina, "La locura durante la Revolución," 68.

78. Michel Foucault, *History of Madness*, ed. Jean Khalfa, trans. Jonathan Murphy and Jean Khalfa (New York: Routledge, 2009).

79. Porfirio Parra, *Ensayo sobre la patogenia de la locura* (Mexico City: Tipografía Literaria, 1878).

80. Ballenger, "Modernizing Madness," 257. Porfirio Parra argued that doctors should not dabble in the metaphysical moral causes of mental illness and should instead concentrate on the physiological ones. See Parra, *Ensayo sobre la patogenia de la locura.*

81. Ballenger, "Modernizing Madness," 259.

82. Ríos Molina, "La locura durante la Revolución," 122–140.

83. Mariano Rivadeneyra, quoted in Ballenger, "Modernizing Madness," 263. See also Rivadeneyra's thesis, "Apuntes para la estadística de la locura en México" (master's thesis, Escuela Nacional de Medicina en México, 1887).

84. Ballenger, "Modernizing Madness," 279.

85. Ibid.

86. Ibid., 270. Cathy Popkin found that the same was true for late nineteenth-century and early twentieth-century hysteria cases in Russia. See Popkin, "Hysterical Episodes: Case Histories and Silent Subjects," in *Self and Story in Russian History,* ed. Laura Engelstein and Stephanie Sandler (Ithaca, NY: Cornell University Press, 2000), 189–216.

87. For more on *pulque* and Spanish and Mexican attempts to control its production, the conviviality associated with it in working-class barrios, and its perceived relationship to cultural degeneration, see Áurea Toxqui, "Breadwinners or Entrepreneurs? Women's Involvement in the *Pulquería* World of Mexico City," in *Alcohol in Latin America: A Social and Cultural History,* ed. Gretchen Kristine Pierce and Áurea Toxqui (Tucson: University of Arizona Press, 2014), 104–130; and Deborah Toner, *Alcohol and Nationhood in Nineteenth-Century Mexico* (Lincoln: University of Nebraska Press, 2015).

88. Clinical file, "Ramona M.," caja 2, exp. 1, June 9, 1909, AHSA.

89. Rivera-Garza, "She Neither Respected nor Obeyed Anyone," 670.

90. Ibid., 661.

91. "De sociedad: Elegantes nupcias," *El Imparcial,* September 13, 1903, p. 2.

92. "Society Notes," *Mexican Herald,* June 12, 1898, p. 8.

93. "Society: Premier Social Event," *Mexican Herald,* March 1, 1908, p. 18.

94. "La Señora Doña Manuela Collantes de R, es la dama encerrada en el manicomio," *El Demócrata,* December 3, 1916, p. 1.

95. "El Dr. Schemonti afirma que nunca ha reconocido a la Señora Collantes," *El Universal,* December 6, 1916, p. 1.

96. "El Sr. Director de la Beneficencia Dr. Sepúlveda, visita a la Señora Collantes en el manicomio," *El Universal,* December 7, 1916, pp. 1, 3.

97. Ibid.

98. "La Señora Collantes de Rivero saldrá pronto del Manicomio de la Castañeda," *El Universal,* December 9, 1916, pp. 1, 3.

99. "El Señor Lic. Collantes rocogera a su hija del Manicomio de la Castañeda: No nos intimidan los poderosos menos podremos callar ante Ramón Rivero," *El Universal,* December 10, 1916, p. 1.

100. Enrique O. Aragón was a prominent Porfirian specialist in psychiatry. He published "Psiquiatría: Los síndromas mentales," *Gaceta Médica de México* 7 (1912): 183–226. In this essay, he catalogued symptoms of various mental disorders, including onanism, nymphomania, and effeminacy in men, rather than any underlying causes of the conditions.

101. "El Dres. Collantes y Ruiz Erdozain no firmaron el dictamen contra la Señora Collantes," *El Universal,* December 17, 1916, p. 1.

102. "El Señor Director del 'Manicomio' dirige una carta a 'El Universal,'" *El Universal,* December 18, 1916, pp. 1, 2.

103. "El Dr. Saldaña dictaminó en favor de la Sra. Collantes cuando era médico del manicomio," *El Universal,* December 19, 1916, pp. 1, 4.

104. Rivera-Garza, "Por la salud mental de la nación," 63.

105. Ibid., 79–80.

106. "El asunto de la Sra. Collantes de Rivero," *El Universal,* December 22, 1916, p. 1.

107. "Rindió se declaración el Director del Manicomio General, Dr. Agustín Torres," *El Demócrata,* December 26, 1916, p. 1.

108. *Diario Oficial,* vol. 70, pt. 2 (1932), https://books.google.es/books?lr=&redir_esc=y&hl=sv&id=biJUAAAAYAAJ&dq=editions%3AOCLC7646514&focus=searchwithinvolume&q=manuela+Collantes+.

109. "En México, la beneficencia pública no hace obra de caridad, sino labor de inquisición," *El Demócrata,* July 26, 1919, p. 1.

110. "¡Se mueren de hambre los dementes!" *El Demócrata,* August 27, 1919, pp. 1, 10.

111. "El Presidente de la Huerta visitó el manicomio," *El Demócrata,* September 11, 1920, pp. 1, 3.

112. Rivera-Garza, "Por la salud mental de la nación," 81.

113. "Las boticas extrañan un serio peligro," *Excélsior,* February 17, 1919, pp. 1, 3.

114. "En breve las boticas dejarán de ser un peligro," *Excélsior,* February 18, 1919, pp. 1, 7.

115. "Inmoralidad de las boticas y las droguerías," *Excélsior,* August 30, 1919, pp. 1, 9.

116. "Una investigación que puede ser sensacional: Los permisos para la venta de medicinas de patente," *El Universal,* February 13, 1930, pp. 1, 8.

117. "Medicinas falsificadas que causan la muerte," *El Universal,* June 21, 1930, sec. 2, pp. 1, 4.

118. "La existencia de arsenicales falsificados," *El Universal,* June 25, 1930, sec. 2, pp. 1, 4.

119. "Recetas con sustancias no exentas de peligro," *El Universal,* July 15, 1930, sec. 2, pp. 1, 4.

120. Niño Fidencio was a folk healer who lived in Nuevo León and had many devoted followers. He died at the age of forty in 1938. See Dore Gardner, *Niño Fidencio: A Heart Thrown Open* (Albuquerque: Museum of New Mexico Press, 1994); and Carlos Monsiváis, "El Niño Fidencio," in *Entre la magia y la historia: Tradiciones, mitos y leyendas de la frontera,* ed. José Manuel Valenzuela Arce (Mexico City: Plaza y Valdés, 2000), 107–120.

121. "Recetas con sustancias no exentas de peligro," *El Universal,* pp. 1, 4.

122. See, for example, the advertisement of Dr. McLaughlin's electric belt in *El Imparcial,* July 8, 1900, p. 2.

123. Advertisements in *El Demócrata,* October 28, 1915, p. 2; and October 14, 1921, p. 3.

## FIVE. DEATH IN THE CITY

Portions of this chapter were published before. See Kathryn A. Sloan, "Death and the City: Female Public Suicide and Meaningful Space in Modern Mexico City," *Journal of Urban History* 42, no. 2 (2016): 396–418.

1. Pérez, *To Die in Cuba.*

2. The deaths of these young men were first commemorated at the beginning of the restored republic, in 1871, and the celebration gained prominence during the Porfiriato. During the revolution, leaders like Francisco Madero and Victoriano Huerta continued to preside over the ceremony. See Enrique Plasencia de la Parra, "Conmemoración de la hazaña épica de los niños heroes: Su origen, desarollo y simbolismos," *Historia Mexicana* 45, no. 2 (October–December 1995): 241–279.

3. In Mexico and elsewhere, it could be argued that a cultural logic existed to explain female suicide. Killing oneself to cover shame or deception in love was understandable. In fact, when a young, single woman killed herself, it was assumed that she had been deceived. Gayatri Spivak analyzes the cultural logic of *sati* (the immolation of widows) in Indian culture. See Spivak, "Can the Subaltern Speak?" in *Colonial Discourse and Post-Colonial Theory: A Reader,* ed. Patrick Williams and Laura Chrisman (New York: Columbia University Press, 1994), 66–111.

4. Michel de Certeau, *The Practice of Everyday Life,* trans. Steven Rendell (Berkeley: University of California Press, 1988); Ben Highmore, *Michel de Certeau: Analysing Culture* (New York: Continuum, 2006), 81. See also Mauricio Tenorio-Trillo, *I Speak of the City: Mexico City at the Turn of the Twentieth Century* (Chicago: University of Chicago Press, 2013); and Néstor García Canclini, *Culturas híbridas: Estrategias para entrar y salir de la modernidad* (Mexico City: Editorial Grijalbo, 1990).

5. Michael Johns, *The City of Mexico in the Age of Díaz* (Austin: University of Texas Press, 1997), 9–11.

6. William H. Beezley, *Mexican National Identity: Memory, Innuendo, and Popular Culture* (Tucson: University of Arizona Press, 2008), 107.

7. Henri Lefebvre, *The Production of Space,* trans. Donald Nicholson-Smith (Oxford: Blackwell, 1991).

8. Ibid., 56. Lefebvre does argue that abstract space must also be ahistorical when social struggle in the production of that space is rendered invisible. Although Porfirian planners attempted to homogenize the public spaces of El Centro, it was difficult to erase a history that had so many markers of pre-Columbian and colonial cultures.

9. Claudia Agostoni, *Monuments of Progress: Modernization and Public Health in Mexico City, 1876–1910* (Boulder: University Press of Colorado,, 2003), 80.

10. Cristina Barros and Marco Buenrostro, *Vida cotidiana: Ciudad de México 1850–1910* (Mexico City: Fondo de Cultura Económica USA, 1996), 14.

11. Johns, *City of Mexico,* 11.

12. Tenorio-Trillo, *I Speak of the City,* 72.

13. Barros and Buenrostro, *Vida cotidiana,* 18.

14. Johns, *City of Mexico,* 32.

15. Tenorio-Trillo, *I Speak of the City,* 289.

16. Susie S. Porter, "'And That It Is Custom Makes It Law': Class Conflict and Gender Ideology in the Public Sphere, Mexico City, 1880–1910," *Social Science History* 24, no. 1 (Spring 2000): 122–123.

17. Ibid., 125.

18. Robert South Barrett, *Standard Guide to the City of Mexico and Vicinity, 1900* (St. Louis: Modern Mexico, 1900), 39–41.

19. Andrea Kristine Moerer, "Changing Chapultepec: Construction, Consumption, and Cultural Politics in a Mexico City Forest, 1934–1944" (PhD diss., University of Minnesota, 2013), 16.

20. Katherine Elaine Bliss and Ann S. Blum, "Dangerous Driving: Adolescence, Sex, and the Gendered Experience of Public Space in Early-Twentieth-Century Mexico City," in *Gender, Sexuality, and Power in Latin America since Independence,* ed. William E. French and Katherine Elaine Bliss (Lanham, MD: Rowman and Littlefield, 2007).

21. Porter, "And That It Is Custom Makes It Law," 124.

22. "Suicidio con estricnina," *El Imparcial,* December 20, 1900, p. 1. Note that is unclear whether the reporter surmised her plan or learned of her strategy from a family member or friend. It was not uncommon for reporters of papers like *El Imparcial* and *El Demócrata* to imagine the psychological state and motivations of young suicides.

23. "El suicidio del ayer," *El Imparcial,* April 27, 1905, p. 1.

24. "Envenenamiento de Ana María Schlonwbits, como intento de suicidio," caja 882, exp. 152549, April 27, 1909, TSJDF.

25. "Suicidio en la Alameda: Despojó del cadaver," *El Imparcial,* May 25, 1897, p. 1.

26. "Dos señoritas elegantes se suicidaron ayer en Chapultepec," *El Imparcial,* November 6, 1909, p. 1; "Dos Sritas. se suicidaron ayer en Chapultepec: Se las encontro por tierra enlazadas en postrer abrazo, se mataron por decepciones de amor," *El Diario,* November 6, 1909, p.1.

27. "Se causaron la muerte por no resistir el deseo de lujo," *El Diario,* November 7, 1909, p.1. Another article agreed that the girls killed themselves because they could not have the pleasures and material riches they coveted, but it also pleaded with reporters to stop covering the "vulgar act." See "Crímenes vulgares: Dos niñas románticas y un asesino," *La Patría,* November 9, 1909, p. 5.

28. "Dos señoritas elegantes se suicidaron ayer en Chapultepec," *El Imparcial.*

29. "Mystery of Suicides Has Not Been Solved Yet," *Mexican Herald,* November 8, 1909, p. 1.

30. "Dos señoritas elegantes se suicidaron ayer en Chapultepec," *El Imparcial.*

31. The newspaper of the expatriate Spanish community reported that Elias Rojas admitted that he was the boyfriend of both girls. "Doble suicidio en Chapultepec," *El Correo Español,* November 6, 1909, p. 2.

32. "Dos Sritas. se suicidaron ayer," *El Diario.*

33. "Girls Drink Poison, and Embracing, Die," *Mexican Herald,* November 6, 1909, p. 1.

34. See, for example, "Anoche se ahorcó . . . era joven y bella, de sus cartas se desprende que murió loca de amor," *El Imparcial,* November 10, 1908, p. 1; and "El suicidio por amor," *Boletín de Policía,* November 7, 1909, p. 9.

35. "Se causaron la muerte por no resistir el deseo de lujo," *El Diario.*

36. "Carrozas blancas condujeron al cementerio a las suicidas," *El Diario,* November 9, 1909, p. 2. For a discussion of cemeteries and class in Porfirian Mexico, see Amanda M. López, "Cadaverous City."

37. "Eranse dos vidas, que un día descubrieron su drama," *El Imparcial,* November 8, 1909, p. 2.

38. Jaap van Ginneken, *Crowds, Psychology, and Politics, 1871–1899* (New York: Cambridge University Press, 1992), 79.

39. "Un doble suicidio por amor," *Boletín de Policía,* November 28, 1909, p. 5.

40. Public parks were chosen sites of other suicides and attempted suicides. See, for example, "Suicidio de Jorge Córdova," caja 0116, exp. 017701, July 7, 1901, TSJDF; and "Envenenamiento de Ana María Schlonwbits, como intento de suicidio," TSJDF.

41. Anton Rosenthal, "The Arrival of the Electric Streetcar and the Conflict over Progress in Early Twentieth-Century Montevideo," *Journal of Latin American Studies* 27, no. 2 (1995): 319–341.

42. John Lear, *Workers, Neighbors, and Citizens: The Revolution in Mexico City* (Lincoln: University of Nebraska Press, 2001), 26.

43. "Encierra todo un indescifrable enigma el suicidio del joven José Amieva," *El Demócrata,* January 7, 1920, p. 1.

44. "A bordo de un automóvil, un joven romántico se arrancó ayer la vida," *El Demócrata,* April 17, 1921, p. 1. The sub-subtitle read: "He had taken a nice ride to

the beautiful Chapultepec Forest, and no would believe that this man would let black ideas take his brain" (Había hecho un agradable paseo al hermoso Bosque de Chapultepec, y nadie hubiera creído que aquel hombre llevara en el cerebro tan negras ideas).

45. "Suicidio en el Bosque de Chapultepec: La Srita. Guadalupe Ponce, por causas que se ignoran, apuró en fuerte veneno en la calzada de las violetas, de aquel pintoresco lugar," *El Demócrata,* March 3, 1916, p. 1.

46. Ibid.

47. "Una cortada y un baño en el estanque de Chapultepec," *El Universal,* August 19, 1930, p. 1.

48. "Suicidio en el Ferrocarril del Valle: Drama en un tren," *El Imparcial,* March 2, 1898, p. 1.

49. "Intento de suicidio: Curiosa escena," *El Imparcial,* May 2, 1899, p. 2.

50. "En averiguación de la causa de la muerte de Luis Garcia Rivero," caja 169, exp. 029825, August 19, 1902, TSJDF.

51. "Suicidio," *El Imparcial,* April 20, 1902, p. 4.

52. "En averiguación de la causa de la muerte de Luis Garcia Rivero," TSJDF.

53. "La tragedia en el Panteón Español, tres entrevistas, amor inmenso, Sin él, ni el cielo!" *El Imparcial,* August 28, 1902, pp. 1, 4.

54. Pérez, *To Die in Cuba,* 157.

55. "Suicidio de Gastón Moreno," caja 2257, exp. 413300, September 6, 1929, TSJDF.

56. "Averiguación sobre el intento de suicidio que cometió Efrén Muñoz," caja 1641, exp. 293547, April 16, 1921, TSJDF.

57. A *ratero* is a pickpocket or petty street criminal. For an excellent study of this classification of urban crime, see Pérez, *To Die in Cuba,* 157.

58. "Suicidio de José Díaz," caja 1055, exp. 175785, March 25, 1911, TSJDF.

59. "Suicidio por amor," *El Imparcial,* May 30, 1897, p. 1. The reporter kept the identity of the girl secret, referring to her only as Señorita E. M.

60. "Desde el tercer piso de una casa de la 5a. Calle de Tacuba se arrojó ayer una joven," *El Independiente,* August 1, 1913, pp. 1, 3.

61. "La Señorita María G. Servín se arrojó desde un tercer piso," *El Univeral,* January 10, 1917, pp. 1, 3.

62. "Efluvios morbosos pueblan la urbe y un mal de suicidio enferma los jóvenes espíritus: La Señorita Matilde Chazaro, a cuyo dijera palabras de muerte un vago fantasma, se lanzó al espacio desde un balcón de su casa, privándose de la vida," *El Demócrata,* March 31, 1920, p. 1.

63. "Intento de suicidio a Manuel Castellano," caja 1792, exp. 323019, June 13, 1923, TSJDF.

64. "Intento de suicidio a Alberto Brusco," caja 2219, exp. 406009, August 18, 1928, TSJDF.

65. The same held true in Cuba. Cuban women who committed suicide were especially likely to choose religious buildings as a place of death. See Pérez, *To Die in Cuba,* 143.

66. "Semana alegre: Influencias de las novelas sobre el hígado—Amores y suicidio a unos metros de altura," *El Imparcial,* June 4, 1899, p. 1.

67. The cathedral in Mexico City's central square was constructed on top of a former Aztec temple. The reporter references a circular stone that was excavated from the site on December 17, 1790, when workers were repairing the cathedral. It has been called a calendar and a sunstone, although most Porfirian-era experts believed that it was a ritual stone used as a sacrificial altar. It was mounted on an exterior wall of the cathedral until 1885 and now sits in the National Anthropology Museum.

68. "Extraordinario caso de suicidio: Señorita que se arroja de una torre de la Catedral," *El Imparcial,* June 1, 1899, p. 1.

69. The article referred to the stone as a calendar, which is what it was thought to have been at the time.

70. "Extraordinario caso de suicidio: Señorita que se arroja de una torre de la Catedral," *El Imparcial,* p. 1.

71. Sloan, *Runaway Daughters,* 124.

72. "Extraordinario caso de suicidio: Señorita que se arroja de una torre de la Catedral," *El Imparcial,* p. 1.

73. "El suicidio de Sofía Ahumada: Libertad de los detenidos," *El Imparcial,* June 2, 1899, p. 1.

74. "Semana alegre: Influencias de las novelas sobre el hígado—Amores y suicidio a unos metros de altura," *El Imparcial.*

75. Ibid.

76. "Teórica del mal, las novelas," *El Amigo de la Verdad,* August 17, 1895, p. 2. The editorial was attributed to "La mensajera" rather than "El mensajero," hence my assumption that the writer was female.

77. "Suicidio de Sofia Ahumada: Desde la torre al suelo," *El Chisme,* June 1, 1899, p. 2.

78. "Desde 'La Torre de los Suicidios' se arrojaron ayer una Sra., una Srita. y un niño," *El Imparcial,* December 21, 1912, p. 1.

79. "El desamor de su padre precipitó el suicidio de la pobre Margarita," *El Imparcial,* December 22, 1912, p. 1.

80. "Desde el torre al atrio," *El Demócrata,* July 23, 1920, p. 1.

81. Ibid.

82. "Por que se privó de la vida la pobre Angelina," *El Demócrata,* July 24, 1920, p. 7.

83. "Se suicidó apurando una fuerte dosis de cianuro de mercurio: El mal de Werther," *El Demócrata,* August 24, 1920, p. 3.

84. Laura Isabel Serna, *Making Cinelandia: American Films and Mexican Film Culture Before the Golden Age* (Durham, NC: Duke University Press, 2014), 47–49.

85. "Apelación interpuesta contra la sentencia pronunciada por el Juez Primero de lo Penal, que declaró no delito que proseguir en el suicidio de Angelina Ruiz," caja 1602, exp. 287224, November 12, 1920, TSJDF.

86. Piccato, *Tyranny of Opinion.*

87. "Suicidio de Sofia Ahumada: Importante declaraciones," *El Chisme,* June 2, 1899, p. 2.

88. Alberto del Castillo Troncoso, "Notas sobre la moral dominante a finales del siglo XIX en la Ciudad de México: Las mujeres suicidas como protagonistas de la nota roja," in *Modernidad, tradición y alteridad: La ciudad de México en el cambio de siglo (XIX-XX),* ed. Claudia Agostoni and Elisa Speckman (Mexico City: Universidad Nacional Autónoma de México, 2001), 329.

89. Enrique Metinides, a crime photographer for *La Prensa* in the twentieth century, photographed a suicide by hanging at Chapultepec Park in 1977. The woman had a photograph of her beloved daughter who, on the day of her suicide, celebrated her quinceañera. Her estranged husband had barred her from attending. She asked someone to point out the oldest tree in the park and was later found hanging from it. See Trish Zeff, ed., *101 Tragedies of Enrique Metinides* (New York: Aperture, 2012), 140–141.

90. "Una criada se suicidó ayer en la Alameda," *El Universal,* January 15, 1930, p. 1.

91. "Una hombre que para matarse hace lujo de precauciones," *El Universal,* June 15, 1930, sec. 2, p. 1.

92. *Excélsior* made the decision to stop reporting blood crimes in March 1930. A series of articles followed in several capital newspapers eulogizing the *Excélsior's* decision. See, for example, "Emilio Rabasa une su elogio por Excélsior," *Excélsior,* March 28, 1930, pp. 1, 10.

## SIX. STAINS OF BLOOD

1. "Semana alegre: Influencias de las novelas sobre el hígado—Amores y suicidio a unos metros de altura," *El Imparcial,* June 4, 1899, p. 1.

2. "Carrozas blancas condujeron al cemetario a las suicidas," *El Diario,* November 9, 1909, p. 2.

3. "La nota trágica de la semana," *Semana Ilustrada,* June 24, 1910, n.p.

4. "Corto sus desesperanzas y amarguras lanzándose desde el tercer piso del correo una hermosa señorita," *El Diario,* January 11, 1914, pp. 1, 6; "El cuerpo de una bella joven fue a estrellarse en el pavimiento quedando en el sin vida," *El Independiente,* January 11, 1914, pp. 1, 3; "La Señorita Sara Ramos se suicidó ayer arrojándose del tercer piso del correo," *El País,* January 11, 1914, p. 1.

5. "Suicidio en el cuarto de la catedral: Un joven se arroja de cabeza al patio," *El Imparcial,* January 9, 1907, p. 1.

6. History of emotions scholarship continues to grow. Lucien Febvre and the Annales school scholars are largely credited with historicizing emotions. See Barbara H. Rosenwein, "Worrying about Emotions in History," *American Historical Review* 107, no. 3 (2002): 821–845; and Lucien Febvre, "Sensibility and History: How to Reconstitute the Emotional Life of the Past," in *A New Kind of History: From the Writings of Febvre,* ed. Peter Burke, trans. K. Folca, (New York: Harper and Row, 1973), 12–26. More recently, Peter and Carol Stearns have advanced the

study of emotionology. See Peter N. Stearns and Carol Z. Stearns, "Emotionology: Clarifying the History of Emotions and Emotional Standards," *American Historical Review* 90, no. 4 (1985): 813–836.

7. Philippe Ariès, *The Hour of Our Death,* trans. Helen Weaver (New York: Knopf Doubleday, 2013).

8. Michel Foucault, *Discipline and Punish: The Birth of the Prison,* trans. Alan Sheridan (New York: Knopf Doubleday, 2012), 74–75.

9. Norbert Elias, *The Civilising Process: Sociogenetic and Psychogenetic Investigations,* trans. Edmund Jephcott (Malden, MA: John Wiley and Sons, 1994), 157–158. This work is also discussed in Shaya, "Mayhem of Moderns," 66–68; and Jan Plamper, *The History of Emotions: An Introduction,* trans. Keith Tribe (New York: Oxford University Press, 2014), 49–50.

10. Elias, *Civilising Process,* 135.

11. Michelle Z. Rosaldo, *Knowledge and Passion: Ilongot Notions of Self and Social Life* (New York: Cambridge University Press, 1980); Lila Abu-Lughod, *Veiled Sentiments: Honor and Poetry in a Bedouin Society* (Berkeley: University of California Press, 1986). See also Catherine A. Lutz and Lila Abu-Lughod, eds., *Language and the Politics of Emotion* (New York: Cambridge University Press, 1990).

12. Paul Ekman, "An Argument for Basic Emotions," *Cognition and Emotion* 6, no. 3 (1992): 169–200.

13. Ruth Leys, "How Did Fear Become a Scientific Object and What Kind of Object Is It?" in *Human Facial Expressions: An Evolutionary View,* ed. Alan J. Fridlund (San Diego: Academic Press, 1994).

14. Plamper, *History of Emotions,* 248–249.

15. William M. Reddy, *The Navigation of Feeling: A Framework for the History of Emotions* (New York: Cambridge University Press, 2001), 106, 125–126.

16. Barbara H. Rosenwein, *Emotional Communities in the Early Middle Ages* (Ithaca, NY: Cornell University Press, 2002), 2.

17. Lomnitz-Adler, *Death and the Idea of Mexico,* 41–43. A "totem" is a unifying emotional symbol that unites a culture. Émile Durkheim argued that totems connected communities to their ancestors and provided primitive societies an entity to integrate community around religion. See Émile Durkheim, *Elementary Forms of Religious Life,* trans. Carol Cosman (New York: Oxford University Press, 2001), 171. This is also discussed in Plamper, *History of Emotions,* 83–84.

18. Eric Hobsbawm and Terence Ranger, eds., *The Invention of Tradition* (New York: Cambridge University Press, 2012). See especially chapter 2 on the highland tradition in Scotland, by Hugh Trevor-Roper.

19. Paul Westheim, *La calavera* (Mexico City: Fondo de Cultura Económica, 1953); Octavio Paz, *The Labyrinth of Solitude: And Other Writings,* trans. Lysander Camp, Yara Milos, and Rachel Phillips Belash (New York: Grove Press, 1985).

20. Lomnitz-Adler, *Death and the Idea of Mexico,* 52.

21. Paz, *Labyrinth of Solitude,* 57–61.

22. Carlos Monsiváis, "Los viajeros y la invención de México," *Aztlán* 15, no. 2 (1984): 201–229.

23. Lomnitz-Adler, *Death and the Idea of Mexico.*

24. Brandes, "Is There a Mexican View of Death?" 138.

25. Ibid., 136.

26. Lomnitz-Adler, *Death and the Idea of Mexico,* 51–52.

27. Robert McCaa, "Missing Millions: The Demographic Costs of the Mexican Revolution," *Mexican Studies/Estudios Mexicanos* 19, no. 2 (Summer 2003): 396. The figure of 1.4 million represents excess deaths and does not take into account other demographic variables like lost births or emigration.

28. Esposito, *Funerals, Festivals, and Cultural Politics,* 23.

29. Ibid., 25; Ariès, *Hour of Our Death;* Philippe Ariès, *Western Attitudes toward Death: From the Middle Ages to the Present,* trans. Patricia M. Ranum (Baltimore: Johns Hopkins University Press, 2010), 66.

30. Octavio Paz famously theorized that the Mexican taunts, caresses, sleeps with, and celebrates death, calling it "his most steadfast love." See Paz, *Labyrinth of Solitude,* 57.

31. Claudio Lomnitz-Adler quoted in Carlos Alberto Sánchez, "Death and the Colonial Difference: An Analysis of a Mexican Idea," *Journal of Philosophy of Life* 3, no. 3 (September 2013): 178.

32. Johns, *City of Mexico;* Esposito, *Funerals, Festivals, and Cultural Politics;* Mauricio Tenorio-Trillo, "1910 Mexico City: Space and Nation in the City of the Centenario," *Journal of Latin American Studies* 28 (February 1996): 75–104.

33. Ma. Concepción Lugo, "Los espacios urbanos de la muerte," *Historias* 40 (1998): 35–45.

34. Scholars have written extensively on tragic death and spontaneous memorialization. Some works include Peter Jan Margry and Christina Sánchez-Carretero, "Memorializing Tragic Death," *Anthropology Today* 23, no. 3 (June 2007): 1–2; Peter Jan Margry, "Performative Memorials: Arenas on Political Resentment in Dutch Society," in *Reforming Dutch Culture,* eds. Peter Jan Margry and H. Roodenburg, 109–133 (Aldershot, UK: Ashgate, 2008); Jack Santino, ed., *Spontaneous Shrines and the Public Memorialization of Death* (New York: Palgrave MacMillan, 2006); and Erika Doss, *Memorial Mania: Public Feeling in America* (Chicago: University of Chicago Press, 2010). Historical works on death and commemoration in Latin America include Lyman L. Johnson, ed., *Death, Dismemberment, and Memory: Body Politics In Latin America* (Albuquerque: University of New Mexico Press, 2004); Esposito, *Funerals, Festivals, and Cultural Politics;* and Lomnitz-Adler, *Death and the Idea of Mexico.*

35. Doss, *Memorial Mania,* 67.

36. Jack Santino, "Performative Commemoratives: Spontaneous Shrines and the Public Memorialization of Death," in *Spontaneous Shrines and the Public Memorialization of Death,* ed. Santino, Jack (New York: Palgrave Macmillan, 2006), 10.

37. Rosenwein, *Emotional Communities,* 25.

38. C. Allen Haney, Christina Leimer, and Juliann Lowery, "Spontaneous Memorialization: Violent Death and Emerging Mourning Ritual," *OMEGA* 35, no. 2 (1997): 162.

39. Piccato, *Tyranny of Opinion.*

40. Harriet Senie quoted in Doss, *Memorial Mania,* 68.

41. Doss, *Memorial Mania,* 67.

42. While not explicitly a history of emotions reader, *True Stories of Crime in Modern Mexico* analyzes sensational crime and media responses and speaks to the formation of publics of readers. See Buffington and Pablo Piccato, *True Stories of Crime in Modern Mexico,* 31–32, 59–60, 224–226.

43. Christiane Voss, "Film Experience and the Formation of Illusion: The Spectator as 'Surrogate Body' for the Cinema," *Cinema Journal* 50, no. 4 (2011): 145. Also discussed in Plamper, *History of Emotions,* 285–286. See also Shaya, "Mayhem for Moderns."

44. José Guadalupe Posada, "El fin del mundo es ya cierto," (Mexico City: A. Vanegas Arroyo, 1899), www.loc.gov/pictures/resource/ppmsc.04579.

45. *El Imparcial,* June 7, 1914, p. 1; *El Imparcial,* July 13, 1910, p. 10; *El Demócrata,* April 17, 1921, p. 1; *El Demócrata,* April 13, 1921, p. 1.

46. Katrin Döveling, "Mediated Parasocial Emotions and Community: How Media May Strengthen or Weaken Social Communities," in *Theorizing Emotions: Sociological Explorations and Applications,* ed. Debra Hopkins, Jochen Kleres, Helena Flam, and Helmut Kuzmics (New York: Campus Verlag, 2009), 315–337.

47. Pablo Piccato, "Homicide as Politics in Modern Mexico," in *Murder and Violence in Modern Latin America,* ed. Eric A. Johnson, Ricardo Salvatore, and Pieter Spierenburg (Malden, MA: John Wiley and Sons, 2013), 117–118, 123. Piccato suggests that media depictions of murder and those who read these depictions contribute to the building of civil society and public sphere for the exchange of ideas.

48. Agostoni, *Monuments of Progress,* 84, 86–87.

49. "Corto sus desesperanzas y amarguras lanzándose desde el tercer piso del correo una hermosa señorita," *El Diario,* January 11, 1914, pp. 1, 6.

50. "El cuerpo de una bella joven fue a estrellarse en el pavimiento quedando en el sin vida," *El Independiente,* pp. 1, 3.

51. "Corto sus desesperanzas," *El Diario.*

52. "La Señorita Sara Ramos se suicidó ayer arrojándose del tercer piso del correo," *El País,* January 11, 1914, p. 1.

53. "Corto sus desesperanzas," *El Diario,* January 11, 1914, pp. 1, 6.

54. Ibid.; "Busco en la muerte el fin de sus penas de amor," *El Imparcial,* January 11, 1914, pp. 1, 5.

55. Susie S. Porter, *Working Women in Mexico City: Public Discourses and Material Conditions, 1879–1931* (Tucson: University of Arizona Press, 2003), 159–186.

56. "El cuerpo de una bella joven fue a estrellarse en el pavimiento quedando en el sin vida," *El Independiente,* p. 1.

57. "Busco en la muerte," *El Imparcial,* January 11, 1914, pp. 1, 5.

58. Ibid., 1.

59. Walter Benjamin, *The Writer of Modern Life: Essays on Charles Baudelaire* (Cambridge, MA: Harvard University Press, 2006), 40.

60. Shaya, "Mayhem for Moderns," 244.

61. "Horrible suicidio en la Calle de Capuchinas," *El Imparcial,* June 7, 1914, pp. 1–2.

62. "Desde el tercer piso de una casa de la 5a. Calle de Tacuba se arrojó ayer una joven," *El Independiente,* August 1, 1913, pp. 1, 3.

63. Photograph, "Lugar donde cayó la suicida," *El Diario,* August 1, 1913, p. 1.

64. "La nota trágica de la semana," *La Semana Ilustrada,* June 24, 1910.

65. "Anoche se ahorcó . . . era joven y bella, de sus cartas se desprende que murió loca de amor," *El Imparcial,* November 10, 1908, p. 1

66. "Abominable asesinato de una joven en la Puerta Falsa de Sto. Domingo," *El Diario,* July 14, 1910, p. 1.

67. "El drama de la Puerta Falsa de Santo Domingo," *El Imparcial,* July 14, 1910, p. 1.

68. "La tragedia de la Puerta Falsa de Sto. Domingo," July 15, 1910, p. 5. Other articles that covered the case include "Amor, locura y sangre," *El Imparcial,* July 13, 1910, p. 1; and "El drama de la Puerta Falsa" *El Imparcial,* July 14, 1910, p. 1.

69. "El suicidio de Sofía Ahumada: Libertad de los detenidos," *El Imparcial,* June 2, 1899, p. 1.

70. Many scholars, essayists, and theorists have debated about Mexican attitudes toward death. One camp argues that there is a uniquely Mexican death way and a concomitant worldview that breeds indifference to death. See, for example, Paz, *Labyrinth of Solitude;* Lomnitz-Adler, *Death and the Idea of Mexico;* and Anita Brenner, *Idols behind Altars: Modern Mexican Art and Its Cultural Roots* (Mineola, NY: Dover Publications, 2012). The opposing camp argues that this idea is myth-making par excellence and is perpetuated by the Mexican tourism industry and Mexico's political leaders to oppress the underprivileged classes. See Roger Bartra, *The Cage of Melancholy: Identity and Metamorphosis in the Mexican Character,* trans. Christopher J. Hall (New Brunswick, NJ: Rutgers University Press, 1992); and Carlos Monsiváis, "Los viajeros y la invención de México," *Aztlán* 15, no. 2 (1984): 201–229.

71. Nancy Scheper-Hughes, *Death without Weeping: The Violence of Everyday Life in Brazil* (Berkeley: University of California Press, 1993).

72. See, for example, John R. Flippin, *Sketches from the Mountains of Mexico* (Cincinnati: Standard, 1889), 271–276.

73. I borrow this phrase from Carlos Alberto Sánchez, although I disagree with his belief, shared by Octavio Paz, that Mexicans have a unique penchant for and indifference to death. See Sánchez, "Death and the Colonial Difference," 11.

## CONCLUSION

1. García Canclini, *Culturas híbridas;* Certeau, *Practice of Everyday Life.*

2. José Vasconcelos, *The Cosmic Race/La raza cosmica,* trans. Didier T. Jaén (Baltimore: Johns Hopkins University Press, 1997).

3. Alfred Adler, *Understanding Human Nature: The Psychology of Personality* (London: One World Publications, 1992).

4. Solomon Lipp, *Leopoldo Zea: From Mexicanidad to a Philosophy of History* (Waterloo, Ontario: Wilfrid Laurier University Press, 1980), 9.

5. Octavio Paz, *El laberinto de la soledad* (Mexico City: Fondo de Cultura Económica, 1963).

6. Paz, *El laberinto de la soledad,* 48.

7. Bartra, *Cage of Melancholy.*

8. Lomnitz-Adler, *Death and the Idea of Mexico,* 483.

9. Anthony Giddens, *The Consequences of Modernity* (Stanford, CA: Stanford University, 1990) 55–63.

10. Series editor and historian Paul Gillingham pointed out this analogy to me. Indeed, penny dreadfuls were not so different from the publications of the A. Vanegas Arroyo press in turn-of-the-century Mexico City.

# BIBLIOGRAPHY

## ARCHIVES

Archivo Histórico de Salubridad y Asistencia, Mexico City
  Fondo Beneficiencía Pública
  Fondo Hospitales y Hospicios
  Fondo Manicomio General
Hemeroteca Nacional, Universidad Nacional Autónoma de México, Mexico City
  Fondo Reservado
Tribunal Superior de Justicia de Distrito Federal, Archivo General de la Nación,
  Mexico City

## PERIODICALS AND NEWSPAPERS (MEXICO CITY)

*Diario Oficial*
*El Amigo de la Juventud*
*El Chisme*
*El Correo Españôla*
*El Demócrata*
*El Imparcial*
*El Nacional*
*El País*
*El Tiempo*
*El Universal*
*El Univeral Gráfico*
*Excélsior*
*Ilustración Popular*
*La Caridad*
*La Ciudad de Díos*

*La Patria*
*La Semana Ilustrada*
*Las Hijas de Anáhuac*
*El Hijo del Trabajo*

## PRIMARY SOURCES

Aragón, Agustín. "Influencia social y moral de la lectura de novelas en la juventud." *Revista Positiva* 3 (1903): 263–273.

Aragón, Enrique O. "Psiquiatría: Los síndromas mentales." *Gaceta Médica de México* 7 (1912): 133–226.

Barreda, Gabino. "Algunas consideraciones sobre el suicidio." *La Escuela de Medicina,* no. 14 (January 15, 1883): 159–163.

Barreda, Horacio. "Estudio sobre 'El Feminismo.'" Pts. 1–4. *Revista Positiva,* no. 103 (January 1, 1909): 1–10; no. 104 (January 29, 1909): 45–60; no. 105 (February 20, 1909): 77–86; no. 106 (March 26, 1909): 109–126.

Barrera Lavalle, Francisco. *Apuntes para la historia de la estadística en México, 1821 a 1910.* Mexico City: Tip. de la vda. F. Díaz de León, sucs., 1911.

Barrett, Robert South. *Standard Guide to the City of Mexico and Vicinity, 1900.* St. Louis: Modern Mexico, 1900.

Beard, George Miller. *A Practical Treatise on Nervous Exhaustion (Neurasthenia): Its Symptoms, Nature, Sequences, Treatment.* New York: E. B. Treat, 1888.

Caraza, Rafael. "Informe que el médico cirujano del Hospital de San Hipólito que suscribe, rinde sobre el estado mental de Marcelino Domingo." *El Observador Médico,* no. 5 (1879): 34–39.

Castañeda, José de J., Máximo Silva, and Carlos Aguilera. "Contribución a la estadística del suicidio en la República Mexicana." Pts. 1 and 2. *La Escuela de Medicina,* no. 7 (November 15, 1885): 90–102; no. 8 (December 15, 1885): 103–108.

*Código Penal para el Distrito Federal y Territorio de la Baja California sobre delitos del fuero común y para toda la República sobre delitos contra la Federación.* Mexico City: Imprenta de Flores y Monsalve, 1874.

Durkheim, Émile. *Elementary Forms of Religious Life.* Translated by Carol Cosman. New York: Oxford University Press, 2001.

Flippin, John R. *Sketches from the Mountains of Mexico.* Cincinnati: Standard, 1889.

Flórez, José T. *Compendio de medicina legal con aplicación de las leyes patrias.* Translated by Alphonse Bertillon. Lima: Imprenta la Industria, 1906.

Fuentes Aguilar, Luis, and Consuelo Soto Mora. "Influencia de los frentes meteorológicos en la incidencia de suicidios en México." *Anuario de geografía* 17 (1977): 209–235.

García, Mariano Ruiz-Funes. *Endocrinología y criminalidad.* Madrid: Javier Morata, 1929.

Gota de Zaragoza, Antonio. "El neurismo creciente de nuestro tiempo." *La escuela de medicina,* no. 19 (October 15, 1909): 488–445.

Guerrero, Julio. *La génesis del crimen en México: Estudio de pisquiatría social.* Mexico City: Viuda de C. Bouret, 1901.

Hidalgo y Carpio, Luis, and Gustavo Ruiz y Sandoval. *Compendio de medicina legal: Arreglado a la legislación del Distrito Federal.* Mexico City: Imprenta de Ignacio Escalante, 1877.

Krafft Ebing, Richard von. "La menstruación como causa de irresponsabilidad mental en la mujer." *La Escuela de Medicina,* no. 45 (November 15, 1894): 935–936.

Lallemand, François. *A Practical Treatise on the Causes, Symptoms, and Treatment of Spermatorrhœa.* Translated by Henry J. McDougall. Philadelphia: Henry C. Lea, 1866.

Lara y Pardo, Luis. *La prostitución en México.* Mexico City: Librería de Ch. Bouret, 1908.

Lombroso, Cesare. *Crime, Its Causes and Remedies.* Boston: Little, Brown, 1911.

Maldonado y Morón, Ignacio. *Estudio del suicidio en México: Fundado en datos estadísticos.* Mexico City: Ignacio Escalante, 1876.

Moran, Jesús. *Ligeras consideraciones sobre el suicidio.* Mexico City: Escuela Correccional, 1891.

Morselli, Henry. *Suicide: An Essay on Comparative Moral Statistics.* New York: Appleton Press, 1882.

Olvera, José. "Discursos sobre causas de las neurosis en México." *El Observador Médico: Revista Científica de la Asociación Médica de Pedro Escobeda* 1, no. 4 (February 1870): 49–54.

Parra, Porfirio. *Ensayo sobre la patogenia de la locura.* Mexico City: Tipografía Literaria, 1878.

Quiroz Cuarón, Alfonso. *Medicina forense.* Mexico City: Editorial Porrúa, 1977.

———. *Tendencia y ritmo de la criminalidad en México.* Mexico City: Instituto de Investigaciones Estadísticas, 1939.

Rojas, Ernesto. "La histeria psíquica: Tesis para sustentar examen de especialista en Psiquiatría." Master's thesis, Escuela Nacional de Medicina, 1909.

Roumagnac, Carlos. *La estadística criminal en México.* Mexico City: Imp. de Arturo García Cubas Sucesores Hermanos, 1907.

———. *Los Criminales en México: Ensayo de Psicología Criminal.* Mexico City: Tipografia "El Fenix," 1904.

United States Congress House Committee on Ways and Means. *White Phosphorus Matches: Hearings before the Committee on Ways and Means of the House of Representatives, Sixty-Second Congress, Second Session on H. R. 2896, January 10, 1912.* Washington, DC: U.S. Government Printing Office, 1912.

Vergara y Flores, Luis. "Neuropatía y aberración intelectual." *Medicina científica* 6, no. 13 (1893): 200–204.

Wilbert, Martin I. "The Sale of Bichloride Tablets." *Public Health Reports* 28, no. 46 (November 14, 1913): 2399–2405.

Abu-Lughod, Lila. *Veiled Sentiments: Honor and Poetry in a Bedouin Society.* Berkeley: University of California Press, 1986.

Adler, Alfred. *Understanding Human Nature: The Psychology of Personality.* London: One World Publications, 1992.

Agostoni, Claudia. "Médicos científicos y médicos ilícitos en la ciudad de México durante el porfiriato." *Estudios de historia moderna y contemporánea* 19 (February–July 2000): 13–31.

———. *Monuments of Progress: Modernization and Public Health in Mexico City, 1876–1910.* Boulder: University Press of Colorado, 2003.

Alba, Francisco. *The Population of Mexico: Trends, Issues, and Policies.* Translated by Marjory Mattingly Urquidi. New Brunswick, NJ: Transaction Books, 1982.

Alva-Rodríguez, Mario, and Rolando Neri-Vela. "The Practice of Forensic Science in Mexico." In *The Global Practice of Forensic Science,* edited by Douglas H. Ubelaker, 199–216. Hoboken, NJ: John Wiley and Sons, 2015.

Anderson, James Maxwell. *Daily Life during the Spanish Inquisition.* Westport, CT: Greenwood, 2002.

Anderson, Olive. *Suicide in Victorian and Edwardian England.* New York: Clarendon Press, 1987.

Andrew, Donna T. "Debate: The Secularization of Suicide in England, 1660–1800." *Past and Present* 119 (1988): 158–165.

Ariès, Philippe. *The Hour of Our Death.* Translated by Helen Weaver. New York: Knopf Doubleday, 2013.

———. *Images of Man and Death.* Translated by Janet Lloyd. Cambridge, MA: Harvard University Press, 1985.

———. *Western Attitudes toward Death: From the Middle Ages to the Present.* Translated by Patricia M. Ranum. Baltimore: Johns Hopkins University Press, 2010.

Armus, Diego. *The Ailing City: Health, Tuberculosis, and Culture in Buenos Aires, 1870–1950.* Durham, NC: Duke University Press, 2011.

Bailey, Victor. *This Rash Act: Suicide across the Life Cycle in the Victorian City.* Stanford, CA: Stanford University Press, 1998.

Ballenger, Stephanie Sharon. "Modernizing Madness: Doctors, Patients and Asylums in Nineteenth-Century Mexico City." PhD diss., University of California, Berkeley, 2009.

Barros, Cristina, and Marco Buenrostro. *Vida cotidiana: Ciudad de México 1850–1910.* Mexico City: Fondo de Cultura Económica USA, 1996.

Bartra, Roger. *The Cage of Melancholy: Identity and Metamorphosis in the Mexican Character.* Translated by Christopher J. Hall. New Brunswick, NJ: Rutgers University Press, 1992.

Beezley, William H. *Mexican National Identity: Memory, Innuendo, and Popular Culture.* Tucson: University of Arizona Press, 2008.

Beltrán Abarca, Francisco Javier. "El suicidio en México: Problema social, individuo y poder institucional (1830–1875)." PhD Diss., Universidad Nacional Autónoma de México, 2011.

Benjamin, Walter. *The Writer of Modern Life: Essays on Charles Baudelaire*. Cambridge, MA: Harvard University Press, 2006.

Berman, Marshall. *All That Is Solid Melts into Air: The Experience of Modernity*. New York: Verso, 1982.

Bliss, Katherine Elaine. *Compromised Positions: Prostitution, Public Health, and Gender Politics in Revolutionary Mexico City*. University Park: Pennsylvania State University Press, 2001.

Bliss, Katherine Elaine, and Ann S. Blum. "Dangerous Driving: Adolescence, Sex, and the Gendered Experience of Public Space in Early-Twentieth-Century Mexico City." In *Gender, Sexuality, and Power in Latin America since Independence*, edited by William E. French and Katherine Elaine Bliss, 163–186. Lanham, MD: Rowman and Littlefield, 2007.

Blum, Ann S. *Domestic Economies: Family, Work, and Welfare in Mexico City, 1884–1943*. Lincoln: University of Nebraska Press, 2009.

Blum, Deborah. *The Poisoner's Handbook: Murder and the Birth of Forensic Medicine in Jazz Age New York*. New York: Penguin, 2011.

Bowman, William. "Despair unto Death? Attempted Suicide in Early 1930s Vienna." *Austrian History Yearbook* 39 (2008): 138–156.

Brandes, Stanley. "Is There a Mexican View of Death?" *Ethos* 31, no. 1 (2003): 129–130.

Brenner, Anita. *Idols behind Altars: Modern Mexican Art and Its Cultural Roots*. Mineola, NY: Dover, 2012.

Bridges, F. S., P. S. Yip, and K. C. Yang. "Seasonal Changes in Suicide in the United States, 1971 to 2000." *Perceptual and Motor Skills* 100, no. 3 (June 2005): 920–924.

Bronfen, Elisabeth. *Over Her Dead Body: Death, Femininity and the Aesthetic*. New York: Routledge, 1992.

Brumberg, Joan Jacobs. *Fasting Girls: The History of Anorexia Nervosa*. New York: Vintage Books, 2000.

Brunk, Samuel. "The Mortal Remains of Emiliano Zapata." In *Death, Dismemberment, and Memory: Body Politics in Latin America*, edited by Lyman L. Johnson, 141–178. Albuquerque: University of New Mexico Press, 2004.

Buffington, Robert M. *Criminal and Citizen in Modern Mexico*. Lincoln: University of Nebraska Press, 2000.

———. *A Sentimental Education for the Working Man: The Mexico City Penny Press, 1900–1910*. Durham, NC: Duke University Press, 2015.

Buffington, Robert, and Pablo Piccato. "Tales of Two Women: The Narrative Construal of Porfirian Reality." *Americas* 55, no. 3 (January 1999): 391–424.

———, eds. *True Stories of Crime in Modern Mexico*. Albuquerque: University of New Mexico Press, 2009.

Bunker, Steven B., and Victor M. Macías-González. "Consumption and Material Culture in the Twentieth Century." In *A Companion to Mexican History and Culture,* ed. William H. Beezley, 83–118. Malden, MA: Wiley-Blackwell Publishing, 2011.

Carey, Elaine. "Selling Is More of a Habit Than Using: Narcotraficante Lola la Chata and Her Threat to Civilization, 1930–1960." *Journal of Women's History* 21, no. 2 (Summer 2009): 62–89.

Castillo Troncoso, Alberto del. "Notas sobre la moral dominante a finales del siglo XIX en la Ciudad de México: Las mujeres suicidas como protagonistas de la nota roja." In *Modernidad, tradición y alteridad: La ciudad de México en el cambio de siglo (XIX-XX),* edited by Claudia Agostoni and Elisa Speckman, 319–338. Mexico City: Universidad Nacional Autónoma de México, 2001.

Certeau, Michel de. *The Practice of Everyday Life.* Translated by Steven Rendell. Berkeley: University of California Press, 1988.

Cházaro, Laura. "Reproducción y muerte de la población mexicana: Cálculos estadísticos y preceptos higiénicos a fines del siglo diecinueve." In *De normas y transgresiones: Enfermedad y crimen en América Latina (1850–1950),* edited by Claudia Agostoni and Elisa Speckman, 55–81. Mexico City: Universidad Nacional Autónoma de México, 2005.

Colt, George Howe. *November of the Soul: The Enigma of Suicide.* New York: Scribner, 2006.

Deusen, Nancy E. van. "Determining the Boundaries of Virtue: The Discourse of *Recogimiento* among Women in Seventeenth-Century Lima." *Journal of Family History* 22, no. 2 (1997): 373–389.

Doss, Erika. *Memorial Mania: Public Feeling in America.* Chicago: University of Chicago Press, 2012.

Douglas, Jack D. *Social Meanings of Suicide.* Princeton, NJ: Princeton University Press, 1967.

Döveling, Katrin. "Mediated Parasocial Emotions and Community: How Media May Strengthen or Weaken Social Communities." In *Theorizing Emotions: Sociological Explorations and Applications,* edited by Debra Hopkins, Jochen Kleres, Helena Flam, and Helmut Kuzmics, 315–337. New York: Campus Verlag, 2009.

Drinot, Paulo. "Madness, Neurasthenia, and 'Modernity': Medico-Legal and Popular Interpretations of Suicide in Early Twentieth-Century Lima." *Latin American Research Review* 39, no. 2 (June 2004): 89–113.

Duncan, Cynthia K. "Juan Mateos (1831–1913)." In *Dictionary of Mexican Literature,* edited by Eladio Cortés, 411–413. Westport, CT: Greenwood Press, 1992.

Ekman, Paul. "An Argument for Basic Emotions." *Cognition and Emotion* 6, no. 3 (1992): 169–200.

Elias, Norbert. *The Civilising Process: Sociogenetic and Psychogenetic Investigations.* Translated by Edmund Jephcott. Malden, MA: John Wiley and Sons, 1994.

Esposito, Matthew D. *Funerals, Festivals, and Cultural Politics in Porfirian Mexico.* Albuquerque: University of New Mexico Press, 2010.

Febvre, Lucien. "Sensibility and History: How to Reconstitute the Emotional Life of the Past." In *A New Kind of History: From the Writings of Febvre,* edited by Peter Burke, translated by K. Folca, 12–26. New York: Harper and Row, 1973.

Forth, Christopher E. "Neurasthenia and Manhood in *Fin-de-Siècle* France." In *Cultures of Neurasthenia: From Beard to the First World War,* edited by Marijke Gijsqwijt-Hofstra and Roy Porter, 329–362. New York: Rodopi, 2001.

Foucault, Michel. *The Birth of the Clinic: An Archaeology of Medical Perception.* Translated by A. M. Sheridan. New York: Routledge, 2012.

———. *Discipline and Punish: The Birth of the Prison.* Translated by Alan Sheridan. New York: Knopf Doubleday, 2012.

———. *History of Madness.* Edited by Jean Khalfa. Translated by Jonathan Murphy and Jean Khalfa. New York: Routledge, 2009.

Fowler, Will. *Santa Anna of Mexico.* Lincoln: University of Nebraska Press, 2007.

Franco, Jean. *Plotting Women: Gender and Representation in Mexico.* New York: Columbia University Press, 1989.

Frank, Patrick. *Posada's Broadsheets: Mexican Popular Imagery 1890–1910.* Albuquerque: University of New Mexico Press, 1998.

French, William. "Prostitutes and Guardian Angels: Women, Work, and the Family in Porfirian Mexico." *Hispanic American Historical Review* 72 (1992): 529–555.

French, William, and Katherine Elaine Bliss, eds. *Gender, Sexuality, and Power in Latin America since Independence.* Lanham, MD: Rowman and Littlefield, 2007.

García Canclini, Néstor. *Culturas híbridas: Estrategias para entrar y salir de la modernidad.* Mexico City: Editorial Grijalbo, 1990.

Gardner, Dore. *Niño Fidencio: A Heart Thrown Open.* Albuquerque: Museum of New Mexico Press, 1994.

Garner, Paul. *Porfirio Díaz: Profiles in Power.* New York: Routledge, 2001.

Garza, James Alex. *The Imagined Underworld: Sex, Crime, and Vice in Porfirian Mexico City.* Lincoln: University of Nebraska Press, 2008.

Geltmaker, Ty. *Tired of Living: Suicide in Italy from National Unification to World War I, 1860–1915.* New York: Peter Lang, 2002.

Giddens, Anthony. *The Consequences of Modernity.* Stanford, CA: Stanford University Press, 1990.

———. *Modernity and Self-Identity: Self and Society in the Late Modern Age.* Cambridge: Polity Press in association with Basil Blackwell, 1991.

Giddens, Anthony, and Christopher Pierson. *Conversations with Anthony Giddens: Making Sense of Modernity.* Stanford, CA: Stanford University Press, 1998.

Gijswijt-Hofstra, Marijke, and Roy Porter, eds. *Cultures of Neurasthenia: From Beard to the First World War.* New York: Rodopi, 2001.

Ginneken, Jaap van. *Crowds, Psychology, and Politics, 1871–1899.* New York: Cambridge University Press, 1992.

Gould, Stephen Jay. *The Panda's Thumb: More Reflections in Natural History.* New York: W. W. Norton, 2010.

Hale, Charles Adams. *The Transformation of Liberalism in Late Nineteenth Century Mexico.* New Haven, CT: Princeton University Press, 1989.

Hallam, Elizabeth, Jenny Hockey, and Glennys Howarth. *Beyond the Body: Death and Social Identity.* New York: Routledge, 2005.

Haney, C. Allen, Christina Leimer, and Juliann Lowery. "Spontaneous Memorialization: Violent Death and Emerging Mourning Ritual." *OMEGA* 35, no. 2 (1997): 159–171.

Henderson, Timothy J. *The Worm in the Wheat: Rosalie Evans and the Agrarian Struggle in Puebla-Tlaxcala Valley of Mexico, 1906–1927.* Durham, NC: Duke University Press, 1998.

Hershfield, Joanne. *Imagining la Chica Moderna: Women, Nation, and Visual Culture.* Durham, NC: Duke University Press, 2008.

Highmore, Ben. *Michel de Certeau: Analysing Culture.* New York: Continuum, 2006.

Higonnet, Margaret. "Speaking Silences: Women's Suicide." In *The Female Body in Western Culture: Contemporary Perspectives,* edited by Susan Rubin Suleiman, 68–83. Cambridge, MA: Harvard University Press, 1986.

Hobsbawm, Eric, and Terence Ranger, eds. *The Invention of Tradition.* New York: Cambridge University Press, 2012.

Hopkins, Debra, Jochen Kleres, Helena Flam, and Helmut Kuzmics, eds. *Theorizing Emotions: Sociological Explorations and Applications.* New York: Campus Verlag, 2009.

Hustvedt, Asti. *Medical Muses: Hysteria in Nineteenth-Century Paris.* New York: W.W. Norton, 2012.

Jackson, Michael D. *The Palm at the End of the Mind: Relatedness, Religiosity, and the Real.* Durham, NC: Duke University Press, 2009.

Johns, Michael. *The City of Mexico in the Age of Díaz.* Austin: University of Texas Press, 1997.

Johnson, Eric A., Ricardo Salvatore, and Pieter Spierenburg, eds. *Murder and Violence in Modern Latin America.* Malden, MA: John Wiley and Sons, 2013.

Johnson, Lyman L., ed. *Death, Dismemberment, and Memory: Body Politics in Latin America.* Albuquerque: University of New Mexico Press, 2004.

Knight, Alan. "The Several Legs of Santa Anna: A Saga of Secular Relics." In *Relics and Remains,* ed. Alexandra Walsham, 227–255. New York: Oxford University Press, 2010.

Kushner, Howard I. *American Suicide.* New Brunswick, NJ: Rutgers University Press, 1991.

———. "Suicide, Gender, and the Fear of Modernity." In *Histories of Suicide: International Perspectives on Self-Destruction in the Modern World.* Edited by John Weaver and David Wright, 19–52. Toronto: University of Toronto Press, 2009.

Laqueur, Thomas W. "Cemeteries, Religion and the Culture of Capitalism." In *Revival and Religion since 1700: Essays for John Walsh,* edited by Jane Garnett and Colin Matthew, 183–200. London: Hambledon Press, 1993.

———. *Making Sex: Body and Gender from the Greeks to Freud.* Cambridge, MA: Harvard University Press, 1990.

Lear, John. *Workers, Neighbors, and Citizens: The Revolution in Mexico City*. Lincoln: University of Nebraska Press, 2001.

Lefebvre, Henri. *The Production of Space*. Translated by Donald Nicholson-Smith. Oxford: Blackwell, 1991.

Leys, Ruth. "How Did Fear Become a Scientific Object and What Kind of Object Is It?" In *Human Facial Expressions: An Evolutionary View*, edited by Alan J. Fridlund. San Diego: Academic Press, 1994.

Lieberman, Lisa. "Romanticism and the Culture of Suicide in Nineteenth-Century France." *Comparative Studies in Society and History* 33, no. 3 (July 1991): 611–629.

Lipp, Solomon. *Leopoldo Zea: From Mexicanidad to a Philosophy of History*. Waterloo, Ontario: Wilfrid Laurier University Press, 1980.

Lipsett-Rivera, Sonya. *Gender and the Negotiation of Daily Life in Mexico, 1750–1856*. Lincoln: University of Nebraska Press, 2012.

Lomnitz-Adler, Claudio. *Death and the Idea of Mexico*. New York: Zone Books, 2005.

López, Amanda M. "The Cadaverous City: The Everyday Life of the Dead in Mexico City, 1875–1930." PhD diss., University of Arizona, 2010.

López, Ana M. "Early Cinema and Modernity in Latin America." *Cinema Journal* 40, no. 1 (Fall 2000): 48–78.

Lugo, Ma. Concepción. "Los espacios urbanos de la muerte." *Historias* 40 (1998): 35–45.

Lutz, Catherine A., and Lila Abu-Lughod, eds. *Language and the Politics of Emotion*. New York: Cambridge University Press, 1990.

MacDonald, Michael, and Terence R. Murphy. *Sleepless Souls: Suicide in Early Modern England*. New York: Oxford University Press, 1990.

Mancilla Villa, Martha Lilia. *Locura y mujer durante el porfiriato*. Mexico City: Editorial Círculo Psicoanalítico Mexicano, 2001.

Margry, Peter Jan. "Performative Memorials: Arenas on Political Resentment in Dutch Society." In *Reforming Dutch Culture*, edited by Peter Jan Margry and H. Roodenburg, 109–133. Aldershot, UK: Ashgate, 2008.

Margry, Peter Jan, and Christina Sánchez-Carretero. "Memorializing Tragic Death." *Anthropology Today* 23, no. 3 (June 2007): 1–2.

Mayer Celis, Leticia. *Entre el infierno de una realidad y el cielo de un imaginario: Estadística y comunidad científica en el México de la primera mitad del siglo XIX*. Mexico City: El Colegio de México, 1999.

McCaa, Robert, "Missing Millions: The Demographic Costs of the Mexican Revolution." *Mexican Studies/Estudios Mexicanos* 19, no. 2 (Summer 2003): 367–400.

Minois, George. *History of Suicide: Voluntary Death in Western Culture*. Translated by Lydia G. Cochrane. Baltimore, MD: Johns Hopkins University Press, 1999.

Moerer, Andrea Kristine. "Changing Chapultepec: Construction, Consumption, and Cultural Politics in a Mexico City Forest, 1934–1944." PhD diss., University of Minnesota, 2013.

Molina Avilés, Jorge. "Psicología y positivismo: La enseñanza de la psicología durante el porfiriato: 1896–1910." In *100 años de la psicología en México 1896–1996,* ed. Juan José Sánchez Sosa, 13–28. Mexico City: Universidad Nacional Autónoma de México, 1997.

Monsiváis, Carlos. "El Niño Fidencio." In *Entre la magia y la historia: Tradiciones, mitos y leyendas de la frontera,* edited by José Manuel Valenzuela Arce, 107–120. Mexico City: Plaza y Valdés, 2000.

———. "Los viajeros y la invención de México." *Aztlán* 15, no. 2 (1984): 201–229.

Morrissey, Susan K. *Suicide and the Body Politic in Imperial Russia.* New York: Cambridge University Press, 2006.

Murray, Alexander. *Suicide in the Middle Ages.* Vol. 2, *The Curse on Self-Murder.* New York: Oxford University Press, 2000.

Palmer, Brian. "The Season of Renewal and Suicide." *Slate,* December 7, 2012. www .slate.com/articles/news_and_politics/explainer/2012/12/suicide_rate_season_ there_more_suicides_in_spring_and_not_during_the_holidays.html.

Paperno, Irina. *Suicide as a Cultural Institution in Dostoevsky's Russia.* Ithaca, NY: Cornell University Press, 1997.

Parascandola, John. *King of Poisons: A History of Arsenic.* Washington, DC: Potomac Books, 2012.

Paz, Octavio. *El laberinto de la soledad.* Mexico City: Fondo de Cultura Económica, 1963.

———. *The Labyrinth of Solitude: And Other Writings.* Translated by Lysander Camp, Yara Milos, and Rachel Phillips Belash. New York: Grove Press, 1985.

Pereyra, Carlos. "La sociología abstracta y su aplicación á algunos problemas fundamentales de México." *Revista Positiva,* no. 3 (August 13, 1903): 351–386.

Pérez, Louis A. *To Die in Cuba: Suicide and Society.* Chapel Hill: University of North Carolina Press, 2005.

Piccato, Pablo. *City of Suspects: Crime in Mexico City, 1900–1931.* Durham, NC: Duke University Press, 2001.

———. "Homicide as Politics in Modern Mexico." In *Murder and Violence in Modern Latin America,* edited by Eric A. Johnson, Ricardo Salvatore, and Pieter Spierenburg, 104–125. Malden, MA: John Wiley and Sons, 2013.

———. *The Tyranny of Opinion: Honor in the Construction of the Mexican Public Sphere.* Durham, NC: Duke University Press, 2009.

———. "Urbanistas, Ambulantes, and Mendigos: The Dispute for Urban Space in Mexico City, 1890–30." In *Reconstructing Criminality in Latin America,* edited by Carlos A. Aguirre and Robert Buffington, 113–148. Wilmington, DE: Rowman and Littlefield, 2000.

Pick, Daniel. *Faces of Degeneration: A European Disorder, c. 1848–1918.* New York: Cambridge University Press, 1993.

Pinnow, Kenneth Martin. *Lost to the Collective: Suicide and the Promise of Soviet Socialism, 1921–1929.* Ithaca, NY: Cornell University Press, 2010.

Plamper, Jan. *The History of Emotions: An Introduction.* Translated by Keith Tribe. New York: Oxford University Press, 2014.

Plasencia de la Parra, Enrique. "Conmemoración de la hazaña épica de los niños héroes: Su origen, desarrollo y simbolismos." *Historia Mexicana* 45, no. 2 (October–December 1995): 241–279.

Popkin, Cathy. "Hysterical Episodes: Case Histories and Silent Subjects." In *Self and Story in Russian History,* edited by Laura Engelstein and Stephanie Sandler, 189–216. Ithaca, NY: Cornell University Press, 2000.

Porter, Susie S. "'And That It Is Custom Makes It Law': Class Conflict and Gender Ideology in the Public Sphere, Mexico City, 1880–1910." *Social Science History* 24, no. 1 (Spring 2000): 111–148.

———. *Working Women in Mexico City: Public Discourses and Material Conditions, 1879–1931.* Tucson: University of Arizona Press, 2003.

Pulido Esteva, Diego. "Imágenes de la locura en el discurso de la modernidad, salud mental y orden social a través de las visiones médicas, criminólogico, legal, y literaria (Ciudad de México, 1881–1910)." PhD diss., Universidad Nacional Autónoma de México, 2004.

Ramírez, Cristina Devereaux. *Occupying Our Space: The Mestiza Rhetorics of Mexican Women Journalists and Activists, 1875–1942.* Tucson: University of Arizona Press, 2015.

Reddy, William M. *The Navigation of Feeling: A Framework for the History of Emotions.* New York: Cambridge University Press, 2001.

Ríos Molina, Andrés. "La locura durante la Revolución mexicana: Los primeros años del Manicomio General La Castañeda, 1910–1920." PhD diss., El Colegio de México, 2009.

Rivera-Garza, Cristina. "Por la salud mental de la nación: Vida cotidiana y estado en el Manicomio General de la Castañeda, México 1910–1930." *Secuencia,* no. 51 (September–December 2001): 57–90.

———. "She Neither Respected nor Obeyed Anyone: Inmates and Psychiatrists Debate Gender and Class at the General Insane Asylum La Castañeda, Mexico, 1910–20." *Hispanic American Historical Review* 81, nos. 3–4 (August and November 2001): 653–688.

Rodríguez Sala de Gómezgil, María Luisa. "Suicidios y suicidas en la sociedad Mexicana." Mexico City: Universidad Nacional Autónoma de México, Instituto de Investigaciones Sociales, 1974.

Rosaldo, Michelle Z. *Knowledge and Passion: Ilongot Notions of Self and Social Life.* New York: Cambridge University Press, 1980.

Rosenthal, Anton. "The Arrival of the Streetcar and the Conflict over Progress in Early Twentieth-Century Montevideo." *Journal of Latin American Studies* 27, no. 2 (1995): 319–341.

Rosenwein, Barbara H. *Emotional Communities in the Early Middle Ages.* Ithaca, NY: Cornell University Press, 2002.

———. "Worrying about Emotions in History." *American Historical Review* 107, no. 3 (2002): 821–845.

Ruggiero, Kristin. *Modernity in the Flesh: Medicine, Law, and Society in Turn-of-the-Century Argentina.* Stanford, CA: Stanford University Press, 2004.

Sánchez, Carlos Alberto. "Death and the Colonial Difference: An Analysis of a Mexican Idea." *Journal of Philosophy of Life* 3, no. 3 (September 2013): 168–189.

Santino, Jack. "Performative Commemoratives: Spontaneous Shrines and the Public Memorialization of Death." In *Spontaneous Shrines and the Public Memorialization of Death,* edited by Jack Santino, 5–16. New York: Palgrave Macmillan, 2006.

———, ed. *Spontaneous Shrines and the Public Memorialization of Death.* New York: Palgrave MacMillan, 2006.

Scheper-Hughes, Nancy. *Death without Weeping: The Violence of Everyday Life in Brazil.* Berkeley: University of California Press, 1993.

Schwartz, Kessel. "The Theme of Suicide in Representative Spanish Novels." *Hispania* 58, no. 3 (September 1975): 442–453.

Scott, James C. *Seeing Like a State: How Certain Schemes to Improve the Human Condition Have Failed.* New Haven, CT: Yale University Press, 1999.

Serna, Laura Isabel. *Making Cinelandia: American Films and Mexican Film Culture before the Golden Age.* Durham, NC: Duke University Press, 2014.

Silkenat, David. *Moments of Despair: Suicide, Divorce, and Debt in Civil War Era North Carolina.* Chapel Hill: University of North Carolina Press, 2011.

Shapiro, Ann-Louise. "Disordered Bodies/Disorderly Acts: Medical Discourse and the Female Criminal in Nineteenth-Century Paris." In *Gendered Domains: Rethinking Public and Private in Women's History,* edited by Dorothy O. Helly and Susan M. Reverby, 123–134. Ithaca, NY: Cornell University Press, 1992.

Shaya, Gregory K. "Mayhem of Moderns: The Culture of Sensationalism in France, c. 1900." PhD diss., University of Michigan, 2000.

Shilling, Chris. *The Body and Social Theory.* Los Angeles: Sage, 2012.

Showalter, Elaine. *The Female Malady: Women, Madness, and English Culture, 1830–1980.* New York: Penguin, 1987.

Sloan, Kathryn A. *Runaway Daughters: Seduction, Elopement, and Honor in Modern Mexico.* Albuquerque: University of New Mexico Press, 2008.

Sluis, Ageeth. *Deco Body, Deco City: Female Spectacle and Modernity in Mexico City, 1900–1939.* Lincoln: University of Nebraska Press, 2015.

Smith, Phyllis Lynn. "Contentious Voices amid the Order: The Porfirian Press in Mexico City, 1876–1911." PhD diss., University of Arizona, 1996.

Solórzano Ponce, María Teresa. "Juan Antonio Mateos (1831–1913)." In *La república de las letras: Asomos a la cultura escrita del México decimonónico,* vol. 3: *Galería de escritores,* edited by Belem Clark de Lara and Elisa Speckman Guerra, 333–342. Mexico City: Universidad Nacional Autónoma de México, 2005.

Sommer, Doris. *Foundational Fictions: The National Romances of Latin America.* Berkeley: University of California Press, 1991.

Spivak, Gayatri. "Can the Subaltern Speak?" In *Colonial Discourses and Post-Colonial Theory: A Reader,* edited by Patrick Williams and Laura Chrisman, 66–111. New York: Columbia University Press, 1994.

Stearns, Peter N., and Carol Z. Stearns, "Emotionology: Clarifying the History of Emotions and Emotional Standards." *American Historical Review* 90, no. 4 (1985): 813–836.

Stepan, Nancy Leys. *"The Hour of Eugenics": Race, Gender, and Nation in Latin America.* Ithaca, NY: Cornell University Press, 1991.

Tenorio-Trillo, Mauricio. *I Speak of the City: Mexico City at the Turn of the Twentieth Century.* Chicago: University of Chicago Press, 2013.

———. *Mexico at the World's Fairs: Crafting a Modern Nation.* Berkeley: University of California Press, 1996.

———. "1910 Mexico City: Space and Nation in the City of the Centenario." *Journal of Latin American Studies* 28 (February 1996): 75–104.

Toner, Deborah. *Alcohol and Nationhood in Nineteenth-Century Mexico.* Lincoln: University of Nebraska Press, 2015.

Tortorici, Zeb. "Reading the (Dead) Body: Histories of Suicide in New Spain." In *Death and Dying in Colonial Spanish America,* edited by Martina Will de Chaparro and Miruna Achim, 53–77. Tucson: University of Arizona Press, 2011.

Townsend, Mary Ashley. *Here and There in Mexico: The Travel Writings of Mary Ashley Townsend.* Edited by Ralph Lee Woodard Jr. Tuscaloosa: University of Alabama Press, 2001.

Toxqui, Áurea. "Breadwinners or Entrepreneurs? Women's Involvement in the *Pulquería* World of Mexico City." In *Alcohol in Latin America: A Social and Cultural History,* edited by Gretchen Kristine Pierce and Áurea Toxqui, 104–130. Tucson: University of Arizona Press, 2014.

Vasconcelos, José. *The Cosmic Race/La raza cósmica.* Translated by Didier T. Jaén. Baltimore: Johns Hopkins University Press, 1997.

Vaughan, Mary Kay. "Modernizing Patriarchy: State Policies, Rural Households, and Women in Mexico, 1930–40." In *Hidden Histories of Gender and the State in Latin America,* edited by Elizabeth Dore and Maxine Molyneaux, 194–214. Durham, NC: Duke University Press, 2000.

Voekel, Pamela. *Alone before God: The Religious Origins of Modernity in Mexico.* Durham, NC: Duke University Press, 2002.

Voss, Christiane. "Film Experience and the Formation of Illusion: The Spectator as 'Surrogate Body' for the Cinema." *Cinema Journal* 50, no. 4 (2011): 136–150.

Weaver, John C. *A Sadly Troubled History: The Meanings of Suicide in the Modern Age.* Montreal: McGill-Queen's University Press, 2009.

Weber, Jonathan Michael. "Hustling the Old Mexico Aside: Creating a Modern Mexico City through Medicine, Public Health, and Technology in the Porfiriato, 1887–1913." PhD diss., Florida State University, 2013.

Westheim, Paul. *La calavera.* Mexico City: Fondo de Cultura Económica, 1953.

Williams, Patrick, and Laura Chrisman, eds. *Colonial Discourse and Post-Colonial Theory: A Reader.* New York: Columbia University Press, 1994.

Williams, Raymond Leslie. *The Colombian Novel, 1844–1987.* Austin: University of Texas Press, 1991.

Zeff, Trish, ed. *101 Tragedies of Enrique Metinides.* New York: Aperture, 2012.

# INDEX

Abogado Cristiano, El, 58, 63
Abu-Lughod, Lila, 178
Acuña, Manuel, 69–70, 87
Alameda (park), 32map, 103, 149, 151–153,
    173–175, 192
alcoholism: as cause of mental illness, 140,
    145; as cause of suicide, 29tab., 78–80,
    133–135
Andrade y Pastor, Manuel María, 72–73
Alva, Ramón L., 76–77
*Amigo de la Verdad, El,* 89–90
Aragon, Agustín, 90
Arellano, Agustín, 37
Ariès, Phillippe, 181
Arroyo, Arnulfo, 54
asylums: admission to, 136–137; and gender,
    127; and medical studies, 65, 110, 123–
    127, 134; criticism of by newspapers, 132,
    138–142, 146; records of, xii, 10. *See also*
    Manicomio General "La Castañeda"
autopsy: causes of suicide determined by,
    60, 64; criticism of autopsy in press, 65;
    forensic-medical experts and, 9, 25,
    40–41; rejection of in suicide notes, 27,
    69, 101. *See also* forensic investigation

Barreda, Gabino, 15–16, 35, 120–122
Barreda, Horacio, 122
Barrera Lavalle, Francisco, 13
Beard, George, 128–133
body: and burial, 44, 65–68; and identity,
    34–35, 46; as text, 5, 36, 58, 163, 166, 181;
    effect of poison on, 24–27, 43, 50;

forensic examination of, 37, 40–42,
    52–53, 59; preparation of, 36, 68–69;
    scopiphilic gaze and the, 9, 171–173;
    scientific views of, 20, 103, 118, 134, 201
*Boletín demográfico de la República Mexi-
    cana,* 13
boticas. *See* pharmacies
Bowman, William, 23
Brierre de Boismont, Jacques François, 39,
    118–120
Bronfen, Elizabeth, 36, 53
Busto, Emiliano, 12–13

Cabaret Regis, 112
Cabrera, Miguel, 54
cadaver, 9, 35, 45, 66, 101; and forensic
    investigation, 34, 40–42, 59, 199; and
    public health, 64–65, 68
Calles, Plutarco, 2
Calzada de Violetas, 47, 50, 158
cantinas, 29, 78; and suicide, 21, 100, 111,
    148, 159–162
*Caridad, La,* 79–80
cathedral: and symbolic space, 148–149,
    173, 182; suicide at, 83–85, 88, 165–170,
    173–176, 188, 195–196, 199. *See also*
    Tower of Suicides
Catholic press. *See* press
cemeteries: burial at, 41, 65, 69, 160–161;
    and class of burial, 65–66, 155; and
    public health, 67; and reform move-
    ment, 66–67, 202; as political space, 183,
    195. *See also* Panteón Dolores

251

13, 25; neurasthenia as, 128–132; suicide as, 74, 77, 93

dishonor, 3, 28, 29tab., 46, 72, 91, 122, 126, 130, 170; and public reputation, 162; failed aspirations and, 119; financial ruin and, 111–112

Doctores (barrio), 31, 32map, 100

Doss, Erika, 183

double suicide. *See* suicide pact

dress. *See* clothing

Durkheim, Émile, 8, 10, 18, 120; and Mexican scientists, 117, 135, 201; and moral statistics, 17; on timing of suicide, 20–21

*Eco de Ambos Mundos, El,* 69

Ekman, Paul, 178–179

Elias, Norbert, 178

emotions: and civilization, 178; and gender, 121, 128; and mental illness, 118; and novels, 90; and reporting on suicide, 35, 76; and suicide motive, 28, 96, 99, 113; community of, 56–57, 77, 177–178, 182–185, 191, 196, 200; history of, 11, 177–178; social construction of, 178–179

Establecimiento de Ciencias Médicas, 37

Escuela Nacional de Medicina: and donation of cadavers, 65; and legal medicine, 37–38; and Manuel Acuña, 69; curriculum of, 40, 134; personnel of, 120, 131; religious critique of, 87

Esquirol, Jean-Étienne Dominique, 17, 118–120, 123–124, 201

Europe: and moral statistics, 13, 16–17; influence on medicine, 118; suicide in, 5, 7, 18, 77, 82, 95

*Excélsior* (newspaper): and la nota roja, 175; critique of pharmacies, 142–143; on suicides, 13, 24, 51–52, 72, 101, 106, 114

firearms: availability of, 24; gender and, 24; suicide by, 23, 45, 39, 48, 54, 59, 109, 112

forensic investigation, 50; and autopsy, 34, 40–42; and legal medicine, 37–39; and the courts, 26, 38–39, 44; in suicide cases, 59, 61, 174, 189, 191, 195. *See also* autopsy

Foucault, Michel, 135, 178

free will: and criminality, 38, 135; religious view of, 79; suicide and, 16–17, 23, 119

Freud, Sigmund, 124, 128, 178

funerals: in public space, 3–4, 67, 91, 177, 181–183; reporting on, 69–70, 87, 155, 172. *See also* mourning

*Gaceta Médica de México,* 134

Gamboa, Federico, 35–36, 53

Gaona, Rodolfo, 58–64, 85–86, 192

gender: and autopsy procedure, 40; and disorder, 3, 6–7, 64, 125, 156; and interpretation of suicide, 10, 57, 59, 87, 173, 199; and mental illness, 121, 136; and suicide, 2, 6, 9, 16, 19tab., 22tab., 30, 73, 102, 151; honor and; and method of suicide, 25tab.; motive for suicide, 29tab. *See also* gender ideology; women

Giddings, Franklin H., 117

Goethe, Johann Wolfgang von (The Sorrows of Young Werther), 77, 90, 154

Gota de Zaragoza, Dr. Antonio, 132

*Gran Sedería, La,* 93–94

Granat, Jacobo, 171–172

Guerrero, Julio, 19–20, 150, 155

Guerry, André-Michel de, 16

guns. *See* firearms

Hale, Charles, 14–15

Hidalgo y Carpio, Luis, 37–42

Higonnet, Margaret, 35

*Hijas de Anáhuac, Las,* 75

*Hijo del Trabajo, El,* 78–79

homicide: and criminologists, 12, 20–21; and view of suicide, 10; forensic investigation of, 26, 39, 43; immorality and, 78; rates of, 29, 78; reporting on, 114; -suicide, 192, 193fig., 195

honor, 3, 21, 92, 100, 125, 172; and death, 10, 45–46, 147; and interpretation of suicide, 61, 71, 74, 119, 155, 167–168; and journalists, 3, 140, 171, 173; and public space, 48, 151, 156, 166, 170, 196; as motive for suicide, 2, 10, 28–29, 72, 99, 112, 122, 154, 174–175; female-, 3, 58, 166, 188; male-, 94, 111–112, 162

Hospital Juárez: and autopsy of suicides, 9, 38, 65, 153, 163, 191; and medical treatment after suicide attempt, 28, 98–99. *See also* morgue

186–187; as symbol of social change, 2; and honorable death, 9–10; rejecting natural roles, 7; rural migrants, 3. *See also* gender; clothing

Wright de Kleinhans, Laureana, 74–76

youth suicides: corrupting influence of reading material, 7, 89–94, 116–117, 167; lack of religion blamed for, 75–76, 79–82; perceived rise in, 22; upbringing and prevention of, 82–85

Zapata, Emiliano, 69, 72

Zapatistas, 140

Zárraga, Dr. Fernando, 131–132

Zea, Leopoldo, 200

Zócalo, El, 32map, 46, 98, 148–151, 153, 156, 173